The Making of a Name

The Making of a Name

The Inside Story of the Brands We Buy

Steve Rivkin and Fraser Sutherland

OXFORD
UNIVERSITY PRESS

OXFORD
UNIVERSITY PRESS

Oxford   New York

Auckland   Bangkok   Buenos Aires   Cape Town   Chennai
Dar es Salaam   Delhi   Hong Kong   Istanbul   Karachi   Kolkata
Kuala Lumpur   Madrid   Melbourne   Mexico City   Mumbai   Nairobi
São Paulo   Shanghai   Taipei   Tokyo   Toronto

Copyright © 2004 by Steve Rivkin and Fraser Sutherland

Published by Oxford University Press, Inc.
198 Madison Avenue, New York, New York 10016

www.oup-usa.org/us/

Library of Congress Cataloging-in-Publication Data

Rivkin, Steve, 1947–
    The making of a name : the inside story of the brands we buy / Steve Rivkin and Fraser Sutherland.
        p.   cm.
    Includes bibliographical references and index.
    ISBN-13: 978-0-19-516872-3 (hardcover : alk. paper)
    ISBN-10: 0-19-516872-0 (hardcover : alk. paper)
    1. Brand name products.   I. Sutherland, Fraser.   II. Title
        HD69.B7R58   2004
    658.8'27—dc22

                                                    2004012206

2 3 4 5 6 7 8 9
Printed in the United States of America on acid-free paper.

A good name is rather to be chosen than great riches.
—Proverbs 22:1

Acknowledgments

The first inkling of a book about brand and trade names as linguistic units came to the mind of Erin McKean, Editor in Chief of U.S. Dictionaries for Oxford University Press, and we thank her for this evolving notion. The authors would also like to thank Kim R. Robertson, associate professor of marketing, Department of Business Administration, Trinity University, San Antonio, Texas, for his insights into desirable brand name qualities; trademark attorney Tara L. Benson, of Red Bank, New Jersey, for her scrutiny of legal matters; Greg Tarallo, president of NetStride Corporation, Newton, Pennsylvania, for his canvass of the "Spinning the Name Web" chapter; psychologist Carol Moog, founder of Creative Focus, Bala Cynwyd, Pennsylvania, for helping us peer into the minds of consumers; Andy Chuang, founder of Good Characters, Fresno, California, for his inspection of Chinese and Japanese proceedings in the "Names Heard Round the World" chapter; Lithuanian scholar Rasa Mazeika of Toronto and Glen Morris, Ontario, for her academic expertise; Pierre Ouellet of Toronto for help with French; and J. K. Chambers, professor of linguistics at the University of Toronto, who generously agreed to read and comment on "The Sound of Sales" chapter. Notwithstanding those who gave us aid, all errors of omission, commission, and conception are entirely the authors' responsibility.

Contents

vaccine against pneumococcal bacteria, was supposed to connote the idea of prevention. *Clarinex*, a Schering-Plough allergy medicine, kept the brand name of an already-successful drug alive for a next-generation product: it was a follow-up to *Claritin*, which is now sold over-the-counter. Names could also tie directly to their maker: Amgen used the -*gen* from its own name for its drugs *Neupogen* and *Epogen*.

Although the drugs were new, there was nothing novel about such naming strategies. In the 1860s, a cheap and hard-wearing floor covering made from flax and oil (in Latin, *linum* and *oleum*, respectively) was named *Linoleum*. Their heirs are such agglomerations of sensible-sounding syllables like *Nortel*, *Telegent*, *Navigant*, and *Navistar*. A computer services firm formed by the merger of Sperry and Burroughs had a chief executive who favored *United Information Systems*, or the initialization *UIS*, but settled for *Unisys*. "Systems" was a key element here, just as some coined names concentrate on important ingredients. *Pepsi* has nothing to do with getting pep from its sugar content, but is derived from *pepsin*, an enzyme that aids digestion by breaking down proteins in the stomach. *Oxydol* (the name of a product whose radio-drama sponsorship gave rise to the term "soap opera") played up its connection to *oxygen* to highlight its whitening and bleaching powers.

Coined names, even those that seem completely new, rely on the hearers' unconscious understanding of the bits and pieces of language, and their ability to transfer those new meanings to the new name. Smart namers choose just enough of these bits to create good feeling, leaving room for people to associate the specifics of their product with the name.

PART TWO

NAMING

Holla your name to the reverberate hills,
And make the babbling gossip of the air
Cry out . . .
                    —Shakespeare, *Twelfth Night*, 1:5

5

BRAINWAVES AND BRAIN STORMS

Consider the brain. (Note: you must use your brain to do so.) This effort's made easier by the fact that the human brain contains about 100 billion busily firing nerve cells. Even taking into account that we often do a good job in destroying the brain cells we have, these are more than enough to handle basic thought.

The cerebrum, the wrinkled, involuted dome that takes up 85 percent of the brain and holds the literal and figurative gray matter, is divided into left and right hemispheres. The left brain controls how we cope with written and spoken language, how we reason, how we understand the ways of science, and how we use our right hand. The right brain has different duties: it's in charge of the left hand, but also is deeply involved in matters concerning insight and imagination, with the perception of three-dimensional forms, and with our awareness of music and the visual arts. Our hemispheric split is between the critical and the creative. Even in the right-handed, the right brain's influence is not to be minimized.

The knowledge management firm Funderstanding offers this table to illustrate the differences between thinking:

Left brain	Right brain
Logical	Random
Sequential	Intuitive
Rational	Holistic
Analytical	Synthesizing
Objective	Subjective
Looks at parts	Looks at wholes

Right-brained or left-brained, we exploit only a small fraction of the potential powers our brains already possess. This is perfectly understandable; the brain has a lot of routine work to do (remembering where we put our keys, keeping us from stumbling, figuring out what 24 Down could possibly be), and it couldn't cope without the established patterns and routines we depend on. But what we gain in efficiency we may lose in effectiveness, and by effectiveness, we mean creativity.

Creativity relies on the shaking up of patterns and being open to chance. Chance is to be welcomed, not feared. Creativity blends random association and rational combination with the creative modified by the critical. The work and play of naming involves both brain functions, and a strong creative sense is essential. Helpful exercises have been devised to permit both free play and controlled work. In one exercise, a small group is put together and divided into left-brain (rational) thinkers and right-brain (intuitive) thinkers. The left-brainers are told to compile practical and conventional names, the right-brainers to conjure far-out names. Then the groups and the left-brain and right-brain names are combined, and the names are randomly linked. Other methods can also generate fresh and combinatorial thinking. Groups can be divided according to gender, work experience, departmental responsibilities in a company, geographical origin, or education. One group could be told to do a free-association list of adjectives and verbs, the other a list of nouns that represent some aspect of the product or service to be named. Then a word is randomly chosen from the first list and combined with a word from the second.

All these exercises are meant to shake up preconceived associations and established patterns. The powers of combination will soon reveal themselves almost in mathematical terms, and in fact a simple software program can do the algorithmic hard work. One example (from Steve Rivkin's and Fraser Seitel's *IdeaWise*) involves a new telephone product to be named. The namers were told to come up with ten words that might apply to it in one way or another, and duly offered:

Access	Direct	Global
Bridge	Express	Link
Clear	Flash	Reach
Connect		

Each word has nine other words to join hands with, and in a computer nanosecond ninety different possibilities presented themselves: *AccessBridge, BridgeClear, ClearConnect, ConnectDirect, DirectExpress, ExpressFlash, FlashGlobal, GlobaLink, LinkReach,* and so on. Admittedly, the left brain had dominated the process: the initial list contained words clearly relevant to the product; the stupid-but-fast computer had combined them, and critical human intervention was necessary to choose the best of the ninety alternatives. But the exercise does illustrate that creativity is essentially combinatorial.

True originality may not in fact exist. Everything we create inevitably will bear some resemblance to what is past or present, since we cannot exist independently of history, the world, or the language by which we understand what is or has been. At the same time, it is impossible to be aware of every possible combination or configuration there is or has been. Only someone outside time and space (God, if you will) could encompass all the possibilities. What passes for true originality is correspondence to what has been outside our ken, beyond our narrow frame of reference. Everything's been done before, in art or in nature. Art imitates nature (the idea for *Velcro* came from the clinging barbs some plants possess), nature imitates art (or at least we read art into nature), art imitates art (every art has a tradition to draw on), and nature imitates nature (which is what evolution does, the ongoing repetition of desirable traits). The always-practical Thomas Edison once said that ideas have to be original only in their adaptation to the problem being addressed.

The creative process involves a tension between ideas and details, and draws on the talents of two kinds of individuals, the top-down and the bottom-up. Top-down people, such as philosophers and theorists, make a priority of concepts and principles, and work their way down to the nitty-gritty of facts and functions. Bottom-up people, such as artists and auto mechanics, work in the opposite direction. They immerse themselves in details and materials, and only later reach a conclusion—if at all. (A conclusion may not even be necessary.) The process of naming shares much with other forms of creativity. The Anglo-Maltese thinker Edward de Bono has built a cottage industry around shaking up accustomed patterns of thought. He invented the term "lateral thinking" in his 1967 book *The Use of Lateral Thinking* (titled *New Think* in the United States). Bono has used the example of the ship captain who put out a fire on his oil tanker by—reversing the proverb—pouring oil on the flames. Instead of feeding it, the oil simply smothered the fire. One of Bono's maxims is "You cannot dig a hole in a different place by digging the same hole deeper," meaning that "trying harder in the same direction may not be as useful as changing direction." He aims to dislodge traditional assumptions about concepts and boundaries.

One by-product of the Bono system is a four-line verse form with an *aa bb* rhyme scheme he calls the "Bonto." Like the limerick, the form has strict rules. The first line sets out some bizarre behavior, the second explains it, the third tells what action resulted from it, and the fourth provides a philosophical summary. Here's an example from Bono's Web site:

He put money down the drain
Because he enjoyed the pain.
He became addicted to loss.
You can if you are boss.

Anything that unshackles the imagination—anything that encourages lateral thinking—is welcome. Intelligence, as commonly measured, may actually hinder successful lateral thinking. To be admitted to the Mensa organization, members have to pass tests to certify they have spectacularly high IQs. But, usually, they are not high achievers in society—maybe they're *too* intelligent. In any event, IQ tests are a crude measure of thinking ability. There are many kinds of intelligence. The ability of a Wayne Gretzky to anticipate what eleven other hockey players are about to do on the ice, or how a Michael Jordan can map instantaneously a basketball court in motion, may not be the stuff to launch a crew of astronauts into outer space. Nonetheless, these are astounding mental feats.

Coming up with a new name demands a specialized intelligence, an intelligence that isn't directly linked to conventional intelligence. Neither is it dependent on advanced education, technological expertise, or specialized training—though all may help to a greater or lesser degree. Naming requires three phases of intelligent and intuitive thinking: *Preparation* (the collecting of information), *Incubation* (the assimilation, often subconsciously, of those data), and *Illumination* (the seemingly miraculous appearance of an effective name).

Preparation for naming can be likened to the training of a track athlete. The training is not just to get the sprinter in great shape but also to enable the sprinter to go on automatic pilot on those days when he or she doesn't particularly feel like running fast. The body knows what it's been taught.

There's much to know. The namer has to know about the product, service, or company, about its good and bad points, about its competitors, about the industry in which it functions, about the names that have "been there and done that." In information-gathering, multiple sources can be tapped: print and online directories of trade names and brand names are ready to hand in large public libraries, small specialized or company libraries, and on the Internet. Other Web sites will search for brand names: type "banana" and a swath of banana product and corporate names will pop up, including, of course, *Banana Republic*. Books like the *Encyclopedia of Associations* and the *National Directory of Trade and Professional Organizations* help target groups that have specialized information—or that may be possible markets. Some firms will search out answers for a fee, and there are competitive-intelligence brokers. Companies may house departments dealing with Corporate Communications, Public Relations, Marketing Communications, and Investor Relations—all of which may yield essential information. Numerous naming firms have home pages on the Web, and Rivkin & Associates' *Naming Newsletter*, online at *www.namingnewsletter.com*, is full of illuminating stories.

This digging largely targets companies, products, services, and their names. Preparation also entails stocking the larder with general reference works that are bound to come in handy later on, like the Goliath of dictionaries, the *Oxford English Dictionary*, available on searchable CD-ROM (or at *www.oed.com* by subscription). Every dictionary has its strengths and weaknesses, many are on CD, and the more one can tap the better. There are plenty of other fine word books available, including Stephen Glazier's *The Word Menu*, an invaluable compendium of topical word lists; *The Synonym Finder* (1.5 million synonyms) by J. I. Rodale; and Robert L. Chapman's *Fifth International Roget's Thesaurus*. Dictionaries of slang, regionalisms, and catchwords, almanacs, and gazetteers can be fertile sources of potential brand names. Any large collection of idioms can be of use because brand names often *are* highly idiomatic. (Idioms are the maddening part of learning a new language. Try explaining to a new speaker of English that *near miss* really means "near collision.") Idioms start with a burst of dissonance ("He spoke *off the cuff? Hey, that doesn't make sense!") and then rapidly broaden our consciousness. These paradoxical pairings can be surprising and playful. They engage the left and right brain at the same moment.

For namers, it's not only a matter of letting their fingers do the walking— it's also the walking. A leisurely stroll around the block or in a mall may reveal the inventive and evocative names local retailers come up with, such as *One Night Stand* (a women's boutique that rents high-priced designer clothing for special occasions) or *Creature Comforts* (a pet groomer). Informal research may serve just as well as the findings of focus groups and consumer panels. A well-known sleep aid was named by a fellow who overheard a group of people leaving the theater late in the evening. "Night all," they called to each other. "Night all." This alert listener had his new name: *Nytol.* Listening to customers also helped the maker of a skin cream. A Baltimore pharmacist, George Bunting, was blending his own brand of skin cream in the early 1900s, selling it in small blue jars labeled *Dr. Bunting's Sunburn Remedy.* Women who never ventured into the sun without a parasol were happy with the cream, but Bunting wanted a broader base of business. One day a man entered the store and remarked that the sunburn remedy had miraculously cured his eczema. From that chance remark *Dr. Bunting's Sunburn Remedy* became *Noxzema.*

The Internet offers an unparalleled sprawl of knowledge at a few keystrokes, but can't offer the same kind of serendipity that can come from poking around the shelves of a public library or used-book shop, or sorting through a box of discards at a neighborhood lawn sale. The purpose is not to research a topic to death or to make it an end in itself, much less to self-defeatingly smother the imagination. It's to get one's mind around the problem and prepare the ground for what will follow.

Namers, after finishing their preparation by drawing on such sources and methods, accumulate more facts than they can ever hope to use. This overload of facts doesn't hypnotize successful namers, however. Instead, they move into the second stage, incubation, and let those facts seep into the subconscious, using dowser's wands to find wellsprings. The wands they use include journals and files of newspaper and magazine clippings, computer files of random jottings, and scrapbooks. Unsystematic, scattershot, seemingly irrelevant to the task at hand, they are the unacknowledged tools of the trade.

Equally important is the mental state in which ideas incubate, which may mean getting comfortable, unpressured by office demands. Long accused of indolence, writers, composers, and painters are always on the job, apparently oblivious yet instinctively watchful for the topics and techniques that will work for them. Any number of innovations and discoveries have emerged from apparent idling. The ideal creative attitude is the seemingly contradictory one of relaxed attentiveness. This distracted but ultimately rewarding medium in which ideas can grow may include something as simple as sitting in a favorite chair, reflecting while petting a cat on your lap, one ear to classical music on the CD player, or just fooling around with items strewn across a desk or tabletop. Pleasurable rote behavior like walking the dog or taking a shower releases some people's minds; others may be stimulated by strolling through a museum or a junkyard. Reflective and calming hobbies such as fishing, sewing, or hiking can free new thoughts; for others, helpful (and creative) endorphins can be unleashed by jogging or working out at a gym. Whatever the environment, it has to be one that says it's acceptable to take chances. But activities like going into a coma-like trance or taking up Greco-Roman wrestling are not meant to be ends in themselves.

After sufficient incubation time, names may appear intuitively, or new connections may be drawn out in some more systematic way. The namers may work separately or as part of a group, but the objective is always to generate as many different names as possible. Computers that mate words and word-elements will spew out lists of possibilities almost without end, and the more possibilities, the better. Nine out of any ten names generated by any method or means fail to get through an availability screening—they've already been claimed by someone else.   .

In the brainstorming phase, there is no such thing as a bad idea. It is right-brain time. (The left brain will get its turn later.) For the adventurous namer, any way to get around predictable thinking or linearity is welcome. The serendipities of randomness can occur by even so simple a method as opening a dictionary to a random page and picking a random word. The mind is sure to make a connection, however slight, creating a potential metaphor. The name of a favorite sports team, the title of the most recent movie they enjoyed, the ingredients for a birthday cake—almost anything, if properly dwelled on, can trigger associations. Namers open their minds to things that have nothing to do with the problem they're working on. They compile lists of unlikely objects, ideas, and people, mixing and matching them. They force connections by imagining what Madonna, Beetle Bailey, or the Pope would call a company or product.

Unexpected combinations of language can create memorable names. They engage the brain on several levels because they were surprising, meaningful, and playful—all at the same time. The educational toy store *Zany Brainy* is a juxtaposition (and a rhyme) one wouldn't expect. Stretching language, and the concepts behind words, can be done through palindromes (a sentence spelled the same forward and backward), acrostics (lines whose initial letters spell out a word or statement), or anagrams (words based on the same set of letters).

A single common word may in turn yield a new name when juxtaposed with another. When George Lucas named his special effects factory *Industrial Light & Magic*, he created something resonant by uniting "industrial" and "magic." Another Hollywood example is the studio name *DreamWorks*, merging the dated utilitarian term for "factory" with images of fantasy and reverie. Several decades ago someone named a computer company *Thinking Machines Corp.*, oxymoronically implying that machines could think. The name was ahead of its time, as was *Soft Logic.* Logic was supposed to be hard and specific, at least until the advent of the useful and versatile concept of fuzzy logic. The creation of these word collisions meant that namers were in the business of coining idioms.

Because stand-alone words, and even synthetically bridged compounds, are soon depleted, a dictionary-load of idioms creates escape clauses from literality. The deodorant *No Sweat* works on several levels, as does the makeup aspirationally called *Cover Girl. Smart Money* magazine was presumably smarter than *Money* magazine. A metaphor was adapted for the name *Close-Up*—the toothpaste that had mouthwash in its formula.

An ordinary word might become the keystone for a category. A category could emerge from the self-definitions of a product or company. A product that needed a name that suggested power, speed, and aggressiveness could yield a list of birds of prey, such as *Harrier* (the jump-jet), *Falcon*, and *Tercel* (the cars). A company that wanted to introduce a new sauce with "Mediterranean-style" seasonings might evoke the characteristics, images, or attitudes found in a list of islands in the Mediterranean. A mythical island accounted for the name of the *Atlantis* on Paradise Island in the Bahamas. In Las Vegas, Steve Wynn created *Bellagio* ("beautiful lake" in Italian), whose namesake was on the shore of Lake Como in Italy. Back in the United States, how might a chain of Italian restaurants create its name? By conjuring a list of "things Italian"—no doubt how *Maggiano's Little Italy*, the *Macaroni Grill, Olive Garden*, and *Spaghetti Factory* got their names. Collectively, those four chains operate nearly 650 restaurants.

The company's self-definition may already be embodied in a theme line, tag line, or positioning statement, as in, say, an instant coffee that tasted and smelled like real ground roast: *Taster's Choice.* A new bath soap had so many oils and softeners that it left the skin silky soft to the touch: *Caress.* A chain of Mexican restaurants had a spicy range of dishes: *The Whole Enchilada.* Leapfrogging linguistic categories is another way to expand the branding mind. The abstract *Amplify* was a tactile, volume-enhancing hair care product. *Hefty* was no longer just an adjective but a noun—a trash bag. *Meridian* was a bank, not a circle of longitude. The interjection *Off!* was an insect repellent, a *Visa* was a credit card. Sometimes the key was to focus on what was being done to or with a product. The name for Campbell's  *Chunky* came as an answer to the question "What would happen if you ate soup with a fork?" There'd have to be chunks in it.

Role-playing namers can imagine themselves as any number of people, real or fictitious. Confronted with having to name a new detergent, what would Albert Einstein, George W. Bush, Oprah Winfrey, or Sherlock Holmes come up with? The namer's sister or brother or significant other? All sorts of other combinations and substitutions are possible. If a company were a Renaissance portrait, what would it look like? If the London *Daily Mirror* wrote a front-page headline about it, what would it say? What title would John Grisham give this product if he wrote a book about it?

Visualization—"imagineering" as those masters of branding, Disney, have it—is an intrinsic part of such imaginative projections. Even the soberest of scientists have used it as part of their method. Dr. Jonas Salk, developer of the Salk polio vaccine, said that "When I became a scientist I would picture myself as a virus or cancer cell and try to imagine what it would be like to be either."

Images are inevitably linked to emotions. The naming firm Landor Associates used what it called "mood boards" to elicit what feelings the brand sought to evoke, flashing images to their clients that were tied to descriptive words, then narrowing them down. What *kind* of strength was desired—hurricane strength? Chain-link fence strength? Namers asked important questions. What could visually represent a company or product? An animal? A color? An ocean? A mountain? Visual concepts led to a name.

A marketer was working on the name for a new sore throat medicine in a spray bottle. For the spray to hit its target the mouth had to be opened fairly wide. This action created the image of a lion tamer sticking his head inside the lion's mouth. The name—*Throat Tamer*—and the concept of soothing the "roar" of sore throat pain weren't far behind. Kollmorgen Corp. introduced a very thin DC motor for certain industrial applications. Its flatness was its advantage. The product's name and essential image? *The Pancake.* Thinking about how a product is used can lead to an image. An expensive pair of running shoes helps to make the wearer faster and more agile. What suggests fast and agile? *Reebok* is the name of a fleet-footed African gazelle, and *Puma* is the Spanish word for a big wildcat. Namers imagine a product in a customer's hands actually being used. A marketer of a new portable dictating machine realized that many people like to dictate on their way to and from work. Voilà! *The Commuter.*

Going against the grain is another effective naming strategy. If everyone else has high-tech names, good namers think low-tech. If the other names seem masculine, they try feminine. A hospital in Arkansas found that its competitors all had serious and straightforward names for their maternity centers—*The Maternity Center* or *The Birthing Center*—so they called theirs *Stork & Company.* Many popular cars have three-syllable names, all ending with the letter "a": *Achieva, Aurora, Celica, Corolla, Cressida, Integra, Maxima* (but not yet *Et Cetera*).

This begs for a contrarian name. *Roadkill* likely wouldn't have done, but it might have been a starting point. Being contrarian can be something as elementary as reversing a conventional word order. The holding company for *Pathmark* supermarkets could have called itself *General Supermarkets*

Corp. Instead, it became *Supermarkets General.* The same tactic served the *Corporation for Public Broadcasting.*

Sometimes the old is new, capitalizing on a legacy. When the American Hospital Association toyed with a proposal to change its name in order to be more inclusive of its membership, it polled the 300 people who served on their regional policy boards and found that 45 percent preferred to stay with the old name; another 45 percent favored including another term with "hospital."

Sometimes naming reflects more common sense than courage. Anheuser-Busch decided to spin off the large commercial baking company, Campbell Taggart, that it had acquired in 1982 and sought a more expressive name for the company. Management selected one of their regional bread **WELLS** brands, redesigned it, and elevated it to the corporate name: **FARGO** *Earthgrains Company.* When Wells Fargo Bank merged with a larger bank generically named *American Trust Bank,* the smaller, more resonant name—and the goodwill that went with it—prevailed.

Imitation is the sincerest form of flattery. It's axiomatic in business that the freshest, most nonlinear, and (of course) most successful ideas will motivate a horde of imitators. Among brand names, this will become obvious when we look at the good and the bad, the beautiful, and the ugly.

6

GIVING A GOOD NAME

Nobody really knows whether a brand will succeed or fail until it reaches the market. There are just too many contingencies. Marketers do know, however, that a good brand name aids and abets a brand or, at a minimum, doesn't get in the way, and there are significant predictors of how brand names will fare. At the crucial start of the marketing process—despite a wide variety of naming styles—there's a consensus, even an aesthetic, as to what constitutes a good name.

Any name, no matter how good, can be bad in the wrong time or place. Even a great name cannot rescue a bad concept. *Lean Cuisine* is a dandy name for a line of frozen entrees. But it only works because consumers were ready for low-calorie gourmet dining. The Edsel was the biggest marketing debacle in automotive history. The car was expensive, plagued by manufacturing defects, and as someone said, it had an ugly front grille that "looked like an Oldsmobile sucking on a lemon." That managers ignored focus groups that said that *Edsel* sounded like "pretzel" was just one more marketing error—even a great name wouldn't have saved that car. (It did have a silver lining, however, in that Ford realized the car market was becoming segmented into lifestyles, not income groups, and this awareness ultimately led to the hugely successful Mustang.) Online delivery services failed because the idea that it somehow made economic sense to dispatch, say, thousands of bags of groceries (or even, in the case of Kozmo.com, single candy bars!) to hundreds of householders rather than make the hundreds of householders come to one store, was a wrong one. All the razzmatazz in the world could not save the XFL, a pro football league mounted by the World Wrestling Federation and the National Broadcasting Company. In March 2001, an XFL game received the lowest rating ever for a prime-time network show. Neither the name, nor the sex appeal, could substitute for bad football. The marketing consultant Jack Trout, author of *Positioning*, notes that the trick "is to be first with a good idea, not a dumb idea. *Frosty Paws* was the first ice cream for dogs. They claimed, 'It's not ice cream, but your dog will think it is.' Now how much does my dog know about ice cream? Not much."

A good name shows that a company knows what it's doing and has a firm and focused fix on what it's offering to the public. For every good name or product there's a bad name; in fact, there are many bad names. *Microsoft* is clumsy, but *Windows* is inspired. Sometimes products with bad names like *Microsoft* arrive with such exquisite timing, or their management is so able, that they triumph in the marketplace. As Trout observes, "The first company into the mind with a new product or service is going to become famous. Whether the name is Lindbergh or Smith or Rumpelstiltskin."  That had been true of Kodak, Xerox, and Coca-Cola. The rewards of first entry guaranteed that Coke had nothing to fear from the secondary connotations of its name: a residue of coal burned in the absence of air or a quick way of saying cocaine. A difficult-sounding name may be meaningful and successful in a smaller, more discerning market. *Byrrh* and *Noilly Prat* are hardly common coin, but they register with drinkers of apéritifs. *The Beatles* and *The Rolling Stones* were corny and clichéd names, but the bands and their brands did rather well.

However superlative the name, it matters not if it can't be legally registered as a trademark. (This, as we'll see in Chapter 15, is no sure thing.) But in this chapter let us avoid such unpleasant subjects—the Hall of Shame is always next door to the Hall of Fame. We will accentuate the positive.

A good name essentially answers a resounding "Yes!" to the following questions about new products:

- Is a specific need fulfilled?
- Is it really an improvement over what already exists?
- Is it easier to use than what already exists?
- Is it safer than what already exists?
- Is there a competitive point of difference?

A good name is also the answer to one last question: "How will you bring your idea to life?" In making a brand name or trade name thrive, no single good element of a product exists in isolation. Overlapping, interweaving, they all work together. What all the elements share is an ability to make the customer recall the name.

A good name delivers an idea, concept, or benefit. It sets up a communications premise, linking the name directly to what's variously called a theme line, a selling proposition, or a marketing platform, and is the start of the positioning process. For example: "Raise your arm if you're SURE" for a deodorant.

Toilet bowl cleaners make for an interesting case study. *Ty-D-Bol* is an example of an older naming practice of using hyphens, and not just for toilet bowl cleaners. With its awkward capitalization and hyphenation, the name did create a sense of history, adding an element of playfulness. The benefit was present, too: a tidy bowl. *Vanish* "fights stains," and if the consumer was worried about dropping nasty chemicals in the bowl there was *Chem-free* (where "technology replaces chemistry"). *2000 Flushes* is what you'll get, in case anybody's counting. There was a different number in *Duette*, a two-in-one bowl cleaner and air freshener. *Lysol Toilet Bowl Cleaner* extends a product-family name for cleaners into this corner of the bathroom. (For *Toilet Duck*, please see the next chapter, "Getting a Bad Name.")

Most great brands have good names, a union of concept and verbal construction. *Cottonelle* is not just cotton, it is cottony and soft. *Dial* is round-the-clock protection. The idea is for the name to say it all. A good example was the idea of one John K. Hogg of Frederick, Maryland, a soap manufacturer. On October 25, 1870, Hogg was the proud registrant of U.S. Trademark No. 9 for *Star Soap*. On the soap's wrapper, he wrote in his application, a star symbol was to be "printed, stamped or impressed upon the outside of each piece of soap." Hogg had got himself a nice blend of naming and marketing: a simple, one-syllable name; a highly meaningful word to convey both his aspirations and the quality of his product; and a powerful physical symbol built into the name.

More than a century later, *Star Soap* was an object lesson for the Logitech company. After the disappointing performance of the company' new scanner, the *Scanner 2000*, Logitech chose a more memorable name, *ScanMan*, which created an emotional link between the product and the user. In eighteen months, sales of the scanner more than doubled, without any extra advertising.

Even blended names such as *Portakabin* (portable offices), *CarryFast* (a road haulage company), and *Northstar* (an aircraft engine) relay a specific message to the customer. The company has greater control over the message it sends than with a single, ordinary word (such as *Star* or *Dial*), and the consumer still has a basis from which to decipher the message. Other good examples of names that blend control and comprehension are *Windex* for window cleaning, *Vaseline Intensive Care* for skin lotion, and *Head & Shoulders* shampoo. Newly minted neologisms such as *Humana, Compaq,* and *Acura* convey meaningful concepts to the consumer without too much effort.

Although odd-looking and odder-sounding names were highly visible on the Internet—*Yahoo!, E*Trade, PSINet*—an analysis of the infoscape reveals many traditional monikers. On the Internet, a longer name, if meaningful and relevant, was often preferable to a marginally shorter, but more obscure name. Founded in 1998, the Baltimore-based *www.TeknoSurf.com,* a banner-ad serving and tracking company, found people couldn't get its spelling right. They bought the *www.Advertising.com* domain name and relaunched in 2000. If the exact dot-com was unavailable for a new name, it could be combined with a second, pertinent relevant word or word-element to gain legal dot-com status, a better choice than a less appealing coinage alone. Entirely shunnable were vague generic or near-generic names.

A good name is straightforwardly appealing, makes itself easily understood, and feels comfortable right away. Joy is an emotionally positive word, and *Opium* in the context of perfumes suggests dreaminess, not a stupor. A name by itself is not a legal contractual obligation, but it is a promise of sorts—sometimes literally so. *Premio* is an Italian sausage brand from the former Garden State Sausage Co. of New Jersey. Rather than opt for "Garden State" (New Jersey's state nickname), which suggested vegetable and farm stands, not sausage, Rivkin & Associates came up with *Premio*, an Italian and Spanish word for "prize" or "reward," with associations in English with "premium." *NutraSweet* could be paraphrased as "sweet nutrition." Another Rivkin-created name, *Second Nature*, identified the renewable energy program for Alliant Energy, which gave consumers the choice of getting all or part of their energy from wind turbines and biomass (methane gas from decomposing landfills), playing on the idea of "something done without any special effort, as if by a natural instinct." A perfume was named *Passion*, an arthritis drug *Enablex*, a cleaner *Soft Scrub*. The name *Harlem Savings Bank of New York* was holding the bank back from expanding, both beyond Harlem and outside of its existing customer base. A new name, *Apple Bank*, severed the old associations with Harlem and set up wholesome, friendly associations with the city's nickname, "The Big Apple."

A good name conveys something real and specific about a company, product, or service. Meaningful brand names *(Slender* versus *Metrecal, DieHard* versus *Delco, Budget* versus *Avis,* and *Sprint* versus *MCI)* have an innate memory advantage. As Adrian Room points out, "word names" are "on the whole more satisfactory, because meaningful, than 'name names' or 'arbitrary names.' They offer much greater scope for inventiveness, wittiness, originality, humor, and 'pointedness' than do names derived from the name of a person or place." Such names track the nature of a business and its target audience: *Champion* sporting goods, *Krispy Kreme* doughnuts. The U.S. inventor Maurice Kanbar, who created Quad Cinema (the  first multiplex) and Skyy Vodka, noted in his book *Secrets from an Inventor's Notebook,* "Was *Dirty Dancing* a successful movie because it was a great film? No. The title brought people into the theater. I doubt they'd have come out for the same film if it were called *Weekend in the Catskills.*" Kanbar observed that "if I had a great name for a product, I'd build a business around the name." He tells the story of how, in 1965, he got a patent for a flat film dental floss that slid between teeth easily and comfortably. He tried to sell it to Johnson & Johnson and Colgate, but found no takers. "I thought about manufacturing and selling it myself, but I couldn't come up with a snappy name—I kept calling it something clunky like Film Floss." Many years later he saw a flat film floss on the market called *Glide*. Ruefully, he wished he'd thought of it. Even *Slide* would have done.

There's a common thread here of concreteness: *Craftsman* (tools), *Check-Up* (toothpaste), *Alley Cat* (cat food), and *Coin* (financial

CRAFTSMAN services) say not only something specific about their lines of business, they have tangible sensory referents. *CoolBrands International*, based in Markham, Ontario, is a maker and distributor of Eskimo Pies, and other products found in corner-store freezers and coolers. Its name blends hipness with literalness. Its brands are cool.

Kim R. Robertson, a professor at Trinity University in Texas, has extensively studied brand names as a marketing tool. He points out that concrete nouns with tangible, visual referents work better than abstract nouns: *"Dove, Mustang, Rabbit, and Apple* should inherently be more easily learned and/or retrieved from memory than abstract nouns such as *Pledge, Tempo, Ban,* or *Bold."* He cites studies that show how high-imagery names across a variety of product categories consistently outscore low-imagery ones. One hypothesis is that there's a distinct memory system for storage of visual images (separate from a memory system for storage of lexical or verbal information). This suggests, Robertson says, that a concrete name *(Mustang, Cougar)* would generate both verbal and visual memory codes but an abstraction *(Triumph, Tempo)* would fall short in generating a visual code. "Memory for pictures is superior to memory for words."

Specificity runs the risk that customers will take a name too literally. But customers are not *that* obtuse. They did not suppose that a real-estate agent from the franchise *Century 21* wouldn't sell a house until the dawn of the twenty-first century, that the Revlon deodorant name *No Sweat* meant they absolutely, positively wouldn't sweat, or that a car from *Rent-A-Wreck* was really a wreck.

A good name uniquely distinguishes a company or service from its competition. Products compete on price, quality, service, or performance, but long-term differentiation in these areas can be difficult. A brand name can be a unique distinction no competitor can match. In the telecom and Internet universes

 certain terms recur with such monotonous regularity—*net, link, pro, tech*—that the names became a blur. A smart company could reach outside this technobox and create a fresh, separable, valuable identity. Such was the case with Sun Microsystems' *Java. Virgin Atlantic Airways* shunned the stodgy names endemic in the airline industry. The first personal computer was the MITS Altair 8800 computer. Most people would guess it was Apple.

Sometimes, branders dilute the value of their most successful names by instituting a welter of sub-brands. Until wiser counsel prevailed, Procter &

Gamble had thirty-one versions of Head & Shoulders shampoo and fifty-two versions of Crest toothpaste. Chevrolet, once the quintessential family car, added so many models and types over decades that in the end *Chevrolet* could mean a "small, big, cheap, or expensive" "car, sports car, or truck." Naturally, each new sub-brand carried a different name, multiplying the confusion. Because of this, Ford replaced Chevrolet as the best-selling automaker. Similarly, Marlboro cigarettes in a plain red-and-white pack lost its cowboy touch when it began to produce *Marlboro Lights, Marlboro Mediums, Marlboro Menthol*, and *Marlboro Ultra Lights*. The company later refocused, returning to its core image of the rugged Marlboro Man, who certainly didn't smoke menthols.

In the case of drug names, distinctiveness is literally vital. Most drug names have little to do with their chemical compounds or the diseases they treat. But patient safety, if nothing else, decrees that they look and sound as different as possible. A distinctive brand name can be effective even when a product is not directly targeted toward an end user but is a tool for firms that targeted other business users. LSI Logic chose the name *GigaBlaze* for their serial data transmission technology. In a market saturated with acronyms and numbers, GigaBlaze created vivid images of hot technology and blazing new trails in the users' minds. Whether the customer was a consumer or another business, a brand name could mimic the effect on the user, as in the name *PayPal*, an online payment service.

In the battery business, the technology shifted from zinc carbon to alkaline. Eveready, the leading brand in batteries, hoped to transfer its name to the new technology, but Duracell captured the alkaline category with its bright new name. By the time Eveready conceived a good brand name of its own *(The Energizer)*, Duracell had seized a commanding market share.

A good name is short, crisp, and concise. Several decades ago, the Harvard psychologist George Miller found that only seven pieces of information—like seven brands in a category, or seven digits in a phone number—could easily be held in short-term memory. This may be why consumers instinctively simplify names: *Chevrolet* becomes *Chevy*, a *Jaguar* becomes a *Jag*, *Coca-Cola* becomes *Coke*. Because we're constantly deluged with new information, we have limited attention spans. On first meeting a simple name, it's easy to "get it," the information settling more easily into our memory. *Advil* is retained better than *Ibuprofen*. Less is more, as *Aim, Ban, Bic, Bold, Off!, Raid*, and *Tide* attest. *Dr. Richardson's Croup and Pneumonia Cure Salve* was a sickly brand until it became *Vicks VapoRub*. Shorter names, like *Oxo* or *El Al*, are more visually balanced and symmetrical.

All things being equal, a short name is better. But just as important are the right vocabulary and register. The level of education and social status of the customer often dictate the most acceptable diction. Scholastic or scientific language might be right for a pharmaceutical product. Queen's English or the spoken language was right for most banking services. Grade-school vocabulary suits many consumer products.

Although acronyms are hard to create, and inherently less meaningful than actual or even coined names, they could capitalize on inherent double meanings, as in *VISTA* (*Volunteers In Service To America*), *MADD* (*Mothers Against Drunk Driving*), and *FAST LANE* (a bank's *Fully Automated Super Teller*). Coinages, too, can possess extra resonance. The computer services firm Unisys derived from the concept of "United Information Systems," though the more abbreviated UIS was wisely abandoned.

Simplicity makes a name easy to say, easy to spell, easy to read, easy to understand, easy to learn, and easy to order or believe in. Coined drug names, long enigmatic, have become simpler and memorable; for one thing, they pop up frequently on TV commercials, simplicity helps doctors remember them, and they yield themselves to word-of-mouth—proverbially the best advertising. From the business viewpoint, cleanness and clarity could also save massive amounts of money, a simple name change setting off a chain reaction of economies. This happened when *Federal Express* became *FedEx*. Some twenty years ago, the word "Federal" was considered an asset, and gave the fledgling company immediate equity, as an unofficial alternative to the U.S. Postal Service. But problems arose as the company grew. "Federal" came to be associated with being slow and bureaucratic. At five syllables, *Federal Express* was rather long. In Latin American countries, the name conjured unwelcome associations with the *federales*. In some parts of the world, people had trouble pronouncing the name.

The solution was obvious: *FedEx*. It was already in the minds and on the lips of customers. It was shorter, crisper, and clearer. It looked good. The design for the shortened name replaced the old 1970s typeface and removed a restrictive purple field around the logotype. The space in the logo between the *E* and the *x* formed an arrow, symbolizing speedy delivery. Company vehicles became moving billboards. *Federal Express* only allowed fifty-eight-inch letters on the side of a trailer. But the letters spelling out *FedEx* could be six feet tall. Airplane logos of it could now be read from across an entire airfield. Eliminating the big purple color field saved up to $1,000 in labor and materials on a single fifty-three-foot tractor trailer—and the company owned ten thousand tractor trailers. Aircraft paint jobs also cost less without purple covering half the jet. Without all the purple, aircraft surface temperatures dropped, lowering energy needed to cool the planes and reducing fuel costs per flight. All these savings came from just clipping off nine little letters.

Corporation

A good name pleases the ear in any language. Auditory memory is more powerful than visual memory, and the most unlikely people can recite the lyrics to thousands of songs. The sound of a name is crucial.

Some letters can sound or seem light or heavy, masculine or feminine, slow or fast, strong or weak, small or large. As we shall see in Chapter 10, plosives—phonemes like B, P, K, C, and T—are powerful, and many brand names begin with them. *Bic, Coca-Cola, Kellogg's, Pontiac, Kool-Aid,* and *Cadillac* benefit from initial and terminal plosives. *Prozac* and *Viagra* combine power and speed. Letters like X or Z are speedy fricatives—no wonder that so many drug names contain them. This is true in English. A globally circulated brand name or trade name must also contend with what is true in other languages. To the English-speaker some Japanese brand names for cars seem irresistibly funny: the Mazda *Secret Hideout;* the Suzuki *Van Van* (which wasn't a van); the Mazda *Bongo Frendi;* the Suzuki *Afternoon Tea;* and the Mitsubishi *Mini Active Urban Sandal,* but they weren't necessarily funny to the Southeast Asians. As the British linguist Tony Thorne said, the mere fact that the names were English and still pronounceable made them trendy.

We'll analyze phonetic considerations later. For now, let's consider *Viagra.* The name combines "vigor" with "Niagara" (Falls) and thus suggests vitality, strength, and natural force. In French it connotes life (*vie*) and the senses of robustness (*gras* as in *Mardi Gras*) or large (*grand*); in English, German, Spanish, Portuguese, and Russian the final four letters can suggest the *agri-* of agriculture, with images of flourishing and growth; it suggests "Grand Street" (*via grande*); in Spanish and Portuguese it hints at travel (*viajar*) and large (*grande*). It has no negative connotations in the top ten languages of business.

At this point, it's worth recalling one of the most unlikely stories in all of word history, which the lexicographer Allen Walker Read unraveled. In March 1839 in Boston, Massachusetts, "O.K." turned up in a newspaper, an abbreviation for the humorous respelling "oll korrect"—the joke was that neither *o* nor *k* was correct. Such orthographic manglings, especially in imitation-dialect form, were a staple of humor at the time. The expression was reinforced in President Martin Van Buren's reelection campaign of 1840, as Van Buren was born in Kinderhook, New York, and was known as "Old Kinderhook." Newspapers began to say, satirically or not, that Van Buren would make "all things O.K." From such obscure and tangled beginnings, "OK" has become the most recognized word in the world. Even if a native speaker in the known universe understands no other word of English, he or she will instantly comprehend "OK." The brand name that is its nearest rival for universal linguistic recognition closely resembles it in sound and appearance:

Coke.

OK?

A good name bundles associations and is rich in implications. When two Norwegian steamship companies—*Bergen Line* and *Nordenfjedske*—merged, they took the name *Royal Viking Line* despite the loathing of management, who did not want to be reminded of their barbarous ancestors. However, research showed that one large segment of the cruise-ship market—wealthy widows—thought that the name and the image it conveyed was terrific. The widows plainly imagined bronzed stalwart Norsemen piloting them safely across the cresting waves. Besides, the Vikings were royal. The raping, pillaging Vikings had been rehabilitated.

If an originally highly negative word can turn out to have largely positive connotations, the same is even more the case for one that was positive to begin with, as we saw earlier in the case of Lucent Technologies. By the late 1990s, with so many Internet companies heading south—in stock market jargon this was *not* a good thing—trade names abruptly veered away from technobabble and became both more semantically and emotively relevant. The new, or at least newly named, companies had to cope with pandemic change and reform their naming solutions. Hybridized names involving *.net* and *.com* fell by the wayside as companies graduated from engineering-driven venture capitalism to the challenges of marketing. As companies got bigger and their markets expanded, it became imperative that their fame would be spread less by personal experience and more by the creation of an image or sound bite. *Covad Communications* was thinking "copper value-added" for their business, which offered high-speed data services over conventional phone lines. Customers may not have got its connection, but the name still worked because it was short and suggested speed. The seemingly tautological *Electric Lightwave* suggested fiber optics, and "electric" offered a familiar and comfortable word that, in combination, did not imply obsolescence. Most important, it conveyed movement and energy.

The collapse of *.net*, at least for brand names that were not part of a World Wide Web address, was confirmed in early 2003, when Microsoft announced that they were dropping the *.Net* label from their servers, replacing the *.Net Enterprise Server* name with the unsurprising *Windows Server System.* By creating the new, or very old, naming convention for all its server products, Microsoft hoped to clarify what the *.Net* name meant. This was as much as admitting that only software developers, certainly not the IT (Information Technology) directors who were its customers, understood it at all.

For new drug names, the trend was toward more evocative morphemes, as in *Celebrex,* a name that linked celebration with freedom from pain. Older, scientifically based names for drugs like *Vasomax, Nembutal,* and *Arthrotec* (which treated erectile dysfunction, insomnia, and arthritis, respectively) gave way to new medicines for those conditions called *Viagra, Sonata,* and *Enbrel.* Patients were more interested in the drugs' effects than in their mechanisms. Solemn pharmaceutical firms sometimes betrayed a sense of humor. After years of study, researchers discovered the **VIAGRA** secrets of the anticoagulants in vampire bat saliva, pointing the way toward a drug that prevents blood clotting. The French company Rhone-Poulenc applied for a patent in at least eighty countries. The drug's code name was *Draculin.*

A good name can build on a perceived weakness as well as strength, or, *You've got to know when to hold'em, know when to fold'em.* In 1985, Colgate-Palmolive bought half of the Hawley & Hazel Co. in Hong Kong, marketer of the best-selling toothpastes in several Asian countries. One of them was named *Darkie,* with a package featuring an image of a grinning black-faced minstrel. (There were actually historical reasons for this politically incorrect laughingstock of the toothpaste world. The minstrel had became part of the design in the 1920s when the company's then-CEO saw the American singer Al Jolson ["Swannee, how I love ya, Swannee"] and thought his big toothy smile would make a wonderful logo.) After the purchase, Colgate-Palmolive was besieged with complaints about the toothpaste's insensitive name and packaging. Religious groups decried the name, and shareholders mounted petitions. *Darkie* obviously had to go, but a totally new name and packaging would have wiped out an identity recognized by customers in Hong Kong, Malaysia, Singapore, Taiwan, and Thailand. The company responded intelligently. In 1989 it renamed the toothpaste *Darlie* and changed the logo to a portrait of a man of ambiguous race wearing a top hat, tuxedo, and bow tie.

In the United Kingdom, the name *Bass* is synonymous with beer, representing more than two hundred years of tradition. But brewing only represented a fifth of the beer-maker's business. When the company sold its brewing interests, it renamed itself to account for the rest of the business—hotels, restaurants, and pubs—considering more than ten thousand possible candidates. *Six Continents*, suggesting a world of hospitality, came by way of an employee competition, though an agency checked the name for all the cultures and languages in which it was to do duty. After more than £300,000, a year of deliberation, and the approval of a special general meeting for shareholders, *Six Continents* became a fact. Soon the company became known popularly as *Six-C.*

Sometimes the answer to a naming dilemma is to do nothing, or even to backtrack. The engineers who come up with a sensational new technology want a correspondingly sensational name for it. But if the new product doesn't have a promotional budget to fully support it, it's better to go with an existing brand or sub-brand, or apply a purely descriptive name. The modem maker U.S. Robotics became part of 3Com when the network equipment maker acquired it. When 3Com spun off its modem business, the new enterprise revived the name U.S. Robotics.

Some names beg to be changed. In the United Kingdom, a defense conglomerate bore the 100-year-old name *General Electric Company Plc*. This GEC had nothing to do with the famous *General Electric* in the United States, and never did, in spite of the fact that people assumed it was the British unit of GE. The British GEC wanted to reinvent themselves as a technology company and was preparing to be listed on NASDAQ. So early in 2000, General Electric Company Plc was renamed *Marconi*, in honor of Guglielmo Marconi, the Italian pioneer of radio transmission who founded one of GEC's predecessor companies.

Understandably, in view of the AIDS epidemic, the American Institute of Decision Sciences, a professional group widely known by its acronym *AIDS*, changed its name to the *Decision Sciences Institute*. A California firm that had been known as *AIDS Ambulance Service* (for *Attitude, Integrity, Dependability* and *Service*) found that its drivers were harassed by people who assumed the vehicles were for AIDS victims only. As well, at least one injured man refused to get into their ambulance. They changed their name to *AME*. The diet-aid appetite-suppression candy Ayds, even with the slightly different spelling, first changed its name to *Diet Ayds* and then disappeared completely. *Sars*, a sarsaparilla soft drink in Taiwan, suffered from association with SARS (Severe Acute Respiratory Syndrome). A spokesperson denied that the trademark owner, the Hey Song Company, would change the name, saying "most people know you won't get SARS simply by drinking Sars."

A bad name could sometimes be a good thing. Smucker's, the makers of jam and jellies—chose not to change its name. In fact, it capitalized on it, playfully and candidly proclaiming, "With a name like *Smucker's*, it's got to be good." Price-Pfister turned its tongue  twister into a memory device, "The pfabulous pfaucet with the pfunny name," and even put the line on the products' hangtags at retailers. Right from the start, the Czech car-maker Skoda overcame the handicap that *Skoda* in Czech means "pity" or "shame," as in "it's a pity, it's a shame." And Orville Redenbacher's homespun name did no harm to his *Orville Redenbacher Gourmet Popping Corn*.

Origins of a different nature became a problem when Philip Morris Companies announced that it would change its corporate name to the *Altria Group*. It was assailed both by antismoking forces, who called it a cheap trick to erect a firewall between its cigarettes and its Kraft Foods and Miller beverage businesses, and by marketing critics, who lambasted the name as weak, uninspired, and faux-Latinate. The media sniped that consultants have been trying to pass off some version of the Latin word *altus* ("high") for years. Hilariously, in view of the companies' cigarettes, beer, and Kraft Dinner, Latin scholars further found that the name suggested *altrix* ("wet nurse"). Philanthropists groused that Philip Morris was trying to hook up with "altruism" via the new name. Then there was the relatively tiny Altria Healthcare Corp. in Birmingham, Alabama, outraged that a big tobacco and alcohol company was adopting an identical name.

The irony was that Philip Morris, in trying to make a naming break from tobacco, the product that had cost it billions in government settlements and civil lawsuits, had even prepared to sacrifice its cherished MO stock-market symbol to achieve this break, but ran smack into a public relations wall. In an interview with the *Naming Newsletter*, Fraser Seitel, the author of *The Practice of Public Relations*, noted that the Philip Morris image was tarnished. "Burnished in the cranium of the public is the gaggle of tobacco company CEOs, right hands raised before Congress, testifying that they had no idea their products caused cancer," he said. "Wrong. They knew. They lied. They were all drummed out. But the damage, it was done. And the industry and its largest manufacturer have been paying the media price ever since."

Seitel observed that "Over time, as long as Philip Morris acts responsibly and truthfully relative to its cigarette business—the attention to tobacco companies generally will dissipate. People will accept that smoking is harmful to you, manufacturers have been fined severely for past indiscretions, and people are free to choose. All of this will be quite separate from the new name." Philip Morris did err in ignoring, or not realizing, that a healthcare company had the same name. But whatever the name, Philip Morris would be a target for abuse. In Seitel's view, the company should stay the course with its new name. Which is what it did.

A good name fits into a family and takes account of the past and future. The names *International Harvester* and *General Motors* may seem dull, but over many decades they have kept pace as their businesses and products evolved. The same flexibility must apply to companies that have a multitude of products. An extra complication is that new trade names sometimes have to take account of the genealogy of predecessor companies. Other companies doggedly stick with names that are at best nondescript. *ICG Netcom* was a tip of the corporate hat to the original name, *IntelCom Communications Group*. When ICG bought *Netcom On-Line Communication Services*, it combined its initials and the Netcom name for marketing purposes.

A company must decide how a new name fits into a long-term strategy. As Randall S. Rozin, Global Brand Manager for Dow Corning Corp., notes, a company should consider whether the name should be "something highly descriptive to play along a narrow front (*Silastic*, for silicone rubber), or a more generic or coined name to allow for brand expansion across categories (*Virgin*)." Roughly, there are four types of naming systems for companies and their products, no one necessarily better than the other. The Procter & Gamble approach puts the brand name front and center (*Ariel, Camay, Folgers, Pampers*) and keeps the trade name buried. Each brand has its own team, budget, and separate identity. Another example is *DuPont*, which can mean anything from herbicides to antifreeze, and which creates specific brand names like *Cordura* and *StainMaster*. Individual brands may even compete in same category.

The megabrand or "family name" approach spirals a family of products around a core concept. With Lysol, the concept might be "serious cleaning." Thus, the megabrand name equally functions as the trade name, as in *Lysol Toilet Bowl Cleaner*. The megabrand name competes in the marketplace against specialized brand names, for example, *Ty-D-Bol*. Other examples: Intuit extended its *Quicken* software name to become the name for a line of related products; and Intel's *Pentium* was the brand name for a range of computer chip performance levels. In 2002, the same thinking lay behind Citigroup's attempt to unify its brand by combining its Salomon Smith Barney investment banking unit with the Citibank corporate bank to produce *Citigroup Corporate and Investment Bank*. *CitiCapital* was the new brand for the equipment finance business; *Citigroup Private Bank* replaced *Citibank Private Bank* for the asset management and private banking group, *Citigroup Asset Management*; *Citifunds* became the main international fund family brand; and *Citigroup Venture Capital* replaced *Citicorp Venture Capital*. *Travelers* was the brand name for the North American insurance franchise, but internationally, it became *CitiInsurance*.

Similarly, at least in form, the "partnership" or "hybrid" approach blends the trade name with individual brand names, as in the Kensington products for computers and workstations. Kensington offers hundreds of different products, each of which gives equal billing to the Kensington name and individual product names, which in turn may range from trademarks to generic descriptions like the *Kensington Turbo Mouse* (trademarked) input device to the *Kensington Slim Screen Premium Anti-Glare/Anti-Radiation Screen Filter* (non-trademarked).

Finally, and least sexily, there's the "company is the brand" approach. For General Electric, *GE* is the brand name, often followed by a descriptive word or two and a model number: GE Model WWA8600G might stand for GE Heavy Duty Extra Large Capacity washing machine. Individual brand names like *Carry-Cool* (a line of portable air conditioners) or *MPI* (handheld two-way radios) could appear, but they played catch-up to the identity and presentation of the trade name.

What Ford did with the name of its flagship minivan illustrated the tensions between past and future when it dropped *Windstar* and adopted *Freestar*. Ford's $600 million 2003 redesign of the Windstar essentially created a new minivan with a larger engine, revamped third-row seating, all-new cabin and instrument panels, side curtain airbags, and hundreds of other new parts. Ford dealers urged the automaker to change the name as a way to express how much the vehicle had changed. The Windstar had an outstanding safety record and outsold its nearest rival, the Honda Odyssey, so there was some risk in changing the name. But an "F" theme figured in the names of Ford models in the past, such as the *Fairlane, Falcon, Fiesta,* and *Focus.* The *Freestar* followed tradition and joined the *Freestyle* SUV, the *Five Hundred* sedan, and the luxuriously redesigned *F-150* pickup truck.

A good brand name is good branding. A name is only one part of the complex process of branding (although we would say it's the most important). In marketing jargon, branding is a matter of "creating a franchise" and "owning a category." One essential characteristic of a good name is a chameleon-like ability to adapt itself to the theme a company is hoping to establish, as in the car rental firm Hertz's slogan, "There's Hertz and not exactly."

Jack Trout has pointed out that many great brand names achieved their dominance through establishing an identity and sticking with it. "McDonald's became the first high-speed hamburger," he told Steve Rivkin. "Coke can lay claim to being the 'real thing' because it was indeed the founder of colas. The first champagne, *Dom Perignon,* became the most recognized name in champagnes." Trout notes, "The most powerful brands tend to own a word in the mind. *Crest* owns 'cavities.' Thirty-five years of 'Look ma, no cavities.'" With this example in mind, it is easy to see that the tanklike *Volvo* owns "safety," *Domino's* pizza owns two words, "home delivery," and *Prego* pasta sauce owns "thick."

The ultimate in branding occurs when a name, image, and delivery system fuse into a seamless unity. Such was the case with *L'eggs* hosiery. The name was short, clear, easy to remember, humorous, and packed in a punning double meaning. The hosiery came in transparent plastic egg-shaped containers, was kept in stock like farm-fresh Extra Large, and was often sold at supermarket checkouts. Hanes, its manufacturer, had not laid an egg.

7

GETTING A BAD NAME

A venerable marketing joke tells of two leather-skinned Texans who find them-selves side by side in a Houston bar. They begin to talk and learn they both own cattle ranches.

"So what's the name of your ranch?" the first rancher asks.

"The Circle K," the second says. "What about yours?"

"Mine's the Lazy L Bar T Q Sleepy C Triangle D."

"Jeez, you must have a ton of cattle!" the second says. "About how many head do you have?"

The first winces. "To tell you the truth, not that many. Most of 'em don't survive the branding."

If your name doesn't fulfill any of the responsibilities of a good brand name (as set out in the previous chapter), you probably have a bad brand name. A bad brand name can become a howler in English (or in any other language). It can build a wall of sales resistance. The most penetrating critiques of brand names do not come from consumers, or even from the Vancouver-based magazine, *Adbusters*, which spoofs ads and creates inventive campaigns against the adver-tising industry. For true pungent criticism, one must look to the professional brand namers themselves, a few of whom in 2002 inaugurated an annual award called the Shinolas, given to the year's worst new brand name. The Shinolas take their name from a former brand for shoe polish and the World War II expres-sion among American servicemen, "You don't know shit from Shinola." Although Oscar-like statuettes for these dubious achievement awards were not actually handed out, the companies were sometimes notified of their wins. Jay Jurisich, one of the awards' initiators and a director of Igor, a naming and branding agency, noted that "The reaction tends to be a letter months later saying something like 'Thank you for contacting Bloggs's Foods. We have forwarded your interesting comments onto the appropriate people who will ignore it for perpetuity.'"

Steve Manning, another Igor director, pointed to wider cultural factors. "We started the Shinolas to talk about the effect of all these names on the lan-guage because we're forced to use them. We wanted to address how these corpo-rations were making these decisions and putting words in our mouths and how it was changing the language and the way we think about things." The awards'

Web site, *www.shinolas.com*, maintains Top Ten lists of naming nightmares in categories like toys, magazines, sports utility vehicles, and junk food, and has conferred Shinolas on *Achieva* (an Oldsmobile model) and *Cruex* (a cream to soothe itching). There is no shortage of new nominees and plenty of winners.

The sponsors of the Shinolas are biased against cautious names and corporate same-think. Steve Manning believes that focus groups are the problem: "the easiest way to get consensus is to take part of a word from Greek and part of a word from Latin and modify it and say to the boardroom 'oh, this part represents power and the other part means cutting edge.' That's why you end up with companies called *Mirant* and *Agilent*."

In late 2003 one advertising company, The Design Conspiracy of London, England, set up a Web site, *www.whatbrandareyou.com*, intended to spoof bad brand names. Visitors were invited to select from a menu of core values like "dynamic" and "passionate" and goals like "global leadership" or "client focus." They clicked and got a supposedly customized name; examples included names like *Accumulo, Bivium, Integriti,* and *Ualeo*. The gullible could not have known that, with the aid of an online Latin dictionary, The Design Conspiracy had cooked up all 150 bad names in the course of one fun afternoon.

With so much money at stake, it's understandable that companies would be uncomfortable with risky, audacious names. The authors of *IdeaWise* have cited the five forms of perceived risks people face in their daily lives.

· *Monetary*: "I could lose my shirt."
· *Functional*: "Maybe the thing won't work. Maybe it won't do what it's supposed to do."
· *Physical*: "The thing looks dangerous. I could get hurt."
· *Social*: "I wonder what my friends will think if I buy this."
· *Psychological*: "I might feel guilty or irresponsible if I do this."

What applies to individuals also applies to companies. The knowledge that these risks are very real shouldn't lead to naming timidity, but instead to a serious appraisal of the potential pitfalls and possible rewards of a new name. In their obsession with novelty, drug namers often ignore real naming risks, and their coinages sometimes come perilously close to those in a 2003 *New Yorker* cartoon parody, "What's New in Pharmacology," that proposed *Confusadril, Revoltin, Mindbenderine, Nothin* (with *Somethin*), *Neo-Sufferin, Ibuproblem,* and *Relapsin*.

A brand name can go wrong in many ways, starting from the very beginning. Julie Cottineau, the Naming Director at Interbrand in New York, has noted some common pitfalls on the Web site *www.brandchannel.com*. Companies can wait too long to start the naming process, underestimating the time needed, and then scrambling when the product is about to be unleashed. She pointed out that this often results in higher legal fees and a second-choice name. "No serious product manager would approach a new product launch without a systematic and clearly defined critical path for product development, concept development, package design, advertising, PR, and distribution." Taking a haphazard approach to naming "reflects a failure to recognize that the name is actually the first act of public branding."

Companies are also wrong to abandon potential names just because the corresponding domain names aren't available. Names can often be bought. (In fact, many no-brainer URLs were snapped up early on by people who bought them speculatively, hoping to sell them later on.) Cottineau cautions against being too wrapped up in an insider's point of view (what she calls "subjectivity") and urges that companies get "impartial feedback from the people who are ultimately going to determine the success of the product or service . . . the target market consumers." Companies should zero in on how a name can communicate key attributes, benefits, and emotions, and how it can distance itself from the competition. (See Chapter 6 for the other responsibilities of a good name.) Cottineau adds that names need to be checked for their effectiveness in many different languages, since, through the Internet, even a product intended for a purely local market can find a far-flung buyer.

Cottineau warns against trying to name a product in-house instead of hiring a naming specialist. "A lot of time, effort and money [can be] wasted and with no agreed to or available names to show for it. . . . Terrible naming blunders have been committed by clients simply because they failed to perform the proper research on their own internally created names." A company needs an executive-led project team with experienced marketing and legal people on it. (But not *too* many people: When a company finally chooses from a short list, it's axiomatic that the fewer people involved the better.)

Since Cottineau ably summed up the general problems that come from poor corporate planning, we can turn our attention to names specifically bad in their nomenclature. Although we'll cite especially egregious cases, badness in names is often merely humdrum, such as names that are bland or hackneyed, generic or meaningless.

New to the ways of capitalism, Moscow store owners following the collapse of the Soviet Union called some of their establishments simply *Shoes, Beer,* and *Food.* These invite a sarcastic response like "So what?" or "Oh yeah?" Sometimes the problem is that the name is so difficult to spell that it begs to be changed, like *Coryphaeus Software,* renamed *Centric Software.* In naming, shorter is generally better: as we saw earlier, changing from *Federal Express* to *FedEx* made perfect economic sense. But the shortening must have impact: were the hefty sums spent by The British Council, an organization whose mandate was to promote its country's culture abroad, worth it? The new name was shortened to *British Council.*

Some miscalculations are due not so much to naming as to misguided marketing. Smith & Wesson, the maker of .357 and .44 Magnums, has a perfectly good brand name—for guns. When they issued a catalog in 2003 featuring gift ideas like cowgirl pillows, silk blouses, and bedding in a "rustic yet romantic print," and later began to sell Smith & Wesson mountain bikes, too, the consumer was bound to wonder what they all had in common. In a more natural extension, Smith & Wesson licensed their name for a line of golf clubs. "The guy who buys a Smith & Wesson handgun is in many ways in the same demographic as the guy who buys golf clubs," said John Steele, Smith & Wesson's licensing manager. Golf equipment (a $2 billion market in the U.S.) is a hotly competitive field dominated by *Callaway* (with their *Big Bertha*), *Taylor Made*, and *Cobra*.

The same analogy might have applied to the AdBusters Media Foundation, which in August 2003, announced that it would begin to market stylish and expensive Black Spot sneakers that would bear an "Unswoosher" anti-logo, pitting itself against Puma, Adidas, and Nike. Nike's techno-driven sneakers already had been under competitive pressure from Puma's and Adidas's low-tech versions. Adbusters, whose magazine had a circulation of 200,000, had earlier urged its readers to deface the storefronts and logos of "the world's biggest, dirtiest corporations" with a black circle with a large black dot in it. That Adbusters would get into the same game as those it pilloried smacked of inconsistency, if not outright hypocrisy.

A bad rebranding can lead to considerable confusion. In 2000, for example, a Web marketing firm announced that it was to be called *Luminant Worldwide*. Luminant Worldwide had previously been *Clarant Worldwide*, which had before that been *Radian Worldwide*, which had earlier been . . . *Clarant*. Wunderman, Ricotta & Kline, founded in 1958, stuck with its newly adopted name, *Impiric*, for sixteen months before reverting in 2001 to Wunderman, the name of one of its human founders.

Change costs money. One of the most costly naming mistakes involved the Royal Mail's decision to rename itself *Consignia*. In 1969, the centuries-old Royal Mail was split into two groups: the Post Office Group for the mail; and what became British Telecommunications, later the BT Group, responsible for phone calls. Then, in March 2002, the British government privatized the post office (though the government was in fact is sole shareholder). That decision required it to add *Plc*, the equivalent of the North American *Inc.*, to its documents, at an annual cost of $2 million. But that was nothing to the $2.9 million and three years of research invested in changing Royal Mail to Consignia.

In the tradition-minded United Kingdom, rebranding is considered suspicious on principle, as when England's best-selling *Marathon Bar* changed names to match its American equivalent, *Snickers*, and another candy, *Opal Fruits*, became *Starburst*. The Royal Mail's new name was derived from "consign," to deliver or entrust, and ultimately from the Latin *consignare*, to mark with a seal, and was analogous to such Latinate names as *Accenture, Corus, Innogy, Amicus,* and

accenture *Centrica.* Consignia quickly became the butt of dinner-party banter, with critics saying that it sounded like a Spanish office for lost luggage. The company's union asked its three hundred thousand workers to boycott Consignia and use *Post Office* instead. Dragon Brands, which had devised Consignia, indignantly protested that the name was only that of the holding company, which also owned *Parcelforce,* a package delivery service. Nothing hindered the tidal wave of protest and, coincidentally or not, the company posted a hefty pretax loss in its fiscal year. In 2002, only fifteen months after the name change, the company announced that henceforward it would call itself . . . the *Royal Mail Group.*

Let's pause a moment for a spot of compassion. Even at the best of times, English is a notoriously difficult language, simple enough to learn and use at a rudimentary level, but devilishly hard to speak and write proficiently. English offers a bewildering range of options for its users. Wannabe English users have to sort out the variants in dialects, notably British and American, cope with punctuation puzzles, decide whether to use double consonants (*instalment* or *installment*), and what to do when a verb, adjective, or adverb is formed from a noun ending in a vowel. David Crystal quotes a clever passage illustrating the last quandary: "I would rather be in a comfortable verandahed house, sitting pjamaed in a duveted bed and being fed puréed fruit by a muumuued beauty, than be bivouacked on a sparsely treed plain, sitting anorak-ed and shivering in the leaden-skiied gloom and eating potatoes that were sautéd yesterday before the power cables arc-ed."

Not everyone goes around equipped with a computer spell-checker. If it's thought that only long words can be misspelled, consider the following one-syllable items from the *21st Century Misspeller's Dictionary* (please note that "misspelled" is often misspelled):

ache	kiln	realm
balm	lymph	sword
cease	maze	thresh
damned	niche	vein
freight	ought	waive
ghost	prize	yacht
halves	qualm	zeal
jibe		

English is an exception-filled language, whose vagaries drove George Bernard Shaw to bequeath a substantial sum for the advancement of spelling reform. The main trouble is that our spelling often bears scant relation to pronunciation. Here are some of the phonetically nonsensical words that maddened Shaw:

although	eye	receive
answer	flood	rough
are	ghost	says
aunt	health	shoe
blood	island	some
climb	juice	sugar
comb	knot	sure
cough	lamb	two
debt	moist	use
does	none	view
done	oath	whole
dough	quay	yolk
drought		

New writers of English have to contend with capitalization (how to choose between *moon* and *Moon*, *earth* and *Earth*). They must reckon with the fact that a common noun can be a count noun (*strings, cars*), a non-count (*music, consent*), or a mass noun (like *flock* and *herd*). Common and proper nouns can be divided into the concrete and the abstract, or stand alone as a clause element ("I love Pepsi"). They don't usually allow plurals (brand names are an exception) except in sentences like "There are several New Yorks" or "Some France goes a long way." Etymology hinders as much as it helps, especially in folk etymology, in which case enough people make a wrong guess about the origins of a word that it becomes an established part of the language: the origin of *bridegroom* has nothing to do with *groom*, but derives from the Old English *brydguma*, from *byrd* "bride" and *guma* "man."

Our idiomatic expressions are copious, and our collocations tricky. Collocations are words that typically mate with other words, like "auspicious" with "occasion." A sequence of words may be further frozen into the form of a short phrase, like "in a nutshell" (perhaps a naming possibility for a health food store), or into culturally determined catchphrases like "Me Tarzan, You Jane" or "Elementary, my dear Watson."

Our verbs are often irregular, our grammar unpredictable, even the pronunciations of native speakers haphazard. One survey of speech conducted in the early 1930s, but no doubt equally true today, found that only one in one hundred thousand could correctly pronounce "data," "gratis," "culinary," "gondola," "impious," and "chic." Homophones and homographs—words that

have the same pronunciation or spelling but different meanings and origins—
abound: I *knew* I could *lead* you to a *new lead* mine." Other words are not strictly
homophones, but sound alike enough to cause confusion. Among *A* words
alone, we have to come to terms with such confounding pairs as:

adverse /averse	amend /emend
advice /advise	apprise /apprize
affect /effect	attain /obtain
afflict /inflict	aural /oral

Apart from pronunciation problems, English has many contrasting pairs of
words in various levels of distinction, such as A/B, Yes/No, fact/fiction, and the
printing measures of em/en. Because they're so often muddled, many of these
binaries, especially affixes, will repay a lookup in a good dictionary.

acri- (top)/basi- (bottom)	intra-(within)/extra-(without)
acro- (top)/bathy- (depth)	maxi-(most)/mini- (least)
ad- (to)/ab- (from)	mega-(big)/micro-(little)
ana- (up)/cata- (down)	mono-(one)/di- (two, double)
andro- (male)/gyno-, gynaeco (female)	mono- (one)/poly- (many)
-androus (male)/ -gynous (female)	neo- (new)/paleo- (old)
ante- (before)/post- (after)	ob- (toward)/sub- (under)
apo- (away, off)/peri- (round, near)	ortho- (straight)/caco- (bad)
auto-(self)/hetero- (other)	patri- (father)/matri- (mother)
bene- (good, well)/male- (bad)	phil- (love)/mis- (hate)
brevi- (short)/longi- (long)	-phile (lover)/ -phobe (hater)
calli- (beautiful)/caco- (bad)	poly- (many)/oligo- (few)
con- (with)/dis- (not, apart)	pre- (before)/post- (other)
endo- (in)/exo- (out)	pro- (for)/anti- (against)
-er (doer)/ -ee (one done to)	pro- (forward)/retro- (backward)
eso- (inside)/exo- (outside)	-ster (male)/ -stress (female)
eu- (good)/dys- (bad)	super-(above)/infra-(below)
giga- (giant)/nano- (dwarf)	super- (above)/sub- (below)
holo- (whole)/mero- (part)	syn- (with)/anti- (against)
homo- (same)/hetero- (different)	-tor (male)/-trix (female)
hyper- (over)/hypo- (under)	uni- (one)/bi- (two)
in- (in)/ex- (out)	uni- (one)/multi- (many)
infra- (below)/ultra- (beyond)	

Although English is a difficult language, it's also a very rewarding one—
sometimes literally, if you can leverage expert knowledge of the way it works to

create a successful brand name. Misusing English, however, can lead to highly unsuccessful brand names.

Is it a man? Is it a bird? No, it's a bad brand name. The Consignia fiasco showed several ways in which a new name could go wrong. One characteristic bad brand names share is inappropriateness. Take the names of condoms, circa 2003. The Durex *Avanti* could have been a car, **TROJAN®** the Trojan *Magnum XL* a car (or perhaps a gun), *Hardcover* a book, and *Sagami Type E* a skin cream. Brand naming is a form of communication, and to communicate well one must say what one means and mean what one says. Unintelligibility is literally a nonstarter. In fact, this is so broad a category of badness that it could subsume all those that follow. A bad brand name sows confusion and bewilderment. Despite a $12 million advertising launch for *Mennen E* that proclaimed, "Vitamin E, incredibly is a deodorant," the product failed because people couldn't figure out how Vitamin E related to their armpits.

Drivers, especially, are often puzzled by inappropriate or confusing names. In aiming for the under-twenty-five market at the 2002 New York International Auto Show, Cadillac tried too hard to get hip with the names *Imaj* and *Vizon.* Toyota's *Scion* assumed, perhaps, a level of erudition that its customers did not have (a *scion* is a descendant of a notable family or one with a long lineage), and Saturn had an astigmatic eye on the youth market with *Ion* ("a charged atom"), also from the Greek for "something that goes." It may not.

Chris Yaneff, a consultant responsible for changing *Brewer's Retail,* the name for a chain of beer stores owned by the province of Ontario, to the decidedly reductivist *The Beer Store,* told a *Globe and Mail* reporter in 2001, "The name has to relate to the business you're in." He noted that that *Clarica Life,* the new name for Mutual Life Assurance, sounded like a hairspray. "Ninety per cent of the names you see now are stupid," he said.

Yaneff might have overstated the problem, but certainly the list of stupid names is long. In 2001 Canadian Occidental Petroleum (often called *CanOxy*), used two identity specialist firms to change its name to *Nexen,* despite the fact there were already several global companies with that name, and the domain name *www.nexen.com* had been taken. The cost was a reported $8 million, but that amount was dwarfed by the $100 million it cost Andersen Consulting, divorced from its mate, the accounting firm Arthur Andersen, to rename itself *Accenture.* Although Landor Associates looked at some 5,500 possible names, the winner—if it can be called that—came from an Andersen manager in Oslo, Norway, who was awarded a trip to the company's golf tournament in Australia. Perhaps coincidentally, the Arthur Andersen parent became one of the great financial implosions of the corporate world. If a name is incomprehensible to begin with, it requires a huge investment of time and money to get the message across, taking resources that the business needs for core operations. Introducing the unpopular new holding company name *Allegis* was the catalyst for the breakup of the former UAL Inc. and the eventual sale of its Westin and Hertz companies.

Regardless of how a company fares financially, there is inherent sadness in the decline of wonderfully evocative names. *Homestake,* the legendary South Dakota gold mine, is no more, having merged into Barrick Gold; the magnificently named Australian mining company *Broken Hill* became the generic *BHP Billiton.* Even *Billabong* would have been better. Utility companies seem to specialize in creating verbal vacuums with their name changes. *Boston Edison* became *Keyspan, Boston Gas* became *Nstar, Cellular One* became *Cingular.* When Bell Telephone, the original "Ma Bell," birthed seven regional "Baby Bells," three of them provided negative lessons. *US West* told its customers where it was based, but gave no immediate sense of what business it was in, and its successor name, *Qwest,* was even more enigmatic (an airline? an insurance company?). Ameritech's name compression ("American Technology") suggested a hundred different possibilities.

In 2002, CompUSA, a computer products store, had nationwide brand recognition in the United States. Expanding to sell a wider range of electronic goods, it sought a new Web address that would point to something more than an online catalog. They rejected the old one, *www.ComUSAnet.com* as well as 20,000 neologisms. The name they settled on was *Cozone*—a name that, like *Lucent,* was "an empty vessel" that could be indefinitely filled. The firm that came up with *Cozone* boasted that "Not only does the name mean nothing in English, it means nothing in any major linguistic group." Six months after it was set up the Web site was dead.

Latin is a language as dead as it can be. It killed the ancient Romans, and now it's killing me. The schoolroom rhyme had a point. In English, morphemes (prefixes, suffixes, word-roots) typically derive from Latin and Greek, and are often foundation stones for new brand names. They always have been. Just as artificial languages like Esperanto and Volapuk tapped the commonality of morphemes among European languages, in the aftermath of World War I, the suffix *-ine* became popular in brand names (*Ovaltine, Vaseline*). **Vaseline®** The suffix's allure was due to its Latin origin, a reversion to the days when the language was universal, at least in Europe. A brand name that used such a suffix sought international appeal.

If morphemes are not in some way meaningful, they remain linguistic fossils. During a BBC radio panel discussion, Tony Thorne, head of the Language Centre at Kings College London, criticized *Navigant, Candescent, Veriton,* and *Vivident* as pretentious names and patronizing to their customers. The shortage of actual words that were not already trademarked drove this trend, together with the fact that Latin names were usually easy to pronounce. Drawing on Latinate or Latin-sounding suffixes like -ent, -int, and -ant, there was a rush to create names like Lucent, Conexant, and Consilient (originally named InfoCanvas) that seemed to add a sense of portentous significance. What militated against them, though, is that in English, Latinate words tend to sound more formal than those with earthier, everyday Old English origins (largely because Latin and Norman French once loomed large in the churches and law courts of England). Thanks to the Norman Conquest of 1066, Latinate words—often via French—today greatly outnumber Old English words. But the latter are far more commonly used. In the phrase "the little words of house and home," for example, each word derives from Old English.

The Latin-derived Romance languages, especially Italian, were not far back in the pack. Car models, which already had names like Sentra, Maxima, Altima, Vitara, Aerio, Spectra, and Optima, now turned to Italian place-names for inspiration: Kia's Sorento and Amanti (Amanti was a glassworks in Murano, Italy), Nissan's Murano, and Suzuki's Verona. As the sardonic commentator who brought these examples to the attention of a Web site said, "Can the Hummer Mussolini be far behind?"

As with every trend, wretched excess plays a leading role, and any new name that seems inventive could end up as insipid, which was the verdict some rivals of Landor Associates handed down in the case of Agilent. Rick Bragdon of Idiom called it the **Agilent Technologies** "most namby-pamby, phonetically weak, light-in-its-shoes name in the entire history of naming. . . . It ought to be taken out back and shot."

Steve Manning agreed, saying it "sounds like a committee name. 'Who's your competition?'"

"Lucent."

"Well, we want to play off Lucent—only we're agile."

These authorities were quoted by Ruth Shalit, who summed up: "In their zeal to professionalize and standardize what used to be a goofy, freewheeling, fly-by-night enterprise, the naming conglomerates tend to produce names that are reflective not of the client's corporate culture, but of their own. The result: a slew of names that are sterile, antiseptic, talcum-powder bland."

Technobabble. Tech talk, geek speak. Also TechnoLatin, a term that Hodskins, Simone, and Searls, a Palo Alto, California, public relations firm, coined for "language that makes things easy to describe but hard to understand." TechnoLatin replaces nouns with "vague and nebulous substitutes." To aid the fuzzy-minded, the firm invented what it called a "Generic Description Table" that listed adverbs, adjectives, modifying nouns, nouns, and combining forms in order to generate random strings of self-important but meaningless terms, for example, "Entirely Configured Commitment-Structured Computing." The firm has allies in its campaign against muddiness. Since 1974 the National Council of Teachers of English in the United States has given out Doublespeak Awards, whose British equivalent is the Golden Bull Awards, for the most flagrant and fragrant examples of euphemistic language or other abuses of plain English. The first winner was a U.S. colonel, a press officer in Cambodia, who told the press in exasperation: "You always write it's bombing, bombing, bombing. It's not bombing! It's air support!"

A study funded and released in July 2003 by Advanced Micro Devices showed that unintelligibly technical terms frustrated equipment users, who didn't get what they wanted most: speed of setup and ease of use. A journalist who reported this finding said that he used to blame engineers, but now didn't, since "few engineers really want to confuse their listeners; most learned very quickly that if they talk like geeks, they don't get a date Friday night." He blamed marketing and sales people: "Talk to engineers about a computer, and they call it a 'box'; the marketing department will elevate it to a 'productivity system.'" Or, "ask engineers if a certain box can handle an increase in traffic and they will say 'yes'; marketers will say grandly that it's 'scalable.' An engineer's 'network' is a marketer's 'end-to-end solution.' What an engineer calls a 'video card' is promoted to a 'visual processing solution.'"

The better way was shown by James Gosling, Sun's inventor of the Java software language, who explained what "Web services" meant: "You know how companies have different software packages that run different parts of their businesses and the packages don't communicate with each other?" he asked. "Well, all the stuff that makes them talk to each other is Web services."

In early 2003 IBM was developing a massive new mainframe computer—mainframes contributed 40 percent of IBM's profits—a major upgrade that involved up to thirty-two processors, new memory, and a revamped operating system. It could process 450 million e-business transactions a day. The buyers would be big banks, retailers, and insurance companies whose older unreplaceable codes could only run on mainframes. The mainframe's  code name was, fittingly, *T-Rex.* Its official name was the *eServer z 990.* This was not an isolated incident. AMD's computer chip, code-named *Sledgehammer,* became *Opteron;* Intel's *McKinley* chip became the *Itanium 2.*

When it came to technology companies, it seemed that anything other than plain forceful English would do. The Internet only worsened the com-tech-net-cyber-dot-link trend of the 1990s. Names blended software shoptalk with street-smart slang, aiming for a combination of the hip and futuristic, the playful and the edgy. Software programming was a stylistic influence: in programming code, words or word segments that run together are often capitalized, because computers cannot read spaces, and the capitals made it easier for human beings to read the code. Everyday rules of capitalization, punctuation, and spelling were ditched. Lowercase *e* (for *electronic*) and *i* (*information, interactive, Internet*) littered the Internet landscape. Intercapitalization got its start with products like *HyperCard* (an early Macintosh database product) and *MacWrite*. When Apple's cofounder, Steve Jobs, started a computer company in 1986 called *NeXT*, the caps-lock key got a further workout. Circa 1997 we had *iVillage, id Software, planetU, D2K, TouchNet, Q-Zar, Alt-imedi, Art4-U, DesignVoX, Dzignlight Studios, eVox Productions, iMOTION*, and *@Climax*, an online seller of adult videos. Even chemical formulas got into the act. In 2001 British Telecom renamed its BT Cellnet mobile phone brand *mmO2*. Customers took the short route, calling it *O2*, as in "CO_2."

The techie symbols were often unintelligible to those who were not insiders, and hard to look up. In some telephone directories, a name like *@Home* was listed as if it were spelled out as "At Home," and the same applied to print editions of the *Wall Street Journal* and the *New York Times*. On the other hand, @Home's stock market ticker symbol was ATHM. Such typographical difficulties had precedents the namers should have known about. Gulf & Western years ago replaced its ampersand with the plus-sign (*Gulf + Western*), but the media didn't obey it in headlines and body copy, and similar fates awaited all-cap names (*XEROX*) and the all-lowercase *adidas*.

But some lessons never stick, especially when designers are given free creative range. For some days in early 2003, the business pages of North American newspapers were dominated by multiple two-page spreads boasting of Hewlett-Packard products' use with other products: "dreamworks + hp" (HP did animation  workstations and servers), "bmw williamsf1 team + hp" (an HP supercomputer designed a racing car and conducted race simulations), "nyse + hp" (servers and storage to handle day trading), "hongkong + hp" (a Web portal that handled citizens' access to government), "fedex + hp" (a method of identifying and correcting potential problems), "birdlife finland + hp" (a bird observation service with mobile phones to send information to a central database), and "gruma + hp" (a new network for the world's largest corn and tortilla producer). Each linkage was keyed to a different Web site. Thus Hewlett-Packard ignored the International Trademark Association's warning that consistency is vital and that typographical gimmickry should be shunned. Potentially, it had undermined the value not only of its own trademark, but the trademarks of others as well.

While it lasted, the techie guessing game was cool—and then it became cold. By the early 2000s, the stew of letters and numerals largely had gone off the heat. For one thing, the stock market crash in dot-coms—Hewlett-Packard was, of course, one of its victims—had given tech companies a negative image, and customers had become wary of them. Ditching the *.com* suffix were such

NASDAQ-listed companies as *Autobytel.com*, an automobile Web site, and it was joined by *Neoforma*, *Activeworlds*, *AdStar*, and *PartsBase*. Namers rediscovered English.

If it sounds ugly, it probably is. We will have more to say later about the potential phonetic tiger-traps that English digs for itself. What sounds bad is often highly subjective and bound to a particular time and place. In August 1946, the U.S. National Association of Teachers of English said the following were the worst-sounding English words: *cacophony, crunch, flatulent, gripe, jazz, phlegmatic, plump, plutocrat, sap,* and *treachery.* Different ones would be chosen today. Certainly, ugly-sounding words are plentiful among brand names. A $10,000 home entertainment system is named *Faroudja.* A model of bathroom-wall spotlight in the IKEA catalog is labeled the *Fartyg.*

An advertising agency called itself Batten Barton Durstine and Osborn (BBD&O), which someone said sounded "like a trunk bouncing down a flight of stairs." The names of small companies are especially prone to punning addiction and terminal cuteness, like those of two Toronto firms, a car-rental agency called *Chariots of Hire*, and a wine- and beer-making supply shop called *Wine Not.* These may be forgiven their self-indulgence, and even offer comic relief from befogging corporate atrocities like the throat-clearing *UNUM* (was that "YOU-numb"or "OOO-numb"?) insurance company. Even the big company's receptionists weren't sure. The name sounded like a grunt or grumble: by comparison, the insurer's previous name—Union Mutual—was a gem.

Latinization had its perils, certainly, especially for trade names ending with *-is*, as in *Allgeis*. The real estate developer Donald Trump said that it sounded like "a world-class disease." The names of numerous diseases and maladies do in fact end that way—*arthritis, gingivitis, encephalitis,* and *syphilis.* The new name for the merger of Rhone-Poulenc and Hoechst gambled that the life sciences could evade the unhealthy context. Their name was *Aventis.* The potential risks of another trend, technobabbling names, was summed up by a quip from Doug Byrnes on the Shinola Web site: "Are we gonna have conversations like: 'Honey? Did you order anything from a company called 6o#LRft?' 'That depends. Is the question mark at the end of your sentence part of the name?'"

A company called 6o#LRft would at least run no risk of becoming a mondegreen. Mondegreens are specimens of creative mishearing, Freudian slips, or auditory dyslexia—take your choice—to which even acute ears are susceptible from time to time. There are entire Web sites devoted to them. In the November 1954 issue of *Harper's*, Sylvia Wright confessed that when she had read two lines from a Scottish ballad:

> They hae slain the Earl of Moray
> And laid him on the green

she heard it as

> They hae slain the Earl Amurray
> And Lady Mondegreen

A useful new word had been added to the language to account for what happens when a listener hears the line of a Jimi Hendrix song, "Excuse me while I kiss the sky" as "Excuse me while I kiss this guy." Kids hear the U.S. Pledge of Allegiance as "I led the pigeons to the flag." Though mondegreens are most creatively employed with phrases, brand names are also vulnerable. One contributor to a Web site devoted to mondegreens reported that when her four-year-old son heard "a Toyota" he commented, "That's not a toy ota, it's a big ota."

Misjudgments about brand names can also result from too much sensitivity to sound. When Nissan originally introduced its cars to the U.S. market in the 1960s, it called itself *Datsun* because *Nissan* was believed to sound too Japanese. Then, twenty years later, the company reverted to its original name because, with the reputation for quality to back it up, to sound Japanese seemed no bad thing. This came too late for another Japanese carmaker, Isuzu. In 1976, with the value of the German mark skyrocketing, Buick decided to replace its **ISUZU** German Opels with cheaper-to-make Japanese ones. It turned to Isuzu, a company partially owned by General Motors, to produce the new car, the Opel-Isuzu. Millions of dollars were squandered trying to turn Isuzu into a big-selling import. In Japanese, *Isuzu* means "fifty bells," a pleasant suggestion. However, in English the name sounded more like a social disease than an automobile. The advertising prepared by Buick's ad agency made fun of the name ("What do Isuzus do?"' asked one ad. "How's your ol' Isuzu?" inquired another) but the dealers were not amused. Out of the planned production of 24,000 units, Buick dealers sold less than 8,000 Opel Isuzus the first year, down from nearly 40,000 Opels the previous year. Sales continued to sink, and this during years when the import market was booming. Toyota, Datsun, and Honda together sold well over a million cars in 1978.

Isuzu decided it could do better on its own, and set up American Isuzu Motors, hiring an advertising agency headed by Jerry Della Femina (ironically, the author of the book *From Those Wonderful Folks Who Gave You Pearl Harbor*). Isuzu was now called "The advanced car with the backward name." Despite increasing ad budgets, sales were dismal. In 1985, the ads keyed on the automaker's sixty-nine-year history, with the theme, "The first car builders in Japan. We're going to teach Nissan, Honda, and Toyota some respect for their elders." That year Isuzu sold 26,953 cars; the younger generation sold 1,561,832. A story began to be told about three guys:

"I drive a Honda," says the first.

"I drive a Toyota," says the second.

"I drive a Japanese car," says the third. He was, of course, an Isuzu owner.

In time, Isuzu found a solution. It dropped its car line and focused all its resources on trucks and 4×4 vehicles sub-branded *Trooper* and *Rodeo*. An unsatisfactory brand name didn't influence purchasers of such vehicles, especially when combined with an attractive sub-brand. Business improved. By itself, Isuzu sounded like a sneeze.

The dot-com cyber rush added its quota to auditory bafflement. In 1997 SprintCellular became *360° Communications*, but how did you pronounce the name? People settled for "Three Sixty," a simple enough solution compared to the quandary posed by *VXTreme*, *ichat* ("itch at" or "eye-chat"?), and *X'iT Group Creative*. Some brand names positively invited consumer rebellion, as in the case of *One2One*, which was nicknamed *One-2-no-One*, or *One2None* by disgruntled customers. It wisely rebranded itself as *T-Mobile*.

Duplicated vowels or consonants can create pronunciation problems. Clearly, *NBA* ("en bee ay," National *B*asketball *A*ssociation) or *NFL* ("en ef el,"

National *F*ootball *L*eague) is an easier mouthful than *AAA* (*A*merican *A*utomobile *A*ssociation), though *AA* (*Al*coholics *A*nonymous) just passes muster. Duplications often require the insertion of the pointers "double" or "triple" before letters, as in *NAACP* ("en double-ay cee pee," National *A*ssociation for the Advancement of *C*olored *P*eople). A different kind of problem is associated with words like *VAT* (*V*alue *A*dded *T*ax) and *WHO* (*W*orld *H*ealth *O*rganization) for which speakers are supposed to go against their natural instincts and pronounce not as words but as separate letters.

Sometimes a bad name is just the natural consequence of a bad product. Consider the case of *Urine Luck Products*, whose Web site advertised "completely undetectable" chemicals that, if added to urine samples, would destroy "unwanted toxins." It takes no great imagination to suppose the additive could help users to cheat on drug tests. Maybe it should have been called—if the user were caught—*Urnotin Luck*. *Whizzinator*, an artificial penis that dispenses fake pee, had a different problem in 2003. Across the span of six months, the sheriff's department in Lubbock County, Texas, caught five suspects attempting to deceive urinalysis by using the Whizzinator. Said the owner of the company that made the device, which also sold dried urine, "How people choose to use it is beyond our control."

Me-Too Nightmares. The perils of the herd mentality are abundantly clear for company names infected by technobabble or Latinity. But me-tooism attends almost any trend, tendency, or movement. If a bar is named *Cheers* soon there will be a *Toots*, a *Waves*, and a *Winks*. Specific words also can become grossly overdone. Like "One," of which there are  many: *Pepsi One* (which fizzled in the market), *Bank One*, *eOne*, *Fiber One*, *Global One*, *Mobil 1*, *Network One*, *OgilvyOne*, *One Health Plan*, *One.Tel*, *OnePoint*, *OneSoft*, *Oneworld*, *PureONE*, *Schwab OneSource*, *Source One*, *Square One*, *VerticalOne*, *V-ONE*, and *Westwood One*. In some instances a term was associated so much with a product that it became generic, as in the tagline "Lite beer from Miller." Beer-drinkers soon could choose from *Schlitz Light*, *Coors Light*, and *Bud Light*. Media and the public quickly corrupted the Miller product to "Miller Lite." Miller had lost its right to exclusive use of "light"and "lite."

Dennis Baron has commented on the "InternalCapitalizationPhenomenon," in which the spacing is dropped between capitalized words. Baron (or "DennisBaron" if the internal capitalization phenomenon extended to personal names) sees the trend everywhere in corporate America, in names such as *ConAgra Foods*, *PeopleSoft*, and *SmartSignal*. In Chicago-area residential complexes and developments alone, there were *WeatherStone*, *LakeBreeze*, *RiverBend*, *EastGate*, *TerraVilla*, *BrightWater*, *NeuTrenton*, and *OakHurst Meadows*. It has followed what Baron calls the "e at the end" trend, which produced subdivisions with names ending with *Pointe* or *Towne*, and "at names," new-home developments with names like *The Trails at Brittany*. In twenty years, he predicts, all such names will seem impossibly dated.

For a short period, there was a penchant for personal names as titles for magazines—one might almost say a *Vogue*—such as the late John F. Kennedy Jr.'s *George* (should it have been called *John John?*), *O: The Oprah Magazine*, and *Martha Stewart Living*. In 2001, the 125-year-old women's magazine, *McCall's*, changed its name to *Rosie*, after Rosie O'Donnell, one of Oprah's TV talk show rivals, who was named its editorial director and had a 50 percent financial stake in the enterprise. Rosie was featured often on its covers. In conflict with its publishers, Gruner & Jahr USA, Rosie quit the next year, and the magazine ended.

Nadirs in sports naming. Although the Atlanta *Braves* and the Cleveland *Indians* baseball teams have been chastised for the supposed political incorrectness of their names, there seems little prospect that they will rename themselves the Atlanta or Cleveland Native Americans. Other sports names could stand some recasting, though, on the grounds of taste alone. The National Hockey League's Anaheim *Mighty Ducks* quacks in the direction of its owner, the Disney Corporation and its animated poultry, Donald Duck and his family. When sports and business mate, it's easy to get jaded about the naming results. After all, Americans lived through the *Sega Sports Las Vegas Bowl*, the *Culligan Holiday Bowl*, and the *Chick-fil-A Peach Bowl*. Over the years, sponsors had snapped up naming rights to championship bowl games, stadiums and its teams, and mascot names. But the sporting name game may have hit an all-time low when a public elementary school sold its naming rights to the local supermarket, and when a minor league hockey team gave itself a nickname for cow manure.

In the first known episode of trafficking in the naming rights for any part of a public school building anywhere in the country, the mayor of Brooklawn, New Jersey, arranged the "sale" of the new gymnasium for his town's only school. For a pledge of $100,000 over the next twenty years to pay the debt service on the $1.7 million gym, Brooklawnians bore witness to the elementary school's *ShopRite of Brooklawn Gymnasium.* Said an embarrassed superintendent of schools: "We've crossed the line and we know it."

Much further west, the Buzzards played in the Western Professional Hockey League in El Paso, Texas. The Buzzards, however, had been dead meat at the box office. So the team's brain trust decided to try a new nickname and see if it would . . . stick. The Buzzards' new nickname: the *Cow Pattys.* (With just that plural—not even the Cow Patties.) Just in case the local hockey fans didn't understand what they were stepping into, there was also a new logo: a cartoon cow holding a hockey stick and wearing a helmet. Behind the cow was a steaming pile of manure.

Semantic Obliviousness. Names are words, and words have meanings. The design of Herman Miller's suite of office furniture extended desk surfaces both vertically and 360°, and was christened *Levity* to express unique vertical capability and freedom. But did Herman Miller really want its office furniture to suggest lightness or fickleness of mind, character, or behavior? *Hotpoint* was a good brand for stoves but was it the right one for fridges? A Montreal company selling Internet security and privacy products called itself *Zero-Knowledge Systems,* which might have had some resonance inside the industry, but suggested ignorance outside of it.

A Minnesota company was named *Sick Optic-Electronic.* (Surely people would not want a sick sensor on their hands.) On the West Coast, the Fluke Corporation made sophisticated handheld instruments, their proud motto: "Serious tools for serious work." One assumed their engineering left nothing to chance or accident, which was how a dictionary would define a fluke. And that they never floundered around (the homonymic "fluke" is a member of the flounder family).

In 2002 *Air Canada* launched a discount carrier called *Zip Air,* which to many suggested not speed, but nothingness. *Con Ed* (*Con*solidated *Ed*ison) was a problematic name, since "Con" could suggest "concentration," "consul," "convict," and "confidence trick." Its accomplice in crime could have been the Toronto *Globe and Mail,* whose *Report on Business* magazine began to be identified as *ROB.* There was also a broadcast channel called *ROB-TV.*

The Taiwan Tobacco and Liquor Corporation was reorganized in 2003 from a government agency to a state-owned agency. This could spell the end of its fifty-three-year-old popular cigarette brand, *Long Life*—a picture of a man and a crane on the pack—because a proposed law would forbid any marketing claim or suggestion that cigarettes were clean, safe, or healthy. The company warned that changing the name would severely hurt business, but others pointed out that young people didn't smoke Long Life, only "middle-aged and older men."

Another Taiwan enterprise, the Hey Song Company, could hardly have known that in the spring of 2003 the SARS (Sudden Acute Respiratory Syndrome) epidemic would kill hundreds and hospitalize thousands in China, Hong Kong, Singapore, Canada—and Taiwan. But there it was, stuck with its root beerlike soft drink Sars, popular since the 1940s and named after its main ingredient, sarsaparilla, which the Chinese favored because they believed it lowered body temperature and prevented sore throats.

In early 2003, *Dr. Pepper/Seven-Up, Inc.* tried to promote its new flavored-milk product, *Raging Cow*, through blogs. But the marketing backfired. Bloggers instantly pointed out that Dr. Pepper/Seven-Up, Inc. might as well be urging its customers to contract mad cow disease.

Some oblivious naming disasters were only narrowly averted. In the mid-1980s, executives at two energy firms, InterNorth of Omaha and Houston Natural Gas, wanted a catchy name for their newly merged companies. Their supposedly world-class choice—*Enteron*—drew attention, but for all the wrong reasons. Numerous callers pointed out that *enteron* is the medical term for the tract through which the human body digests food and disposes of waste. The company's name was hastily changed to *Enron*. (Considering Enron's later fate as a colossal bankruptcy, they might have been right the first time.)

In 1997, Reebok tripped over its laces with its new women's running shoe, *Incubus*. Only after putting the shoe on the market did it discover that the word denoted a demon that visited women while they were sleeping and ravished them. Reebok discontinued the shoes. Another 1997 offering was a line of bas-ketball shoes called the *Jackal*, which can mean: a small doglike mammal, a per-son who performs menial tasks for another, or a lackey who aids in the commission of disreputable acts. Presumably the Jackal-wearer fouled out of the game. Something about athletic shoes inspires ahistorical amnesia in namers. Until an official at Simon Wiesenthal Center pointed out the howler in 2002, Umbro, the British company that outfitted the English national soccer team, had been selling shoes inside boxes labeled *Zyklon:* crystalized Zyklon B had been the active agent in Nazi death camp gas chambers.

Umbro's absentmindedness was horrific, but there can be less obvious gaffes. African American speech and youth slang can hold linguistic booby traps for those not familiar with it. The number "51" seems innocuous enough, for instance, but it is also slang for a cigarette that is part marijuana and part crack cocaine. Yet America's Hobby Center had a pending trademark for *Area 51* for radio-controlled flying saucers, and Ames International registered *51* for a line of denim shirts. *Sapphire* is the name of a lovely blue gemstone and has been used as a trademark for greeting cards, gin, citrus fruit, and flashlights. But it was also a derogatory slang reference to a black woman, from a character in the *Amos 'n' Andy* radio and TV programs. Sapphire on the show was a stereotyped loud, complaining, emasculating black woman.

Verbal gridlock. Here we have the traffic pileups. The giant Japanese company Nippon Telegraph & Telephone has a wireless unit called *NTT DoCoMo*. It's also seen in the pileup lunacy of a name such as *Morgan Stanley, Dean Witter, Discover & Company*. A lack of vowels can produce an impenetrable jungle of letters, as in the case of *MSDW* (the investment firm Morgan Stanley, Dean Witter). In fact, any merger of two or more organizations can create collisions of initials that resemble car wrecks. It's the jammed-together ego trip of *LVMH Moët Hennessy-Louis Vuitton*. It's the telephone receptionist agony of *BankAmerica Robertson Stephens*. The Frankensteinian name *PricewaterhouseCoopers*. (As if to atone for its sins, PricewaterhouseCoopers announced in 2002 that its spinoff consulting arm would be named *Monday*.)

Banks especially did not practice due diligence about their name changes, moving from straightforward names to obscure or unintelligible ones. In Canada, for example, Canadian Imperial Bank of Commerce changed itself to *CIBC*, and the Bank of Nova Scotia to *Scotiabank*. The U.S. brokerage arm of RBC (ex–*Royal Bank of Canada*) was *RBC Dain Rauscher*, and its U.S. retail bank *RBC Centura*. By 2002 the Bank of Montreal (founded in 1817) had become the *BMO Financial Group*, and the Toronto-Dominion Bank became the *TD Bank Financial Group*. Arguably, *Scotiabank* was an improvement, but *CIBC* pointed to another variant of gridlock, the pileup not of separate words, but of enigmatic initials.

Consider the movies playing on the screens of the nearest megaplex. Long ago and far away, *Jaws* said it all in four letters; *Chicago* and *Spider-Man* in three syllables. By the summer of 2003, movie titles were long enough to tell half the plot—and they seldom fit on the theater marquee.

Pirates of the Caribbean: The Curse of the Black Pearl (fourteen syllables)

Lara Croft Tomb Raider: The Cradle of Life (eleven syllables)

Terminator 3: Rise of the Machines (ten syllables)

Legally Blonde 2: Red, White & Blonde (nine syllables)

These windy titles might add a whiff of literary pretension to whatever Hollywood is peddling, but they don't exactly speed up the ticket line. No wonder moviegoers devise their own shorthand: "Tomb Raider 2" or "T-3."

The telecommunications world trembled in 1997 when WorldCom bought MCI Communications in a $37 billion deal. Temporarily, *MCI WorldCom* was the moniker for the merged colossus, a name berated as flat and cumbersome. *WorldCom* had scope, clout, descriptiveness, and simplicity. But *MCI* stuck, a clumsy set of meaningless initials, little known outside the United States, and a perennial runner-up in terms of image and reputation. In 2002, the company made the largest bankruptcy-court filing in U.S. history—and when they restructured, reverted to *MCI* and ditched *WorldCom*.

Initialisms seldom work, unless the company was a well-established giant, such as *IBM, GE*, or *GM*. The eighty-five-year-old magazine of decoration and gardening, *House & Garden*, had a solid, comprehensible name. In 1987 the magazine sought to attract a younger readership and rechristened itself *HG*. Cancellations flooded in, and the magazine was forced to close in 1993. But a decade later its owner, Condé Nast, announced that it would resurrect the magazine. The new name? *House and Garden*.

Something about the corporate mentality makes it addicted to "agglomerese," the clever term coined by the *New York Times*'s Robert C. Doty in 1959 to denote speech or writing that is loaded with numbers and abbreviations—the bane of much technical writing. The copious use of initials assumes that the reader or hearer will readily know what's being talked about. The practice more often leads to confusion, though, since two or more entities may well reduce their names to the same anagram. Thus, only context can help someone know whether *AAA* represents the *Amateur Athletic Association*, the *American Automobile Association*, or the *Australian Automobile Association*. Such overlaps, real or assumed, can also impinge on ethnic sensibilities. In the United States, a predominantly white audience might associate *CNBC* with the cable TV and Internet subsidiary of NBC. But for African Americans, *CNBC* may suggest the *Congress of National Black Churches*, a coalition of eight historically black denominations, representing more than 60,000 congregations and 20 million worshipers. There's even a chance of unwanted ambiguity, since initials feature in classified personal ads. Imagine, for example, a company whose initialized name is *JDF* (*Jewish Divorced Female*), *WSM* (*White Single Male*), or even possibly *BDG* (*Black Divorced Gay*). The tricky aspect of acronyms can be illustrated by supposing that a company was called *Metro Environmental Systems & Services*. A sensible enough name, but any name with thirteen syllables is most likely to be shortened to its initials. The name could become a real MESS.

Sometimes social changes, like changes in eating patterns, dictate changes. To allay, or perhaps evade, fears about the animal fats in their products, billboards for Dairy Queen began to refer to something called *DQ*, and in 1991 Kentucky Fried Chicken began to call itself *KFC*. In any case, studies have shown that all-initial names are as much as 40 percent less memorable than names that use actual or made-up words. This proposition can be tested by looking at the all-initial names of companies in the Fortune 500 list, names like *TJX* and *SPX*. How many of the following do you recognize?

CVS	TJX	SPX
HCA	AES	CNF
AMR	FPL	USG
TXU	CSX	

Names such as *TXU*, *AES*, and *CNF* are the corporate equivalent of a disguise.

As for run-on, jawbreaker names, lawyers couldn't be blamed for the multisyllabic mess often created by corporate mergers, even though old-time law firms produced their own share of them. Senior managers stood convicted of refusing to deal with the marketing or communications reality that such names were confusing to the client, annoying to the prospective customer, ugly to the eye and the ear, impossible to remember, and sure to be changed.

8

SCRABBLE'S SCRAMBLE: HOW NAMES ARE CONSTRUCTED

Language is composed of small units called *morphemes*, though much scholastic debate rages about how these should be defined. A morpheme is a minimal unit of meaning and is distinguished from a phoneme, which is a minimal unit of sound. So far so good. The difficulty sets in when we try to subdivide the morpheme into a grammatical unit (for example, a pluralization or an inflection of a verb) and a lexical unit (often called a *lexeme*), which may also involve separate forms of a single word (the lexeme *bring* includes *brought* and *bringing*).

Being academic cowards, and at the risk of committing loose talk, we will only deal with morphemes in the broadest possible sense. A morpheme can be free or bound: the former exists in freestanding isolation, the latter is bound to another morpheme: in *builder*, the *build* is a free morpheme (note the lack of a hyphen!); -*er* is bound to it. Here we're concerned not so much with the content of brand names—what one or more of the morphemes that structure them might mean in a grammar or dictionary—as with their form. Whether it involves words or parts of words, the process by which these bits and pieces are shifted across the brand-name construction site include marking, borrowing, affixation, compounding, reduction, and ordering. We'll look at them in sequence.

Marking. If you squint your eyes, any language is just an agglomeration of marks. For want of a better word, "marking" is the respect people in general, or namers in particular, pay to these tiny separate units. Among the units that attract extra attention are punctuation, numerals, special characters and symbols, and diacritical marks.

In brand names, diacritical marks usually are inserted for a visual rather than a phonetic effect, creating a faux-foreign impression (like the umlaut in *Häagen-Dazs*), or to lend themselves to logos, like the biacron—an *i* with a circle instead of a dot—as in *Factîva*, the replacement name for *Reuters–Dow Jones Interactive*. The *i* with a circle over it is the international symbol for information. Seeking to distinguish itself from *Agilent* and *Navigent* (both of which accent the letter *i*), the online data-mining company *Naviant* also embraced the biacron. A spokesperson for the firm that named Navigent noted that "Consumers will come to associate it with endless inspiration, endless possibility." Unless, one commentator noted, "they associated it with googly eyed teenage girls who dot their *i*'s with hearts and smiley faces."

The exclamation mark was once much favored for revues and musicals like *Oklahoma!* and *O Calcutta!* The hyphen used to be more popular in brand names than it is today. *Sun-Maid*, *Star-Kist*, and *Sani-Flush* all date from the 1920s, although they're now more likely to be marketed as *SunMaid*, *StarKist*, and *SaniFlush*. As John Benbow remarked in his book, *Manuscript and Proof*, "If you take hyphens seriously, you will surely go mad."

Coca-Cola, *Bristol-Myers*, and *Rolls-Royce* have remained hyphenated since 1886, 1899, and 1906, respectively (the second formerly *Bristol, Myers*), and their famous names remain stable. But the *Times-Mirror Company* (parent company of the *Los Angeles Times*), the *Erie-Lackawanna Railroad*, and the *Knight-Ridder* news agency became the *Times Mirror* (1962), *Erie Lackawanna* (1963), and *Knight Ridder* (1998). By early 2000, the at-signs (@), slashes (/), and all the other bizarre punctuation from the personal-computer and dot-com decades began to seem almost creaky. More enduring were ideophonemes—alphanumeric combinations—in such names as *7 UP*, *7-Eleven*, *Union 76*, *V8*, *2-4-1 Pizza*, and *Drugs 4 U*.

Any typographer knows that individual letters or characters have physiques and personalities of their own, and you don't have to be a typographer to recognize the effectiveness of the childlike reversed *R* in Toys "Я" Us. Letters may have frequent companions, like *w* with *h*, and *q* with *u*. The brand-name compiler Adrian Room has pointed out that by itself *O* is a perfectly rounded form visually, the circle offering a target and drawing the eye to its center, and not surprisingly is often associated with the human eye and mouth. *X*, visually, has a regular, uniform shape with balance and symmetry, and like *O* it's a target letter, drawing the eye to the central point at the cross of two diagonals. Thus, on visual grounds alone, a name like OXO has double appeal. In their spelled-out, Greek-letter versions, the names Alpha, Delta, and Omega lend a touch of classical prestige.

Alphabetical letters drastically differ, not just in their conformation, but in the frequency with which they begin ordinary lowercase words. The following crude and wholly unscientific table shows how the frequency with which such letters begin ordinary words differs from those beginning brand names and trade names. The first column is drawn from a page count of letters in a dictionary that does not include proper names, the *Chambers Maxi Paperback Dictionary*. The second column shows the frequency in two long lists of brand names, and the third shows the frequency of trade names on the New York Stock Exchange. Some initial-letter words are so close in frequency-count that they're clustered.

Dictionary Frequency	Brand Name Frequency	Trade Name Frequency
S	C	A, C
P	S	S
C	M	B
T	A	T
B, M	B	M, P
A, D, R, W	P, T	D, E, F, G, H
F	O	N, R
E, G, H, I, L	D, L	I, W, L
O	H	K, U
N	F, G, R	J, O, V
U	E, V	Q
V	K	X, Y, Z
Q	I, W	
J, K	J, Z, Q, U, X, Y	
X, Y, Z		

Even more than the table indicates, initial S-words outrank others in ordinary usage, and it's a truism that a lexicographer cannot be confident a dictionary he or she is working on will ever get finished until the S block is done. Among brand names and trade names, S-words rank a distant second. L-words rank eighth in frequency in all three categories, and X- and Y-words are at the bottom in all three. P-words are second in dictionary occurrences, but fifth among trade names and sixth among brand names. C-words tie for the top in brand names and trade names. A-words are at the top for trade names, but are fourth among brand names and sixth in dictionaries. If a lesson can be drawn from these data, it may be that the contrarian-minded would be well advised to concentrate on J, K, X, Y, and Z as the first letter of a brand name.

The same lesson can apply to the frequency of letters wherever they occur in a word. Here is the frequency of letters in the words—1.5 million of them—in the *Cambridge Encyclopedia*, edited by David Crystal. The count may be a little more reliable than most letter-frequency tabulations, since it includes proper nouns—like brand names. In any count, "e" is always the most common letter in the English language.

e	r	c	g	k
a	s	m	b	x
t	l	u	y	j
i	h	f	w	z
n	d	p	v	q
o				

Apart from bringing to bear visual and quantitative influence, letters of the alphabet can be grammatical morphemes. An -s, for example, can pluralize nouns (cats), the names of games (billiards), and involuntary conditions (giggles). It can be a suffix for a hypocoristic, which is an uppercase noun that is a pet name or nickname (Fats). It can mark the third-person singular active indicative (walks, talks). It can form adverbs (unawares). Such single-letter morphemes also bear bundles of connotations and associations important in brand names.

Take the first letter of the alphabet. For all of its history, A has been the first letter, which is perhaps why it signifies a top mark or grade. It is seldom doubled and then only in words loaned from another language (aardvark, Aaron). The a- or -a can signify: a phonetic spelling for "of" (cuppa, lotsa); a feminine singular ending (cinchona); a feminine ending of personal names (Roberta); an oxide of a chemical element (alumina); a plural ending (phenomena); a prefix meaning "away or from" (avert); "a point of action at the beginning or end" (abide); "on, in, or into, to or toward" (afoot, afar); and "not," a negative, or just absence (amoral, atonal). And, as we've noted, an armada of automobile names end in a.

A often gives a brand name a foreign, exotic, feminine, Romance-, or classical-language look.

Aga	Granada	Oceana
Agfa	Honda	Omega
Bata	Konica	Ribena
Cessna	Lada	Ryvita
Cona	Lancia	Sabena
Corona	Leica	Simca
Cortina	Lufthansa	Skoda
Fanta	Matsushita	Tia Maria
Fiesta	Mazda	Toshiba
Formica	Minolta	Toyota
Fujica	Nivea	

O covers a multitude of functions and meanings as well. Grammatically, it can be a connective (speedometer). It can mean "facing, toward, to, on, over, against, reversely, or inversely" (omission). It's often found in informal or slang words (ammo, combo, limo, blotto); as a pejorative ending (cheapo, sicko); as an informal ending in addressing someone (cheerio); to shorten a proper name, affectionately or otherwise (Jacko); or in fact to shorten many words (photo, memo, video, disco). It appears before the final element of a word that was at least scientific to begin with (thermometer), and can mean "egg" (oidium).

O is linked to words from Romance languages like Italian and Spanish (*amigo, bambino*) and, further back, to Latin and Greek, not just in words themselves but in their cultural referents (*Scorpio*), and generally to an exotic background (*mikado*). We connect it with musical terms (*concerto, allegro*). We use it in spoken words to attract attention, to express surprise or delight ("Oh, look!," "Oh, yes!"), as an apostrophe in poems ("Oh to be in England, now that April's here"), or to convey a short succinct message or emotion (*Hello!*). *O* frequently occurs as a combining vowel in ethnic terms, whether spelled with a hyphen or not (*Anglo-American*), in scientific and technical terms (*electromagnetic*), and in expressions related to literature or culture (*socio-comic*). Given such abundance of connotation it's unsurprising that a prominent *O* has been popular in brand names since the nineteenth century, and sometimes even pops up more than once in the same name: *Bronco,* **VOLVO** *Omo, Polo, Volvo, Yo-Yo.*

Aero	Cinzano	Milo
Alfa-Romeo	Day-Glo	Sanyo
Allegro	Eno	Sirocco
Biro	Glaxo	Tesco
Bisto	Jell-O	Typhoo (tea)
Brasso	Marlboro	Velcro
Brillo	Meccano	Yo-Yo

A rival to *O* in brand-name visibility, though certainly not in frequency, is *X.* It figures as the prefix *ex-*, beginning many words (*ex-President*) and can mean "out, from, or derived from"; often begins words of Greek origin and ends Latin ones; finds itself a phonetic or shorter spelling for *-cks* or *ex* (*sox, pix, Xtra Large*); and serves as the sign for Christ, the Cross, and Christians (*Xians*). "X marks the spot" where something is to be found, and it's the mark a person makes in casting a vote, as well as a substitute for the personal name of someone who cannot write a signature. It may be a symbol for an unknown quantity (*Mr. X*), a symbol to denote the strength of ale in the United Kingdom (XXXX is extra strong—no wonder that an Australian beer calls itself *XXXX*). It's an adults-only category of film, a personal sign for a kiss, and an indication of a wrong answer (the opposite of a check or tick mark). It's a symbol for "multiply," for a capture in chess, for a drawn game in British football pool coupons, for a sexual hybrid in horticulture (*Aceras x Herminium*), for a female in genetics (*X chromosome*), for magnification in photography. It's ten in Roman numerals. Perhaps its most distinctive solo appearance in marketing is as "Brand X," the hapless product that is always unfavorably compared to a name brand in TV commercials. To the puzzlement of many, especially your authors, the no-name *Brand X* actually has been trademarked as the honest-to-no-goodness identifier for household cleaning items, for safety goggles, and even as the name of an advertising agency in Milwaukee.

Steve Manning of the brand-naming firm Igor has noted that *X* is associated with science fiction, high tech, computers, automobiles, and drugs. As a brand name, it does double duty in *Exxon*, *Ex-Lax*, and *Xerox*. It may be a classical element to lend prestige (*excellent*) or texture (*Spandex*). Its marketing virtues have been exploited since the 1920s in many brand names, including such extinct ones as *Kanotex*, *Footex*, *Pointex*, and *Pinex*. At this writing, the following brand names are still being used:

Ajax	Kleenex	Playtex
Cutex	Kotex	Pyrex
Dexedrine	Lux	Rolex
Durex	Miramax	Timex
Electrolux	Perspex	Westclox
Ex-Lax		

K has often been favored in names—including *Kleenex*, *Kodak*, *Kotex*—since it's distinctive-looking and, phonetically spelled, can double in sound for the hard *c* and, in combination, for *q*: *Krispy Kreme* doughnuts, *Krazy Glue*, *Kwik Kopy*. In English, it regularly appears in words with exotic associations (*sheikh*, *batik*, *karate*, *koala*), turns up in foreign personal names (*Khrushchev*), the names of aliens (*Klingons*), and in humor (*Keystone Kops*). *K* may also suggest a vitamin, as in *Special K*. When George Eastman coined *Kodak*, he said, "The letter *K* has been a favorite with me—it seemed a strong, incisive sort of letter."

The letter *V*, which outranks *W* in brand name frequency, has useful associations with *victory*, *vital*, and *virile*. *E* is for excellence, the drug ecstasy, and effort. *F* is for academic failure, loudness (*forte*), and obscenity (the euphemistic *effing*). *Y* can add a jaunty note (*Speedy Muffler King*). The exotic *Z* often turns up in loan words (*zombie*, *bazaar*, *mazurka*). Strangely, this Zorro of a letter is not only Spanish for "sly" or "crafty," but can also mean sleep, as in "catch some Zs."

Borrowing. As a mongrel language, English is notorious for its ability to assimilate, appropriate, absorb, and even downright steal from other languages. Brand naming frequently indulges in such borrowing. Sometimes a single word or phrase may be stolen, like *Volare*, *Quattro*, *Montero*, *Samurai*, *El Pollo Loco*,

Encanto, and *Fuego.* Borrowing plays an even bigger but subtler role in the origins of prefixes and suffixes.

Affixation. Affixation is the use of prefixes, the rare infixes (an infix is a part that comes in the middle of an otherwise inseparable word, and in English these are usually found in oaths: *abso-damn-lutely*), and, especially, suffixes. To standard affixes may be added vowels that bind together a word's elements, such as -*o*-, -*a*-, and -*i*-, or such wordlike connectors as *bio*- and *Euro*-. One comprehensive list of affixes includes 386 different prefixes and 322 suffixes, excluding variants.

Suffixes come in many guises and levels of formation. One way that words are created is through derivation, a type of which involves the process of forming more complex words from less complex ones, often including a change in the part of speech, such as *engraver* from *engrave* or *realness* from *real.* Another word-making method is *conversion,* in which an adjective can become a noun (a *natural*), a noun can become a verb (*refereed* the game), as can an adjective (*emptied* the bottle), and a noun can become an adjective or another modifier (*cotton* blouse). Grammatical function words and prepositions can become verbs (she *upped* the ante) or nouns (the *how* and *why*). Affixes can also become nouns (*ologies, isms*), as can phrases (a *free-for-all*).

Affixes are versatile. They may be inflectional, as in plurals (quizz*es*, carr*ots*); possessives (dog*'s*); verb-tense markers, sometimes contracted (see*s,* shout*ed,* ongo*ing,* doesn*'t*); pronoun endings (some*body,* any*thing,* her*self*); and comparatives or superlatives (bett*er,* kind*est*). They may also be derivational, forming abstract nouns like front*age,* star*dom,* farm*ing,* or friend*ship.* Or they form concrete nouns like book*let* or engin*eer.* They may form adverbs, as in quick*ly* or down*ward,* or adjectives, as in Portugu*ese* or left*ist.* They can turn verbs into nouns, as in break*age* or act*or,* or into adjectives, as in wash*able* and attract*ive.* They can turn adjectives into nouns, as in happi*ness,* and nouns into adjectives, as in use*ful,* foo*lish,* and hair*y.*

Suffixes often derive from Latin or Greek. *Pentium,* Intel's fifth generation of computer chips, combines the Greek word for "five" with the suffix for such elements on the periodic table as *uranium* or *titanium.* That -*um,* the ending of Latin second declension neuter nouns and neuter adjectives, also occurs in coined names like *Librium* and *Valium* or as an ending of a genuine Latin element, as in *Aquascutum* (*scutum,* shield) or *linoleum* (*oleum,* oil). In *Postum* it is unusually appended to a personal name, *Post,* after the beverage's inventor, Charles William Post. It's often used to name medicines, as are the suffixes -*in,* -*ine,* and -*ene,* predictable enough since in ordinary English they're often attached to terms for chemical substances (*penicillin, quinine, benzene*):

Aspirin	Dramamine	Ovaltine
Benzedrine	Listerine	Plasticine
Dexedrine	Methedrine	Vaseline
Disprin		

The suffix *-oid*, "resembling or having the form of," as in *Polaroid*, began to be used commercially in the late nineteenth century and got its impetus from *celluloid* and *tabloid*, both originally trademarks. Then there are the oily suffixes, *-ol* and *-ola*. Ordinary *-ol* words usually denote chemical compounds, especially those involving alcohol (*glycerol, phenol*). Besides this meaning (*Dettol, Skol*), brand names expand the senses to include oil, its by-products, or something that uses them, as in *Castrol*, **CLAIROL®** *Clairol*, and *Cuprinol*.

The *-ola* suffix has had a more complex career. It turns up as a jocular ending (*crapola*) and in a word for bribery or covert payments (*payola*). In commercial coinages it can mean oil as in *Mazola* ("maize oil"), or can be a quasi-Italian diminutive: *Pianola, Victrola*. More obliquely, it turns up in *Coca-Cola* and *Pepsi-Cola*. The *-on* or *-lon* suffixes have been used mostly for subatomic particles (*neutron*), molecular units (*codon*), and more generally for substances (*interferon*). Apart from a few exceptions (*Canon, Exxon,* and *Mogodon*), in brand names they are used largely for synthetic fabrics, on the model of the generic words *rayon* and *nylon: Ban-Lon, Chinon, Dacron, Orlon*. As a feminine suffix, *-elle* adds grace and softness (*Cottonelle, Trielle*), while *–ette* suggests femininity (*Vassarette*) or substitution (*Chinette*).

The suffix *-scape* is an old one and shows no signs of going away. It dates to seventeenth-century Dutch and German in *landschap* (now our word *landscape*). The same suffix shows up in a number of standard dictionary entries, including *cityscape, dreamscape, seascape,* and *skyscape* ("to give the sense of looking over a broad terrain"). Formations with *-scape* thrive on the Internet. *Netscape* is the obvious example, but there are also *Medscape, Globalscape, Seniorscape,* and *Travelscape*.

NETSCAPE

Obviously, coined names make affixation more than a walk-on part in a morphemic play. The following highly selective table shows some other typical affixes and a representative brand name or trade name associated with it.

-able	Quicken ExpensAble	aero-	Aeroflot
ac-	Accenture	ana-	Anadem
-ac	Prozac	ant-	Antabuse
ad-	Adrenalin	-ant	Cendant
-ad	Covad	aqua-	Aquafresh
-ade	Gatorade	-ar	Pixar

arthro-	Arthrotec	lum-	Lumenaré
astro-	Astroturf	-max	Betamax
-ator	Purolator	max-	Maxager
auto-	Autoharp	-max	Vasomax
-centric	Concentric	mega-	MegaDrops
cine-	Cinerama	micro-	Microlux
co-	Comergent	neo-	Neosynephrin
-co	Tesco	omni-	Omniva
col-	Coldon	-or	Zocor
com-	Compaq	-ped-	Expedia
-com	3Com	plex-	Plexiglas
con-	Consilient	poly-	Polyfilla
cor-	Corian	pre-	Previa
duo-	Duotang	pro-	Prozac
dura-	Duracell	san-	Sanotogen
electro-	Electrolux	-scope	Cinemascope
en-	Enbrel	-set	Letraset
-ence	Vividence	-ster	Dumpster
-ent	Agilent	supr-	Supra
-er	Breathalyzer	sym-	Symantec
exo-	Exocet	-sys	Unisys
-im	Altim	tech-	Technicolor
-in	Lanoxin	-tel	Nortel
-in-	Lumina	tele-	TelePrompTer
-ine	Listerine	-tron	Icotron
inter-	Internap	ultra-	Ultrasuede
-ion	Halicion	uni-	Unilever
-ite	Arborite	-ure	Accenture
-ity	Genuity	-us	Velocitus
-le	Boxxle	-val	Miraval
-lin	Adrenalin	ven-	Venator
log-	Logitech	ver-	Verbex
luc-	Lucite	veri-	Verigold

As kinds of abbreviation, some suffixes, like -*y*, -*o*, -*er*, and -*s*, can produce lexemes that are highly informal in tone. The -*y* or -*ie* turns up in *baddy* and *daddy*, in *auntie*, *Susie*, *Billy*, and the British *telly*. The -*o* appears in *ammo*, *weirdo*, and in *aggro* (British for "aggravation") and doubled in *smasheroo*. The British favor -*er*: *boner* (a blunder) and *rugger* (rugby football). The -*s* ("Moms and Dads") also figures in the British *preggers* (pregnant) and *starkers* (stark naked), and in relics of English upperclass slang from between the two world wars, such as *champers*.

Suffixes can go through periods of increased popularity, just as words do. In the early 1960s there was a brief vogue for *–nik,* after the Soviet Union's launch of *Sputnik*. The Watergate scandal of the early 1970s opened the way for *Irangate* and *Nannygate*. Then, in the 1980s, other affixes came to the fore, like *mega-* (in words like *megatrendy, megaplan, megacity, megabrand*), *-friendly* (as in *user-friendly,* but also *customer-friendly* and *ecofriendly*), new *-isms* (like *heightism* and *ageism*), and *-aid* (deriving, of course, from *Band-Aid*).

New brand names are neologisms, and the lexicographer Victoria Neufeldt has called neologizing "the linguistic collective unconscious of the speech community." Neologisms, she notes, need not be flashy newcomers like *McJob* or *couch potato*. (Or even the 2004 American Dialect Society Word of the Year, *metrosexual*.) They can also use old suffixes, like *-ize,* to make new words, like *texturize,* and add suffixes to old words in new ways. Here are some of the productive suffixes that she lists:

-(a)holic	-ese	-safe
-adelic	-head	-something
-appropriate	-meister	-speak
-averse	-neutral	
-capable	-oid	

We can add *-friendly* to her list, as in *user-friendly,* and that favorite of the supermarket, *-fresh,* as in *garden-fresh*. Because they include familiar elements, such new words, like *multitasking,* gain quick acceptance. *Multitasking* creates a new *multi-* compound, Neufeldt said, as well as a new function for the word *task* by assuming an intransitive verb that hadn't existed before, and also invents a new gerund, *tasking*.

Brand namers routinely engage in multitasking. Not content with using standard affixes, they constantly add new ones to the lexicon, especially for pharmaceutical products (although many of their "new" affixes reach back to Greek or Latin origins). Here are some of them, each with an associated product:

accu-	Accutane	ben-	Benadryl
achro-	Achromycin	cal-	Calidus
adria-	Adriamycin	cele-	Celebrex
alba-	Albamycin	cepa-	Cepacol
aldo-	Aldomet	cere-	Cerebyte
alt-	Altoids	chem-	Chemdex
amy-	Amytal	cor-	Corian
ata-	Atabrine	dem-	Demerol
aureo-	Aureomycin	dent-	Dentegra
avo-	Avosure	dexe-	Dexedrine

dram-	Dramamine	neutro-	Neutrogena
elasto-	Elastoplast	novo-	Novocain
epo-	Epogen	nutra-	NutraSweet
-exant	Conexant	opt-	Optima
ico-	Icontron	osmi-	Osmiroid
larg-	Largactil	plexi-	Plexiglas
laundro-	Laundromat	suda-	Sudafed
libr-	Librium	thora-	Thorazine
lycr-	Lycra	tyl-	Tylenol
mercuro-	Mercurochrome	val-	Valium
meri-	Meritel	vivi-	Vividence
nem-	Nembutal	zix-	Zixoryn
neu-	Neupogen	zyr-	Zyrtec

Compounding. For brand names specifically, compounding is a very important technique. Like affixation, compounding expands the range of words. Affixation spreads the roots of words; compounding involves combining whole words. The result may be spelled as one word (*buckshot*), separated by a space (*buckler fern*), or with a hyphen (*buck-tooth*). (No one ever said that English was consistent.)

English relentlessly compounds itself, and many monosyllablic words can be girders in the *Meccano* set. Here are some common ones:

aid	eye	jet	pal
bank	fast	joy	path
base	file	jump	prime
best	find	king	pure
big	fine	land	queen
box	first	light	real
cap	flow	line	room
check	form	live	scale
choice	free	look	scan
clean	friend	love	score
clear	full	main	set
click	fun	mate	share
cool	gain	mind	soft
craft	go	more	sound
day	great	most	source
desk	head	my	space
door	heart	net	speed
dream	home	now	star
drive	jack	one	suite
eat	jazz	pack	sun

sure	touch	walk	world
talk	track	wave	yes
team	tree	web	you
time	true	well	zone
tool	up	wise	
top	voice	work	

A quick skim through a catalog or the *Yellow Pages* will show how often the above one-syllable words wed each other, and the result is only multiplied when one includes unions of words with more than one syllable—computing alone gives us *LaserJet, PowerBook, PageMaker,* and *ImageWriter.*

Reduction. However you cut it, reduction entails shortening. The shortening process is related to the broader techniques of compounding and derivation, and is an old story in etymology. The historical process of word formation inevitably involves various forms of alteration, if only changes in spelling. But there are more dramatic forms of change. *Back-formation,* for example, is the creation of a new shorter word, often in fact a new part of speech, from a longer form, which accounts for the appearance in English of *enthuse* from *enthusiasm, laze* from *lazy,* and *liaise* from *liaison.* A *blend,* also called a *fusion,* is the joining of two separate words into a new one. Lewis Carroll called such forms "portmanteau words" in his classic book *Through the Looking Glass,* because they suggested the traveling bag that opened into two separate parts. He was a master at making them: he blended *slimy* and *lithe* to make *slithy, snort* and *chuckle* to make *chortle.* Blending, already a common practice (*smog* from *smoke* and *fog, motorcade* from *motor* and *cavalcade*), is increasingly on the rise, due to the necessity of shortening unwieldy technical and scientific terms.

Clipping sheds word elements, usually one or more syllables, as in *pro* from *professional.* Fore-clipping lops from the beginning of a word, as in *(ham)burger* and *(tele)phone.* Back-clipping shears the end of words, as in *ad(vertisement), fan(atic), deli(catessen), cab(riolet),* and *curio(sity).* Front-and-rear clipping plays both ends against the middle, as in *(in)flu(enza).* Commonest of all are initialisms and acronyms (*Amoco, Nabisco*)—the corporate and organizational worlds could not live without them. What these different kinds of shortenings share is a tendency to make a formal word informal, though perhaps *United Airlines* got too chummy with the name of the discount airline it launched in February 2004: It was called *Ted*—short for *United.*

Among brand names, the shortening may be something as elementary as deleting the space and a repeated letter between two words, as in *Eveready, Travelodge, DirecTV,* and *ReaLemon.* A brand name may become a nickname, or at least a friendlier version of the old form, as in

Pan-Am(merican) and *Jag(uar)*. Front-clipping accounts for *Genuity*, the e-business operation of GTE: *Genuity* is "ingenuity," with a little off the top. Another front-clipper is *(in)Candescent Technologies*, though what is being purveyed is thin CRTs for notebook computers, not lightbulbs. As blends, *Spam* and *Intel* stand, respectively, for "spiced ham" and "integrated electronics." Back-clipping generates *Essent(ial) Healthcare*, a for-profit hospital chain, and *Intuit(ive)*, the maker of personal finance and small business accounting software.

In the long-and-short of brand names, no easy or sharp distinction exists between clipping, blends, and acronyms. Amalgams and alloys abound, as exemplified in *Cambozola* (a cheese that combines Camembert and Gorgonzola), *Bisquick*, *NutraSweet*, and *Qualcomm*.

Ordering. Because brand names are often composed of only one word, the ordering of words, that is, syntax, is relatively unimportant, although much can depend on whether the specifically branding term is placed before or after the generic one (*Budget* Garden Supplies, *Superior* Propane, *Bargain* Furnishings, *Mr.* Muffler, *Dial-a-Winner* vs. Pharma *Plus*, Pizza *Hut*, Business *Depot*, Find-*All*). Even the ordering of letters can be significant. Names with doubled letters are visually more pleasing than without them: *Allegro*, not *Alegro*.

Most interesting of all are the semantic constraints implicit in phrasal brand names like *Jaws of Life* or *Spic and Span*. Such constraints often result in the first element becoming associated with *here* ("here and there," "in and out"), *now* ("now and then," "sooner or later"), *adult* ("mother and daughter," "father and son"), *male* ("man and woman," "king and queen"), and *solid* ("field and stream," "land and sea"). Space-axis constraints also intervene: vertical precedes horizontal ("height and width," "North, South, East, and West"), and high usually precedes low ("rise and fall," "hill and dale"). Search high and low, some brand names are *Head & Shoulders* above others.

All these techniques—using unusual letters or characters, borrowing foreign words and phrases, attaching affixes, converting words from one part of speech to another, making new compounds and cutting old words down to size, and rearranging phrases—have been used successfully to make new words in English for hundreds of years. Successful brand namers realize the value of these techniques in making new, interesting, evocative names that still "read" as English to the consumer.

9
FIGURES OF BRANDSPEAK

The word *rhetoric* often collocates with *mere* and *empty*, as in "empty rhetoric." *Rhetorical* collocates with *question*, as in the rhetorical questions "Why should I do a damn thing?" or "Do you have to slam the door every time you leave?" *Rhetoric* lugs heavy pejorative baggage.

Yet we could not talk to each other without using rhetoric. Poetic devices, tropes, and figures of speech may have poly-handled names stemming from their ancient Greek origins, but (for the most part without being aware of it) we use them every day. Rhetoric is a necessary part of the art of persuasion, and the art of brand-naming is the art of persuasion.

Rhetoric alters and extends meaning, and rhetorical speech has real effects on those who hear or read it. To be comfortable with rhetorical devices, we have to first understand certain types of lexical relationships. *Hyponomy* involves sets of superordinate-subordinate orderings. A set may be a superset (*hyponym*) or a subset (*hypernym*). Thus, *plant* is a superset of *fruit*, and *fruit* is a superset of *orange*. Working backward, *orange* is a subset of *fruit* and *fruit* is a subset of *plant*. There are also part-to-whole relationships: a *cell* is part of the whole, called a *prison*. *Synonymy* is sameness of meaning, and *antonymy* is oppositeness of meaning. Antonyms can be complementary (you're either *single* or *married*, *male* or *female*), converse (in which one implies the existence of the other, such as *husband*/*wife*), or gradable (really *hot* or not too *cold*, quite *big* or unusually *small*). *Monosemy* and *polysemy* refer not to marital arrangements, but to whether a word has one or several senses.

Brand names may not offer as much scope for the time-honored stratagems of classical rhetoric (often called *schemes*) as an entire speech, advertisement, or TV commercial, but they often expand into slogans. *Slogan* comes from the Scottish Gaelic for "army shout," a battle or rallying cry. From these beginnings we come to "A glass of Guinness is a cheerful sight" or the more famous "Guinness is good for you," "All Aboard Amtrak," "America Runs on Bulova," "Beautiful skin begins with Noxzema," and "Fly the friendly skies of United."

Schemes of balance or parallelism contain the same number of words, syllables, or word-length: *Coca-Cola* and *Pepsi-Cola* are balanced names, with *Coca-Cola* being just a bit more even with its four-four letter arrangement. Antithetical schemes set up oppositions, as in the slogan "difficult to design, easy to perform." *Chiasmus*, a rhetorical device where word order is inverted, also makes for good slogans: "Guard your youth with Youth Garde" for a skin moisturizer; "If it's Madewell, it's well made" from Taunton Knitting.

For namers, *tautology* (saying the same thing twice in different words), ordinarily a weakness in writing, can be put to good use, the theory behind most advertising being that something is more effective if said over and over again: *Crown Royal* whisky and *Royal Crown* (later *RC*) cola. Confusing ambiguity is to be shunned in clear writing, but in brand-naming it can be fruitful: *Hawaiian Punch.*

Hyperbole comes from a Greek word meaning "flung too far," and indeed this form of exaggeration flings its net wide. Do *Merry Maids*, whose slogan is "Homes That Sparkle from People Who Shine," merrily polish furniture all the livelong day? Is *Ambrosia*, the rice pudding made by Bovril, truly the food of the gods? Is *Miracle Whip* truly miraculous, and *Magic Marker* magical?

Hyperbole's antonym is *litotes*, understatement. Instead of bragging about itself, the brand name timidly suggests that just possibly you might want to buy it. Thus one finds an antiques store called *The Little House on the Parking Lot* and the self-limiting and punning *Just Desserts*. A brand name like *Simply Good Food*, although quietly proud of its own merits, pares the persuasive message down to a bare minimum. A variant of litotes is a brand name that pokes fun at itself or refuses to take itself seriously, like *Silly Putty* and *Krazy Glue.*

Metaphor, which symbolically identifies one thing as another, applies to numerous allusive names. *Metaphor*, a brand-naming company, is itself a

metaphor. *L'eggs* are pantyhose, not eggs; *Ivory* soap can only be carved by kids; and *Greyhound* will take you to Cleveland, not the dog races. The simile, metaphor's less flamboyant sibling, is insignificant in brand names, although it shows up in slogans: "Like a Rock."

Reduplication (more a linguistic than a rhetorical device) is the repetition of a syllable or other element, either exactly or with a slight change (*fuzzy-wuzzy, helter-skelter*). Reduplication is an important part of a rhetorical scheme of balance, the *isoclon*, and is almost a naming cliché for pizza chains offering two-for-one specials: *Pizza Pizza* and *Double Double* (best enjoyed at the Las Vegas casino-hotel named *Circus Circus*). A different kind of balance asserts itself in the form of *merism*, in which two synonyms or related words are linked by conjunction, such as "aches and pains," "fine and dandy," and "new and different." The quick and easy brand-name example is *Spic and Span.*

Oxymorons are the juxtaposition of apparently contradictory terms. They seem to cancel each other out, as in that hallowed example, "giant shrimp." They are such ill-assorted pairs as *Dry Ice*, *Krispy Kreme*, and *Metal Lumber*. The same surprising contrast is at work in *Soft Logic*. "Logic" is meant to be crisp and specific, not soft and fuzzy. But here, too, technological thinking overtook incongruity. Fuzzy logic, the concept that something may not be true or false, black or white, on or off, but instead occupy many intermediate states, is extensively used in artificial intelligence and the design of control systems.

Prosopopeia, or personification, endows an abstraction or collective sphere of activity with human or humanoid qualities. The advertising universe is rife with such creatures, such as *Merry Maid* with her dowdy but still jolly sister *Molly Maid* and her juice-drinking cousin *Minute Maid*. There's the cake-baking *Betty Crocker*, the pristine *Mr. Clean* ("Mr. Clean! Mr. Clean! Mr. Clean!"), the ice cream–dispensing *Dairy Queen*, the *Jolly Green Giant*, and such figures of commercial folklore—sometimes termed "anthropomorphics"—as the Bibendum tire blimp from Michelin and the debonair Mr. Peanut.

Namers can never resist a good or bad pun in the attempt to pose some form of helpful ambiguity. "Nothing runs like a *Deere*" went the old slogan for John Deere tractors. *Cover Girl* makeup alludes to the idea of a magazine "cover girl," but also implies covering the face with makeup; the deodorant *No Sweat* is both literal and figurative in meaning; a dog grooming and exercise service called *Dogs Pawsitive*; a furniture company called *Suite Dreams*; a lawn-care company called *Lawn Rangers*; and a chain of cosmetic stores called *The Body Shop* to which one takes one's skin, not a rusty heap you hope to refurbish.

Synecdoche uses a genus for a species, or a species for a genus, the part for a whole, or matter for what is made from it. In British usage, *America* means the whole of North America, not the part that is the "United States of America"— much to the annoyance of Canadians and Mexicans, but perhaps to the satisfaction of brands that hope to capture the entire continent. As Kim R. Robertson notes, the use of synedoche as a trope—more for less, less for more—is clearest when an entity is based on something significant about, and directly associated with, the other. Thus, we say *threads* and *wheels* for "clothes" and "car," and speak of infantry on the march as *foot*, just as we use *hands* rather than *foot* for people who work at manual labor. Trade names typically make an implicit substitution of the whole for the part; after all, *General Electric* and *General Motors* cover a multitude of—quite literally—parts. Among brand names related to the part for the whole, synedochics are often restaurant chains: *Red Lobster* for seafood; *The Keg* for steaks; *The Whole Enchilada* for Mexican dishes. If "The" precedes a name, the chances are it's this type of synecdoche.

Under the general heading of synecdoche also fall *antonomasia* and *metonymy*. Antonomasia is the substitution of an epithet or title for a proper name (the "Great Emancipator" is Abraham Lincoln). Antonomasia can also include the use of a proper name to express an idea or attribute (a miser is a "Scrooge"), and indeed some brand names can include a cluster of associations, like *Disneyland*. Metonymy substitutes the name of an attribute or adjunct for that of the thing meant, for example, "the ring" for the sport of boxing. A *metonym* is a word, name, or phrase used as a substitute for something with which it is closely associated, such as *Moscow* for the government of Russia ("Moscow today announced it would take steps to reduce the level of corruption in the country") or *Silicon Valley* for the electronics industry. *Fudge Stripe* is the name of a Keebler cookie. The stripes of fudge are actually rather small, but it's an effective metonymic association.

But language does not just make statements about the world; it also describes actions or occurrences. Verbs are not indispensable in brand names, but they are in advertising texts. Since there are far more nouns than verbs, most dictionaries and thesauruses stress the former. (The exception is Henry G. Burger's thesaurus-like *The WordTree*, which lists words backward toward causes, or forward toward effects. The basic listing element in the book's first half is the transitive verb—Burger finds 26,400 such verbs—and other parts of speech are directly related to it: "FASTEN upon JOINING = Attach." The other half of the work arranges items by levels of abstractness in a hierarchy of concepts that he calls a "cladistic": "PENETRATE & DIVIDE = CUT." It's a new, refreshing way of looking at language.)

A language has function words that do not directly carry meaning, but which help us to manage syntax. They may be helping verbs like *do* or *are*: "We *are* not naming a brand right now." Notoriously hard to define in dictionaries, they may be grammatical terms for parts of speech, like *adjective* or *adverb*, or labels like *transitive* or *intransitive*, to indicate whether a verb takes an object or not. But language also performs more subtle actions. Scholars have pointed out that every utterance has three functions. The *locutionary* function involves what the expression means, literally. The *illocutionary* function entails how an remark behaves as a speech act, which philosophers of language define as an utterance considered as an action. Words not just are, they do. *Perlocutionary* functions include all the effects an utterance has on the receiver. Brand names, like other words, use all three functions. We've discussed meanings and their effects, but not as yet the second speech-act function, the illocutionary.

The reigning authority on the subject, John R. Searle, has identified five basic types of speech acts. They perform several bits of business in brand names.

Representatives commit the speaker to the truth of the expressed proposition: they swear, believe, report, assert, or conclude. *Toys "Я" Us*. A pet day care and boarding establishment called *Pets Preferred*. Although *Sea-Doo* and *Ski-Doo* have an unfortunate association with children's euphemistic word for excrement, they also imply doing. The name of action is also built into two other Canadian brands, the discount airlines *Canjet* and *Jetsgo*.

Directives attempt to get the addressee to do something: they request, command, urge, or question. *Guess* jeans. Brand names are commonly imperatives:

exhorting, commanding, or urging. A dance studio called *Jump to It*; a chain of paint shops called *Color Your World*. The insect repellent *Off!* and a Microsoft imaging software product called *Picture It!* add exclamation points to their commands.

Commissives commit to some future course of action: they promise, threaten, offer, vow, or undertake. A deodorant is called *Ban*; a shampoo, *Amplify*. A software product is called (and may) *Excite*. Or one may undertake to *Hide-A-Bed*.

Expressives express a psychological state: they think, apologize, welcome, or congratulate. *Glad* trash bags, or a brand of shoes, *Happy Feet. Aim, Cheer, Joy,* and *Comfort* are not just products; they're states of being.

Declarations or *performatives* perform immediate changes in a situation and often rely on the cultural context: they excommunicate, baptize, declare war, or dismiss from employment. The TV comedian Johnny Carson marketed a garment brand called *Here's Johnny,* after the catchphrase that opened his talk show. It's not exactly a performative like "I now pronounce you husband and wife," but it does bring Johnny from your TV to your back.

In strictly literal terms, a brand name has, of course, just one function that it wants the customer or client to perform: buy a product or service. But under-neath the surface of glossy names, a lot more is going on. Now that you know the rhetorical tricks good namers use, think of what lies underneath *Piggly Wiggly, Bed, Bath and Beyond, Nice 'n Easy, Ball Park Franks, Gain* detergent, and *Crunch 'n Munch* popcorn. Would you like to buy them? It's a rhetorical question.

10

THE SOUND OF SALES

About 60,000 years ago, human beings, or facsimiles thereof, began to use speech, the first of several great communications revolutions. The first use of script happened about 5,500 years ago, and the invention of movable printing type only 500 years ago. As individuals, we repeat the same sequence: speech comes first, then handwriting, then words on the page or screen. Not only do we use speech first in life, but we're likely to hear and speak more words than we later read or write.

Language use came to human beings late in their evolutionary history. Recent research by Simon Fisher at the Wellcome Trust Center for Human Genetics in Oxford, England, and Svante Paabo at the Max Planck Institute of Evolutionary Anthropology in Leipzig, Germany, has dated key mutations in genes involved in neuron activity that could have aided and abetted the acquisition of speech to just about 200,000 years ago.

The Danish linguist Otto Jespersen has outlined no less than five theories of how speech originated, each with evocative labels:

The *Bow-Wow*: Speech arose because people imitated the sounds of nature around them like animal calls, giving rise to onomatopoeic words like *snap*, *crackle*, and *pop*—this could in fact be called the Rice Krispies Theory.

The *Pooh-Pooh* (which may also be called the *Ow-Ow*): Speech arose when people began making instinctive sounds inspired by their emotions. Thus were born interjections like *Ah!* and *Oh!*

The *Ding-Dong*: Speech arose because people made sounds that imitated or harmonized with their environment, creating auditory symbolism. This theory gains some support in that a few common words, like *mama*, have a similar sound linked to meaning in many languages.

The *Yo-He-Ho*: Speech arose because peoples' physical efforts in work produced accompanying grunts, which eventually became chants and other rhythmic, regular sounds.

The *La-La*: Jespersen himself favored the idea that speech arose from sounds, and later songs, that were associated with love and romance, playfulness, and poetic feeling.

Once people had control of their tongue and facial muscles, all of the above may be true. What's incontestable is that language has always had social purposes. Robin Dunbar of Liverpool University has noted that, during much of human development, language had an analogous function to grooming among monkeys, strengthening social ties between individuals and bonding tribes. Dunbar's research suggested that "early humans indulged in a lot of chanting and choral singing."

Given the primacy of speech around the tribal campfire, it's sometimes thought that the written word is a poor cousin and clumsy imitation of the spoken word. In fact, they are related but separate languages, and accordingly have different rules and practices. The morpheme, the smallest basic unit of meaning, is echoed in speech by the phoneme, the smallest basic unit of distinguishable sound. Phonemes together form syllables, which in turn form words. Whether the special kind of words called brand names are spoken more often than they're seen may be debatable. In any case, we hear brand names so often—on radio and TV, in movie theaters, by word of mouth, in spoken requests—that the commercial importance of how they sound can hardly be overstressed.

The novelist Anthony Burgess sounded the right note when he titled his excellent short introduction to linguistics *A Mouthful of Air.* The ways by which the human body moves air to make sounds begins with the lungs. They take in the air, which then exits the body, making pit stops at the larynx, glottis, palate, tongue, lips, teeth, and nose. To a pure linguist, sounds have no meaning: they are just physical sounds. Phonetics and phonology have evolved highly technical terms for how the body produces sound, and how those sounds are patterned in speech. Care for a *bilabial, labiodental, alveolar, postveolar, retroflex, palatal, velar, uvular, pharyngeal,* or *glottal* consonant, anyone? Fancy a *close, mid-close, open-mid,* or *open* vowel? How about a nice *suprasegmental*? Phonetics even has its own alphabet, the International Phonetic Alphabet, which somewhat resembles, but is far from identical to, the English alphabet. Longer, and speckled with special characters, it attempts to represent every possible speech sound in any language. We will not delve deeply into technical arcana, much less write this chapter in IPA. But we will give a hearing to phonetic and phonological features most relevant to brand names.

Whether one agrees with the theories of Noam Chomsky—who, in historical importance, is to linguistics what Charles Darwin is to biology—that we are hardwired for language competence, and that there is a universal grammar that all speakers use, it's certain that unspoken rules govern all our speaking. Intrinsic rules of construction would not permit in English new words like *mlit, lpang,* or *wmelt*—though the brand names of some pharmaceuticals make one wonder. According to Kim R. Robertson, phonological constraints (the physical limits of what's pronounceable) emphasize consonants at the expense of vowels in such phrases and compounds as "stress and strain," "trick or treat," *fiddle-faddle, criss-cross, zig-zag,* "fair and square," and "vim and vigor." More than habit governs how these sounds are sequenced: "square and fair" sounds odd, and "cross-criss" would baffle anyone who heard it. Without going into too much detail, suffice it to say that if your name "sounds wrong," it's more than likely not just you.

About sound symbolism, one is tempted to use the mantra that concludes many an academic paper: "more research needs to be done." Within cultures, people attribute meaning and connotation to phonemes. James L. Dettore, president of the Miami-based The Brand Institute, coiner of the drug names *Lipitor, Clarinex, Sarafem,* and *Allegra,* has said that the letters *X, Z, C,* and *D* are "phonologics," adding that "The harder the tonality of the name, the more efficacious the product in the mind of the physician and the end user."

Phonemes can sound light or heavy, masculine or feminine, slow or fast, strong or weak, light or dark, small or large. As the linguist and anthropologist Edward Sapir said, "Sounds have a certain feeling-significance, they have a certain meaning in themselves . . . when we hear a word for the first time, it is never neutral, but rather it embodies certain values and echoes already residing in the mind." The psycholinguist Cynthia Whissell of Laurentian University in Sudbury, Ontario, adds that "Most phonemes have a distinct emotional character." The Stanford University linguist Will Leben of Lexicon Branding puts it another way: "Sounds have meaning. There is a relationship between speech sounds and emotions."

Traditional brand naming has neglected phonetics in favor of semantics. Leben notes that, in the past, namers used sound symbolism inadvertently. Chevrolet came up with *Corvette* and *Camaro* for semantic reasons but, says Leben, the General Motors division "found that it tested well on the attributes they wanted customers to associate with the product." One reason was that the names' hard *k* consonants evoked "daring" and "active." It could not have hurt either that, as Adrian Room has pointed out, the sound of the hard *k* is associated with words denoting "a quick, clean, or efficient action," among them many beginning with *cl-: clean, clasp, clever, click, clinical, clip, clock.* (Auditory connotations can be taken too far: GM did not call its cars *Clorvette* and *Clamaro.*) Lexicon, which came up with the *BlackBerry* name for the wireless device made by the Canadian firm Research In Motion, saw that a BlackBerry's tiny buttons looked like seeds. *Strawberry* was proposed. However, *straw-* was a slow syllable, and Research In Motion wanted to connote something fast. But *-berry* had the right effect: Lexicon's research indicated that people associate the *b*-sound with both reliability and relaxation—there were two *b*'s in *BlackBerry*—and the short *e* suggested speed. The two short syllables at the start lent crispness and dispatch;

moreover, there was a painless aspect; the alliteration in the syllables conveyed playfulness—like *Kit Kat* candy bars. The namers may also have been thinking of the final *y*, which is, says Whissell, "very pleasant and friendly, which is why you often find it in nicknames." Voilà! *BlackBerry*.

Kim R. Robertson usefully sums up what linguistic and marketing literature has to tell us about the connotations of phonemes. To make sense of his summary, we need to gloss a few terms. *High* means producing a vowel sound relatively near the palate (the roof of the mouth), and *front* means raising the tongue in order to do this. *Low* means a sound articulated low in the mouth, and *back* means the sound articulated at the back of it. Among consonants, a *plosive* sound is one that is produced by stopping the flow of air (using the lips, teeth, and palate) and then suddenly releasing it. A *guttural* sound is one produced in the throat.

Size: high, front vowel sounds (*i, e*) connote a small size while low, back vowels (*a,o,u*) indicate a large size (e.g., *Zee* versus *Koss*).

Movement: high, front vowel sounds indicate dynamic movement while low, back vowels are associated with slow or "heavy" movement. The consonant combination *sl* indicates a gliding or slipping movement. (The children's toy the *Slinky* is slinky by name and slinky by nature.)

Shape: the acute sounds associated with the high, front vowel sounds indicate sharp, angular shapes while the flat sounds associated with low, back vowel sounds indicate roundish shapes.

Luminosity: high, front vowel sounds and the consonants *k, s,* and *l* indicate light while the low, back vowel sounds and the consonants *d, m, gr,* and *br* connote darkness.

Youth: the consonants *j, g, ch,* and the semivowels *y* and *w* connote youthfulness and joy (as in *Joya* and *Jovan*).

Gender: masculinity is associated with plosive and guttural sounds (as in *tiger* or *cougar*) and with the low, back vowel sounds, while femininity is associated with the soft sibilants *s* and *c*, weak *f* sounds, and the high, front vowel sounds (e.g., *Silk-Ease, Zephyr,* and *Cerissa*).

Each alphabetical letter or phonemic set conveys auditory effects and implications, and may have regional and national variations of how it is said. *H*, for example, may or may not be sounded (usually not sounded in British English) in words like *homage* and *herb*. *R* has a greater variety of sounds than any other consonantal letter, and so is much more liable to regional variation. In fact, regional dialects are often classed as being *rhotic* (sounding the *r*'s) or *non-rhotic* (not sounding them). The *z* may be pronounced "zed" in British and Canadian English, or "zee" in American English. Stuart Berg Flexner has pointed out that Yiddish-derived *sch-* words connote repugnance or deflation (*shmaltz, schlemiel, schmuck, and schmo*). Differences may also vary with the individual. As a phoneme, *t* is made the same way as *d*, but the vocal cords change for *d*, but not for *t*—which is strenuous enough that many people utter one for the other.

Though Ford might disagree, one contributor to *Verbatim: The Language Quarterly* found in the letter *f* "something weak, dark and unmanly." He found a disproportional number of words for unpleasant objects or attributes and twice as many negative than positive words, including such phonetically allied cases as *phobia, phoney,* and *phlegm.* They included *defile, deformation, defect,* and *refuse.* In synonymic pairs *f* words were more potent: *filthy* versus *dirty, fickle* versus *changeable, flee* versus *run.* The F section of the dictionary contained many odd words: *fussbudget, flimflam, flibbertigibbet.* As an unvoiced labiodental fricative, it was the opposite of the plosive. F for *false, failure,* and the *f*-word. The writer concludes, "*F,* more than any other letter, encapsulates the experience of failing and death and brings these fatal redolences, like hovering ghosts, to many a shadowed word."

The sounds of the short *i* as in *tip* and the long *e* as in *teeny* tend to suggest smallness. Anthony Burgess points out a word like *little* is formed "by narrowing the passage between the front of the tongue and the palate, suggesting that only something very small could creep through. The long *e* sound makes "the space between tongue and palate only big enough for something microscopic to creep through. With *teeny-weeny* we are on the borders of invisibility." On the other hand, the *o* in *omega* sounds large, as does the *a* in *broad, tall,* and *large.* Adrian Room points out that *x*, or its surrogates *-cks* and *-ks* (*Daks, Horlicks, Volkswagen*), is incisive and businesslike. In the case of *k*, four letters of the English alphabet have the sound **Maalox.** *k* (*q* as in *Quink,* the hard *c* as in *Black Cat, x* as in *Maalox,* and *k* itself). One of the commonest spelling variants is *-ck,* as in *clock* and *clack.* All of which is sufficient reason why many brand names begin with a *k: Kleenex, Kodak, Kotex, Kit Kat.* They are quite different from the hissing sibilants (*s, sh-*), which are often unpleasant sounds ("shuddering sinister snakes"). But they can have their uses, as in lip-smacking *Hershey's Kisses* or the slinky *Salon Selectives.*

In the movie comedy *The Sunshine Boys,* two elderly vaudevillians are discussing comedy itself. "Words with a *K* in it are funny. Alka-Seltzer is funny. *Chicken* is funny. *Pickle* is funny. All with a *K. L*'s are not funny. *M*'s are not funny." Those old-timers were unwittingly discussing plosives. A plosive pops out of your mouth and draws attention to itself. A plosive is a "stopper" in language. A plosive makes us pause for emphasis when we say it. Plosives possess power: think "ex-plosive."

The consonants *b, c, d, k, p,* and *t* are all plosives. Several studies of the top two hundred brand names have made the point that brand names beginning with a plosive have higher recall scores than nonplosive names. *Bic, Compaq, Coca-Coca, Kellogg's,* and *Pontiac* benefit from their initial or terminal plosives. The plosives of *Kodak* are bookends. In fact, a disproportionate percentage of brands start with the same three plosive letters: *C, K,* and *P.*

One of the most successful drugs in recent decades has been the anti-depressant fluoxetine, much better known as *Prozac.* The name has nothing to do with the drug's chemical makeup or how it is to be used. It has other things going for it. It begins with the positive associations of *pro-* and, just as important, with a punchy plosive. Having built up force, it links to *z,* evoking speed (except for "zzzz," of course, though that, too, may be an element in the drug's success) and then pops out another plosive, *k,* at the end. The drug plainly sounds as if it would work.

The startling prevalence of *v, x,* and *z* in pharmaceutical brand names *(Paxil, Zoloft, Nexium)* is also perfectly rational. They are fricatives (as in the letter *f* in *Five Alive*), a consonant made by the friction of breath in a narrow opening, producing an unsettled airflow. The *v* in *five* brings the active lower lip near the passive upper front teeth (labial-dental) and is voiced. A voiced consonant like *v* and *z* makes a buzzing sound in the larynx by vibrating the vocal cords or folds by bringing them close together. Touch your Adam's apple with your fingertips and sound *v* or *z* loudly, and you'll feel what this means. A voice-less consonant (such as *p, t, k,* and *s*) pulls the vocal folds apart and lets air through unimpeded.

The potency of these factors has much to do with the success of the name *Viagra,* the drug for men who have trouble getting erections. Because *Viagra* rhymes with *Niagara,* it suggests splendid vigor and a natural marvel. It begins with a voiced fricative and suggests speed and power *(velocity, vroom).* The *g* is a voiced stop, a consonant that momentarily blocks the airstream, which could be a plosive or else an affricative (like the *ch-* in *choose*). The sonorant *r* is voiced and implies the fullness of *roundness, resonance,* and *rolling.* The vowels do a job, too. The first *i* is a diphthong, a sound that is formed by the tongue moving from one position to the other in the mouth, producing two sliding vowels combined in a single syllable, as in words like *coin, loud, side, beer, bore, house,* and *my.* Anthony Burgess calls it a "sound-journey from one phoneme to another somewhat different." In *Viagra,* a long *i* sound gives way to a subtle but audible long *e* sound. The two *a*'s are looser and rounder, creating a sense of relaxation. These phonetic gymnastics produce a tripartite rhythm that Viagra's namer rather self-importantly says "suggests preparation, action, and release or rest, yielding a pseudo-chronology of the desirable potency effect itself."

Stress and length figure in the sounds of male and female names. Female first names tend to be longer than those of males in syllable count. Males are much more likely to have a monosyllabic first name *(Bob, Jim, Fred, Frank, John)* and are much less likely to have name of three or more syllables. There are a few monosyllabic female names *(Ann, Joan, May)*, but many are trisyllabic or longer *(Katherine, Elizabeth, Amanda, Victoria)*. Female familiar names are longer than male *(Jackie* for either sex, but *Jack* for male; *Bill* vs. *Billie; Bob* vs. *Bobbie)*. Overwhelmingly, male names strongly stress the first syllable; fewer female names do. Few male names stress the second syllable *(Jerome* and *Tyrone* are exceptions). The stressed syllables of female names make much more use of a high front vowel *(Lisa, Tina, Celia)*; the male equivalent is far less common *(Steve, Keith, Peter)*. Female names are much more likely to end in a spoken vowel, as with *Linda, Tracey, Patricia, Deborah, Mary,* and *Barbara.* If not a vowel, the last sound is likely be a continuant (a sound made with an incomplete closure of vocal tract), especially a nasal *(Jean, Kathleen, Sharon, Ann).* Plosives are more likely in male endings *(Bob, David, Dick, Kurt).*

Repetition of consonants is called *consonance* or, more loosely, *alliteration:* *Weight Watchers, Dunkin' Donuts, Roto-Rooter, Planters Peanuts, Brooks Brothers, Chris-Craft, Green Giant, Rice-a-Roni.* A cardboard wraparound for hot beverages is called a *Java Jacket,* and a pest-control service is called *Critter Control.* It also figures in some former tried-and-true brand-name slogans like "Better Buy Buick" and Levi Strauss's "Don't forget that Koveralls Keep Kids Klean."

Repetition of vowels is called *assonance:* Toyota *Avalon, Kal Kan.* Many car models have three-syllable names, all ending with the letter *a,* and vowels pleasingly alternate in *Fruit of the Loom. Onomatopoeia* is the imitation of a sound made or suggested by its referent, like *buzz* or *squawk,* and so we get the detergent *Wisk,* a day care center called *Choo-Choo Nursery,* and a cellular telephone store called *Blah Blah Blah Wireless.*

Brand names often have phonetic spellings, such as *Rice Krispies* and *Jell-O. Lo* for *low, Tru* for *true, Nu* for *new, Lite* for *light,* and *Kool* for *cool* are omnipresent. The word *easy* is a case in point: it's turned up in ads, if not always in names, spelled *eazy, eezi, eazi, ezey, e-z, eezy, ezy, easi, ese,* and even *eeez. Chef Boyardee* is the phonetic spelling of its founding foodie, Hector Boiardi, an Italian restaurateur in Cleveland who cooked up a recipe for canned spaghetti and meatballs. The slip-on loafer is believed to have evolved from a Norwegian shoe called the clog. Henry Bass, a cobbler from Maine, named his loafer the *Weejun* after the final two syllables of *Norwegian.*

English has an odd phrasal category that some have called *word-chains, concatenants,* or *phonopedes.* These contain three words or wordlike forms each, with one to three syllables per word, and linked by two of the following: rhyme, alliteration, and word-repetition. To this class we owe "healthy, wealthy, and wise," the comic war cry "abba dabba doo," "hickory, dickory, dock," and "kitchy, kitchy, koo," not to mention "bag and baggage," "birds and bees," "dribs and drabs," and "facts and figures." We live and learn by leaps and bounds. Add to these another charming category, the rhyming reduplicatives

OshKosh like "hanky-panky," "fuzzy wuzzy," and the Yiddish-derived
B'gosh "fancy-schmancy." The latter chime in many brand names: *Handy Andy, Humpty Dumpty, Piggly Wiggly, Pall Mall*, and *Osh-Kosh B'Gosh*. More conventional rhyme appears in *Shake 'n Bake, Lean Cuisine*, and *El Pollo Loco*, and a children's furniture shop called *123 Mom and Me*.

The last example, longer than most brand names, reminds us of how often rhyme has been used in commercial slogans, sometimes functioning as a pronunciation guide.

"Aetna, I'm glad I met ya" (Aetna Life & Casualty insurance)

"An inch of Pinch, please" (scotch whisky)

"A sweater is better if it's Huddlespun" (Herald Knitwear)

"Be sure with Pure" (Pure Oil Co.)

"Your Water Should be Pur" (water filters)

"Be Wiser—Buy Keiser"(shears)

"For all kinds of insurance in a single plan, call your Travelers man"

"You work hard, you need Right Guard" (Gillette)

"Everything's better with Blue Bonnet on it"

"Fresh up with 7 UP"

"Kitchenaid. For the way it's made" (Kitchenaid Appliances)

"Beinz Meanz Heinz"

The *Grabbajabba* chain of coffeehouses combines rhyme with phonetic spelling. *PayPal* benefits from short syllables, plosives, and alliteration. Simple repetition, special emphasis, and some punning account for the old slogans "Mar-*VEL*-ous" for Vel, a soap product from Colgate-Palmolive, "REMember this REMarkable REMedy . . . *REM*," and "RELy on *REL* for real RELief" for remedies from the Maryland Pharmaceutical Co. This tactic reminds us of Spike Milligan's line, "He walked with a pronounced limp, pronounced *l, i, m, p.* "

As we've observed, English is a slippery language, strewn with homonymic banana peels, slapstick mondegreens, and tongue twisters. Even fluent speakers of English constantly make mistakes. V. A. Fromkin once analyzed 12,000 spontaneous verbal slips and set out the following categories—which don't even include Freudian slips.

Slips of the Tongue or Brain

Type of Error	Meant as	Said as
Initial consonant anticipated	reading list	leading list
Initial consonant perseveration	black boxes	black bloxes
Consonant reversals	well made	mell wade
Final consonants	king, queen	king, quing
Consonant deletion	tumbled	tubbled
Consonant movement	pinch hit	pitch hint
Consonant clusters	damage claim	damage dame
Consonant clusters divided	fish grotto	frish gotto
Vowels	fill the pool	fool the pill
Vowel + r	foolish	farlish
Single features	spell mother	smell bother
Errors within words	whisper	whipser
Stress change	*sim*ilarly	simi*lar*ily
Word reversals	tank of gas	gas of tank
Telescopic errors	Nixon witness	nitness
Derivational affixes	often	oftenly
Blends	person/people	perple
Word substitution	chamber music	chamber maid
Other grammatical errors	It looks as if	I look as if

The patterned qualities and features of sounds in language—length, rhythm, pitch, tone, and loudness—are called *suprasegmental phonology* among American specialists; but we prefer the term *prosody*, used in British phonetics. Brand names use prosody in a less specialized and more traditional sense, the study and use of versification, especially meter and metrical feet. We speak here of the names themselves, not such immortal verse of the early TV era as:

> You'll wonder where the yellow went
> When you brush your teeth with Pepsodent

The terms for metrical feet derive from Greek prosody. A foot, a combination of stressed (accented) and unstressed syllables, has most commonly two syllables, occasionally three, and very rarely, as many as four. *Iambic pentameter* is a verse line of five iambic feet. The iamb is the most common foot in English prosody and indeed in English speech, and it has an unstressed syllable followed by a stressed one ("da DUM"). The galloping *anapest* has two unstressed syllables followed by one that is stressed ("da da DUM"). Anapests are rare: if "In the Mood" were a brand name, it would be an anapest. Here is a list of typical metrical feet, followed by brand names that use them:

Iamb	da *DUM*	Cascade, Tercel
Spondee	*DUM DUM*	Brylcreem
Trochee	*DUM da*	Aga, DaimlerChrysler, Volvo
Amphibrach	da *DUM da*	Callixa, Zamboni
Bacchic	*DUM DUM da*	Turfmaster
Cretic	*DUM da DUM*	Pepsodent, Benadryl, Cadillac
Dactyl	*DUM da da*	Wurlitzer
Molossus	*DUM DUM DUM*	IBM

Like many other three-syllable abbreviations, the colossus *IBM* is a molossus. *Sara Lee, Sara Lee,* we roll along. On a certain level, this discussion of brand name metrics is not so much DUM as dumb, because poetic feet are only meaningful when they march with other feet. But it's a useful reminder that brand names have their own music.

Not only do namers have to be aware of the literal meanings of their names and their connotations, they also have to be aware of the unconscious associations that speakers of English make between sound and meaning, know whether a name is easy or difficult to pronounce, and strive for a name that has an internal poetry and flow.

11

SYMBOLS AND THEIR BENEFITS

We feel an emotion and then find words to fit it. If you hit your thumb with a hammer, you first feel shock and anger—at yourself or at the hammer. Only then do you enter the verbal realm with a string of curses.

Brand namers seek to convey overwhelmingly positive connotations and denotations. After all, the key to powerful brand names is contained in how they convey the idea of reward for clients and consumers. This is not to say that negative factors can't get an airing, but, in most cases, namers seek to convert a negative experience into a positive one. Death is supremely negative, so a name for a chain of funeral parlors will endeavor to translate grief into dignity and consolation. The anger of ghetto youth may be harnessed by brand names with "attitude."

Negative or positive, the process is the same. In the words of the slogan bannered by a household magazine, "It takes Emotion to move merchandise. . . . *Better Homes & Gardens* is Perpetual Emotion." This is true outside homes and gardens. Carol Moog, a practicing psychologist and adviser to advertisers and agencies, notes, "When you name something, you are bridging an unformed emotional reaction into the start of cognitive control. A name without an emotional non-verbal correlative is useless—it does not stick in the mind." Symbols and images that condense emotional content create what Moog calls "a symbiotic relationship between a name and the non-verbal correlative." The "strongest mnemonic for remembering a person's name is to imagize that name." She nominates **DieHard** *DieHard*, for example, as a brand name that characterizes a stubborn, tenacious person who will not give up. "Without the emotional connective tissue, a brand name is worthless."

Our experience always informs our opinion of a brand name. As U.S. Supreme Court Justice Felix Frankfurter said in 1942, in a case involving the Mishawaka Robber and Woolen Mfg. Co. *v.* S. S. Kresge, "If it's true that we live by symbols, it is no less true that we purchase goods by them." Symbols are not paint-by-number qualities or characteristics; they are dynamic relationships. Moog observes that words "will always carry—unless they are complete fabrications, just a bunch of letters tossed together—emotional associations based on experiences and imagery that is pre-existing." Moreover, the visual frame within which a name is perceived—say, the logo that goes with it—is not stronger than the name itself: it is part of the same thing. The mind takes in both the visual and the verbal, and if a product is called, say, *Tripod*, the word cannot be said without visualizing its form. "If the user doesn't understand what the word means," says Moog, "then the marketer has to create enough imagery and enough texture and enough experience so that the word will have an emotional linkage. If people don't know what something is, they will bring in pre-existing meanings and associations."

These ideas are reinforced in *The Meaning of Things*, a 1981 book by two Chicago sociologists, Mihaly Csikszentmihalyi and Eugene Rochberg-Halton. They noted "the enormous flexibility with which people can attach meanings to objects, and therefore derive meanings from them." From objects, "At least potentially, each person can discover and cultivate a network of meanings out of the experience of his or her own life."

What is true of objects is equally true of emotively charged brand names. To understand them, hard science only goes so far. We know that people read with both the eye and the ear. We know that, within the brain, specialized areas deal with language. Wernicke's area in the temporal lobe analyzes and interprets sounds and words; Broca's area in the frontal lobe analyzes the arrangement of words, coordinates mouth movements, and converts letters into sounds producing speech. The angular gyrus of the parietal lobe converts a visual pattern into sounds and words. Neurosurgeons know them all, and, using mechanistic language, cognitive psychologists attempt to describe what happens as the brain processes information.

To get an overview of how brand names make an emotional impact, some courtesy calls on the past century's great psychologists may prove instructive. We need not believe in Freud's triumvirate of id, ego, and superego, much less the Oedipus complex, to realize that there is much we do not know about ourselves, and much that we resist knowing. We need not subscribe to Jung's theories about the collective unconscious to realize that religion, mythology, and folklore, our dreams and visions, have been constants in our history and prehistory, universals of what makes us human. The psychologists offer metaphors for how the mind works. Pharmacology may seem to have made their insights obsolescent, but drugstores have their limitations. The vast popularity of what's loosely called New Age spirituality is one sign that people instinctively know that it takes more than a pill to make us happy.

We are creatures of needs and wants, and are liable to confuse the two. The humanistic psychology of Abraham Maslow sought to establish a hierarchy of what were in fact needs. Unlike Freud, a student of the irrational who studied neurotics, or the behaviorist psychologists who studied how animals responded to stimuli, Maslow dwelt on people of great achievement and how they led their lives. He believed that human beings are motivated by unsatisfied needs, and that lower needs must be satisfied before higher ones can be. He thought that people are basically good and self-governing, and that violence resulted when human needs were thwarted. However, some needs have to be satisfied before a person can act unselfishly, and blocking their gratification makes us sick or evil. As one need is satisfied, a higher one emerges to take its place.

The first level of need involves such basic body requirements as air, water, food, sleep, and the sexual instinct. When the rudiments of survival are ensured, we can move on to safety needs, such as the security of home, family, and personal relationships. We want to live free from abuse and fear, and this, he thought, might be one reason why people seek the comfort and security of a religion. The need to belong is next on the ladder, and thus humans join communities of all kinds: religious congregations, clubs, societies, work groups, gangs. We need to be approved and accepted by others. Performers yearn for applause; beer commercials stress camaraderie, not solitary drinking.

Esteem needs comprise competence or mastery of a task, and the attention, recognition, and admiration that come from others. This relates to the need to belong, of course, but it also involves a need for power. People who have lower needs satisfied may drive luxury cars or own multiple homes because it raises their level of private and public esteem.

Self-actualization occurs at the top of the ladder when subsidiary needs are satisfied. People are then free to achieve what they are capable of becoming and go in quest of knowledge, peace, artistic expression, oneness with God, or embrace some cause like world peace or environmental protection.

Choosing among brand names is the least of one's concerns if one is scrambling to find food and water, seeking shelter in a snowstorm, or dodging bullets. The same is true at the other end of the ladder: a person who strives for spiritual enlightenment couldn't care less about the right deodorant.

The many ways in which commerce attaches itself to needs are not hard to spot. Brand names necessarily appeal to the yearnings and hungers that Maslow outlines. Basic bodily requirements are answered by the sleep aids *Nytol* or *Sominex* (from the Latin *somnus*). Safety comes on duty with the *Sentry* brand of electrical surge suppressors, *Master-Lock*, and *Reliable* Locksmiths. Love and togetherness is whispered by *Sweetheart* containers, and by perfume brands such as *Romance, Joy*, and *Eternity*. Approval or acceptance extends a hand in an insurance company, *Amica*, and a brand of printing papers or a TV channel called *Bravo*. Self-actualization may seek products, New Age or not, that seem to answer spiritual needs. Marketers have not  been immune to the siren song of "New Age." Those two words have appeared in more than 150 U.S. trademark filings. (Our favorite is a Bangladeshi applicant seeking ownership of *New Age Mime*.)

Looking at it the Maslow way, we also see how products or companies can appeal to a need in his hierarchy, especially when associated with a potent graphical symbol. Thus, we have *Bon Ami* cleanser, with its logo of a newly hatched chick; the old *RCA Victor* with its faithful dog, ears attuned to the horn of a *Victrola*; or the vision stated in the *Coopers* company's slogan, "It's not *Jockey* brand if it doesn't have the Jockey boy." The graphics can be even simpler, as in the slogan "I ♥ New York," one of the most imitated devices in promotional history.

Maslow's own hierarchy is illustrated with a ladder or pyramid. Symbols express needs, and symbol making is itself a need. Symbols can carry a positive charge, like the six-pointed Star of David, or a negative one, like the swastika. Brand names symbolize benefits. Symbols take the basic geometrical forms of the circle, square, and triangle, expressed in advertising design and specifically in logos. As a graphical device, the circle or square encloses many brand names. We have the star of *Texaco* and *Mercedes-Benz*, the triangle of *Delta* airlines, and the diamonds of *Sprint* and *Mitsubishi*. The triangle itself may take such shape as the pyramid, trident, or trigram. Less common shapes can be evocative, too, like the namesake chevron of *Chevron* and the *lemniscate*, the figure eight–shaped infinity symbol of Fujitsu. The *mandala*, the squared circle, fascinated C. G. Jung, who understood it to express the wholeness of the self. The cross becomes the Red Cross, the crescent the Red Crescent. The square may become a cube or a magic square, or dispose itself into more intricate arrangements like a chess or checkerboard. The circle may morph into an ellipse, a disk, a ring, a chain, a wheel, a globe, a dome, a curve, a spiral, or a loop. Knotwork fascinates the Japanese, nets psychically ensnare almost everyone else, and the rectangle is transformed into the flag, an icon of a people or nation.

Chevron

MITSUBISHI
MOTORS

Understanding symbols entails taking account of the work of Sigmund Freud and those who at first followed him. Freud's ideas have inspired at least one artistic movement, surrealism, and are now tightly woven into our cultural fabric. But it is to Jung, the leading apostate from the Freudian sect, that we turn for the most fertile ideas on symbolism. Jung's impact on psychiatry, psychotherapy, art, and literature has been less pervasive than Freud's, but some of his concepts have expressed themselves in surprisingly practical ways. His idea about a higher power influenced the founding of Alcoholics Anonymous, and his table of psychological types has led to such commonly used personality tests and questionnaires as the

Meyers-Briggs and the Keirsley-Bates. The dreams that he and Freud analyzed have loomed large in culture, as witness the many people who record their own dreams and take part in dream workshops and seminars. There's a huge public fascination with such Jungian themes as the symbolic or inner journey or quest.

In Jung's theory, the personal unconscious rests on the collective unconscious, a vast holding pen for inherited archetypes and the processes they set in motion. Images, metaphors, symbols, and fantasies make up its language. As he depicts it, the human psyche is a busy place, populated by figures like the *anima*, the repressed inner figure of woman held by a man, and the *animus*, the equivalent figure of man in a woman's psyche. Anima and animus express themselves in such collective forms and figures as Aphrodite, Athena, Helen of Troy, and the Virgin Mary, or as Hermes, Apollo, Hercules, Alexander the Great, and Romeo. They may be projected onto sports and entertainment celebrities, accounting for their fans' fervor.

In Jung's scheme, repressed parts of the unconscious can burst through in the form of visions, symptoms, or dreams. Dreams can be understood causally, but they could also be purposeful, and even unconsciously anticipate the future, though only as a preliminary blueprint. For Jung, symbolic archetypes are not static emblems, but structuring patterns. They appear in folktales, create exemplars in lives of heroes and heroines, and express themselves through myth as the Great Mother or Earth Mother, the supreme Sky God, the Wise Old Man or Wise Old Woman, the idealistic Young Lover. Figures like these possess *Mana*, from a Melanesian word denoting the supernatural power that flows from certain persons, objects, actions, and events, as well as from dwellers in the spirit world—*charisma* is the modern word for it. Mana suggests the presence of a primal source of growth or magical healing. In its ability to attract, repel, destroy, or heal, it is a power possessed by the magician, priest, saint, or holy fool, a personality like Don Juan, the figure made famous by Carlos Castaneda. Jung himself had a lifelong chummy relationship with one such figure, Philemon, with whom he painted and had long conversations.

Archetypes link body and psyche, instinct and image. Archetypes cluster around the basic and universal experiences of life such as birth, marriage, motherhood, death, and separation. They carry a powerful energy that is hard to resist. The archetypal qualities of symbols account for their fascination, usefulness, and recurrence. Gods are metaphors of archetypal behavior and myths are archetypal enactments. The encounter with God images entails trust in a transcendent power, consistent with the ideas expressed in the theologian Rudolf Otto's *The Idea of the Holy*. Abraham Maslow, a humanist not a theologian, called such encounters "peak experiences." It may seem a plunge from the sacred of the numinous experience to the profane of brand names, but belief in a product necessarily involves a level of faith and trust.

Even earlier than Jung, Alfred Adler broke with Freud. Adler started a school of Individual Psychology—something of a misnomer, since he came to stress that the psyche is motivated not by the desire for pleasure but by the need for self-esteem that, under the influence of anxiety and inferiority complexes, degenerates into a striving for power. Adler thought that the healing of collective and personal ills required arousing the ability to cooperate and communicate as a social being. While he was still an orthodox Freudian, Adler proposed the idea of "organ inferiority," in which a person may overcompensate for some physical deficiency. A surprising proportion of great painters have had eye troubles, and some great composers (Beethoven, for one) have had serious hearing problems. That this has a bearing on market psychology is obvious when one sees a small man driving a muscle car, or a suburbanite piloting himself around in an SUV. Or for that matter, an everyman glancing at *Magnum XL*, the extra large size of condoms on the shelf. (He may wish to reject the adage that "one size fits all.")

This scramble through the thickets of twentieth-century depth psychology may seem to take us far from the practical business of naming brands. But has it really? Affirming the emotional connection a brand name must have, Steve Manning lifts a term straight out of Jung: "Any time you put something on the table that has meaning, somebody will object, so the easy route is to pick something that doesn't mean anything. We believe you're better off using words and images that already exist in the collective subconscious."

In his book *Motivation in Advertising*, Pierre Martineau emphasized the importance of a product's "psychological label," noting that it set up symbolic interpretation. However, Kim R. Robertson cautions, "While linguistic scholars may uniformly agree that the Greek root *Nike* . . . means 'victory,' there is no guarantee that a consumer exposed to the running shoe brand name Nike is going to incorporate the concept of 'victory' into his or her meaning perceptions."

No guarantee, perhaps, but a greater likelihood. How could it be otherwise when myths and archetypes saturate every culture? They encompass Europe and the Middle Eastern culture, Judeo-Christian and Greco-Roman histories, the cultures, religions, and traditions of Asia and Africa, not to mention the traditions of native peoples in Australia, the Pacific Islands, and the Americas.

The Swiss linguist Fernand de Saussure sharply separated what he called the *signifiant* (the signifier, the word) and the *signifié* (the thing signified). Psychologically, things represent symbolic value and visual or auditory impact. Named, they contribute to popular culture. Sometimes art imitates life, which in turn imitates art. The J. Peterman Company, founded in 1987, produced a catalog that advertised such costly items as *Windowpane* blazers, *Dylan Thomas* turtlenecks, and *Indian Elephant* caftans. In difficult financial straits, J. Peterman filed for Chapter 11 protection in 2000. But after the immensely popular TV sitcom *Seinfeld* made the company and its founder, John Peterman, the subject of hilarious satire, the company rebounded, and by the summer of 2001 Peterman was selling his autobiography, *Peterman Rides Again*, and running ads that featured spokesperson John O'Hurley, the actor who had portrayed J. Peterman in *Seinfeld*.

The Marlboro Man was a purer invention. The man on horseback content-edly puffing a Marlboro cigarette was launched in 1954 and by 1993 had become the longest-running ad campaign in history. The brand's slogan was "Come to Marlboro Country," a place that had a  cousinly relationship to the blessed land to which myths have given terms as various as *Eden, Paradise, Elysium, Utopia, Valhalla, Camelot,* and *Avalon*. All you needed to get there was a cigarette and, perhaps, a horse. As well, Marlboro Man was one of the many personifications of products and companies. Here is a cast list of some past and present little and not-so-little folk:

Ann Page	Jolly Green Giant (Green Giant)
Aunt Jemima	Juan Valdez
Basset's Liquorice Allsorts	Little Green Sprout
Betty Crocker	Mr. Bubble
Bibendum (Michelin Tire)	Mr. Clean
Cap'n Crunch	Mr. Peanut (Planters)
Charlie the Tuna (Star-Kist)	Mr. Whipple
Can·D·Man (Scott-Bathgate)	Old Grand-Dad
Chiquita Banana	Pillsbury Dough Boy
Chef Boyardee	Poppin' Fresh
Count Chocula	Puffy Pete Popcorn
Elmer the Safety Elephant	Quaker Puffed Pals
Elsie the Cow	Ronald McDonald
Frito Bandito	Smokey Bear
Joe Camel	Spuds MacKenzie
Joe Isuzu	

Such creatures suggest traditional figures of folklore, as do androids, robots, extraterrestrials, and the other imaginative creatures of fantastic, science, or speculative fiction on or off the movie and TV screens. The names of products, companies, and causes bring to life a horde of creatures and fictional characters. As well, brand names enjoin the real-life or archetypal impulses of humanistic or depth psychology. "Nowadays in dreams we often find that the car and the aircraft have taken the place of the monsters and fabu-lous animals of the distant past," Jung noted. Consider some of the names in the automobile category of SUVs:

Buick Rendezvous
Chevy Blazer, TrailBlazer, and Tahoe
Dodge Durango
Ford Escape, Explorer, Excursion,
  and Expedition
Jeep Liberty
Hyundai Santa Fe

Lincoln Navigator
Mercury Mountaineer
Nissan Pathfinder and Xterra
Oldsmobile Bravada
Range Rover Discovery
Toyota Highlander

The themes of adventure and quest implicit in such names connect not only with Maslow's body and social needs, but also with what Joseph Campbell calls *The Hero with a Thousand Faces* in his eponymous book.

Animals in nature and mythology figure in numerous brand names, especially of aircraft and motor vehicles—the *Cougar, Impala, Jaguar, Mustang, Pinto, Sting Ray, Firebird,* and *Thunderbird.* In 2002, Buick roamed the jungle with *Bengal*—another way to put a tiger in your tank—and was named the "best concept car" by *AutoWeek.* Animal imagery rises in the Borden cow, the Dreyfus and MGM lions, and the Playboy bunny. The cow, after all, is proverbial for maternal nourishment, the lion for royal authority, strength, and wisdom, and the rabbit for fecundity—and sexual appetite.

In anthropological terms, animals are often totems adopted as guardians or guides. Any big dictionary of symbols will show that many creatures have other than zoological significance, including such collectives as *flocks* and *herds,* and animal communities such as *hives* and *reefs.* Nor should we forget gender distinctions like *buck, stag, doe, cock,* or *hen,* or the parts and products of animals like the *horn, wing, feather,* and *shell.* Not for nothing is an oil company called *Shell.*

Many species of fauna are inextricable from the idea of food, not just as basic sustenance, but as religious or cultural symbols: eggs, honey, milk, bread, and wine. Flowers, and roses in particular, have a sophisticated language. They involve not just laudable qualities, but historical allusions and religious and geographical loyalties. Symbolic significance flowers in many plants, like the lily's connotations of purity, the oak leaf's of bravery, the olive branch of peace. They may be tied to Greek or Roman gods, as the laurel for Apollo, or even named after mythological characters, like the narcissus. They may be national emblems like the leek for Wales, the maple for Canada, the shamrock for Ireland, and the thistle for Scotland. Spanning many cultures and countries are fruits, nuts, and berries, and groupings that range from gardens and forests to those that are held in the hand or worn, like the garland, bouquet, sheaf, or wreath.

Minerals and the forms they take, as well as such human necessities as salt and industrial products such as steel, have their own language and symbolism. Jade is significant to the Chinese as the purest and most divine of natural materials. Certain organic substances or derivatives, like ivory and pearl, also have special meanings. They not only point to attributes but also to celestial bodies and signs of the zodiac, which in turn carry their own symbolic charge. In brand naming, *Gold* is a leader, followed by *Crystal* and such gemstones as *Diamond*, *Ruby*, *Sapphire*, *Topaz*, *Amethyst*, and *Turquoise*.

The themes of animal, vegetable, and mineral are just the tip of the iceberg. Abstract or metaphysical categories turn up in *heaven*, *heavenly*, and *infinity*. Cycles of the seasons (*Spring*, *Summer*) may appear in names, too, as well as the stages of human life (*youth* and *young*: *Youth Dew* perfume). Some vocational categories, each with their symbolic job descriptions, figure in the acrobat (think *Acrobat* file-conversion software) and magician (*Wiz* or *Wizard* have become clichés of software application names). At work, such people will use the tools of their trade; a musician, for example, may come equipped with a drum, flute, harp, or trumpet. A worker may use a *Workmate*; a student may write with a *Magic Marker*. They wear characteristic costumes, uniforms, or garments, or, for more casual wear, a *Windbreaker*. They may toil at a *Depot*, *Factory*, or *Mart*. It's not all work, though. They may have fun at a *Club*, *Fiesta*, *Circus*, or *Fair*.

 The buildings and other structures in which people live or work, and the furnishings in them, can be branding symbols. We've already seen that allusive brand names commonly draw on the emotive connotations of royalty (*Rex*) or even royal families like Windsor and York. The King and Queen, Emperor or Empress—perhaps the Dairy Queen herself—may live in a *White Castle*. Here is a naming cluster with regal associations:

Count or Countess	Monarch	Sovereign
Crown	Palace	Throne
Duke or Duchess	Prince or Princess	Tiara
Imperial	Royal	Viscount
Knight	Scepter	

A house, even the humblest, holds the ideas of "comfort," "domestic," "hearth," or "hearthstone," and most of all, home (as in *Home Hardware* and *Home Depot*). Even a hovel will have windows, or perhaps *Microsoft Windows*. It will have some means of creating or conveying heat. Fire or flame is a major symbol in itself, radiated in brand names like *Hotpoint* and *Firestone*.

Outside may be a garden or fountain, even conceivably a tower. All have symbolic import.

Domestic articles and utensils are often containers. *Box* is common in brand names. Even a book, and by extension a library, is a kind of container. If the householder is very lucky, he or she may have possess a cornucopia, the horn of plenty—or *Pot of Gold* chocolates.

Weapons are a kind of tool, whether used for defense or offense, and these are present in brand names, too, as in the *sword* (*Wilkinson Sword* razors) and *arrow* (*Arrow* shirts). *Shield* deodorant soap defends against malodorous molecules. Used in work or play will be other tools, especially a key to unlock the house. (*Key Bank* may in fact lead you to a home loan.) Some, like the peace pipe, may be used for ceremonial or diplomatic purposes, but mostly they have utilitarian purposes, like the anvil, axe, hammer, lamp, torch, and yoke. Secure

 indeed is the *Anchor Savings Bank*. Some figure in coats of arms, and indeed heraldry has its own symbolic schemes of color and configuration, as do Freemasonry and gnostically derived semisecret orders like the Rosicrucians, or come-one, come-all fraternal orders like Rotary, the Kinsmen and, the Lions Club.

To make sense of human existence, we can turn to the great scriptures or books of wisdom, each one dense with symbolism (the *Bible*, the *Talmud*, the *Torah*, the *Qur'an*, the *I Ching*, the *Adi Granth*, the *Bhagavad-Gita*) or the spiritual makers of the cosmos or historical founders of religions. Allah is given ninety-nine different names in the Qur'an, and Jesus an almost equal number in the Bible. Although the use of religion in the names of products for a universal market may seem too sensitive or limiting, a sweet wine is called *Lachrymi Christi* ("Christ's tears").

To make sense of a personal destiny, one can delve into the symbolism of palmistry and other forms of fortune-telling, or to the enigmatic hexagrams of the *I Ching*. Of special psychological note are the seventy-eight brightly colored cards of the Tarot pack that represents an complex symbolism that Jung and others have identified as representing the two coinciding struggles of human life, that of establishing oneself in a social position and occupation, and of real-izing an inner sense of the self. Put another way, it's the split or balance of action and contemplation.

The Greek elements of earth, air, fire, and water have been brilliantly psychoanalyzed by Gaston Bachelard. They have traditionally associated body fluids and attributes of humor (blood = sanguine, phlegm = phlegmatic, yellow bile = choleric, and black bile = melancholic). The Chinese have their own system of elements (water, fire, wood, metal, and earth) with linked attributes, among them number, human character, domestic animal, body organ, color, and emotion. The organs and other parts of the body have symbolic extensions, including Freud's beloved phallic images, and the idea of the media as extensions of the human body and nervous system is the core concept of Marshall McLuhan. Beginning with the heart, our organs and physical features figure—some of them may be treated with *Head & Shoulders* or cosmetics from *The Body Shop*.

Breath itself relates to sound and song, to the magic of one's own name and its echo, to magical spells and verbal formulas (*abracadabra*, incantations, litanies, curses, and anathemas), and may take metaphysical form, as with the word *Amen* and the Hindu mantra and the sacred syllable *om*. It may take physical form, too, as a talisman to promote good or an amulet to ward off evil. It may express itself in such supernatural appearances as the aura, aureole, or halo, and a doll, manikin, or puppet that takes on a life of its own. The adoption of consumer goods as our own can become psychosexual fetishes and totems, and avoidance of them, taboos.

Weather, atmospheric conditions, and the changing appearance of the night sky and celestial bodies are true universals, hence their frequency as brand names (*sun, moon, star*, and the planets—from *Mercury* to *Pluto*). *Thunder* and *lightning* imply more than a decision on whether we will need umbrellas. They may take metaphysical dimensions in the idea of the great flood or deluge, and the ark that allowed humanity to survive it. They are inside a *SkyDome*, on supermarket shelves as *Star-Kist* tuna, and could be bought off the car lot as a *Sunbird*.

Kinship relations are universals, too. The strongest ties that bind are those of the family, of mother, father, and child, and their extensions in clan and tribe. This is ultimately why **Uncle Ben's**® so many products begin with *Mother, Aunt*, and *Uncle*.

From an anthropological viewpoint, many rites and rituals are linked to the age-old rhythms of the agricultural year until transplanted to town and city. The weekdays, months, and seasons of the year are connotative, and the divisions of the day as well from dawn to night. Jews, Muslims, and Hindus organize chronology and history in their own traditional calendars. The Chinese and Japanese have distinctive zodiacs, and the Western world's zodiac is the stuff of innumerable books and daily newspaper summaries. The Western zodiac has twelve parts, representing the zone of the sky that includes the apparent paths of the sun, the moon, and the major planets. Each sector corresponds to about 30°, each part named for a constellation, represented by a sign, often given the name of an animal, and classified as Earth, Air, Fire, or Water. Here are the signs, their common names, and the kind of personalities popularly attributed to them, based only on the position of the sun at the time of their birth.

Sign	Name	Personality Type
Aries	The Ram	Energetic, enthusiastic, adventurous. Can be selfish.
Taurus	The Bull	Empathetic, patient, persistent, giving. Can be jealous and possessive.
Gemini	The Twins	Active, communicative, widely knowledgable, adaptable. Can be superficial.
Cancer	The Crab	Highly sensitive to others, sentimental, thoughtful, protective. Can be very moody.
Leo	The Lion	Generous, competitive, enthusiastic, creatively organizing. Can be interfering and bossy.
Virgo	The Virgin	Modest, reserved, practical, hardworking, perfectionistic. Can be indecisive, complaining, and critical.
Libra	The Scales (The Balance)	Accommodating, diplomatic, compromising, easygoing. Can be gullible.
Scorpio	The Scorpion	Secretive, seeking inner motives and purposes, analytical.
Sagittarius	The Archer	Sociable, optimistic, honest, dependable. Can be careless, reckless, and tactless.
Capricorn	The Goat	Prudent, careful, disciplined, methodical, patient. Can lack self-confidence.
Aquarius	The Water Bearer	Independent, friendly, idealistic, optimistic, future-minded, unconcerned with others' opinions.
Pisces	The Fishes	Imaginative, intuitive, creative, impractical, self-sacrificing, living in both the dream world and reality

Larger chronological periods like decades, historical eras, and centuries are dense with connotations. Even leaving aside the complexities of numerology, the cardinal numbers (one to ten), ordinal numbers (first to tenth), and zero mean much more than their numerical or mathematical values, as do such multiples or descriptors as double, binary, and treble. Nor is the impact of numbers exhausted by one to ten; many others have an extra punch of meaning. The significance of numbers of course varies from culture to culture. In Japan, the fortieth, sixty-first, seventieth, seventy-seventh, and eighty-seventh birthdays are celebrated with special solemnity. In the case of Western wedding anniversaries, dates are linked to materials as suitable gifts in a twinned significance, from paper for the first to silver for the twenty-fifth to platinum for the seventieth.

Some personal names get a symbolic boost because they're associated with sovereigns, biblical figures, or saints. Patron saints each have their own feast day, iconography, and set of attributes linked to a place or occupation, and we've encountered them in the names of hospitals and medical centers like *St. Joseph* and *St. Francis*. No patron saint of brand naming exists, but there is one of advertising. It is not, as one might imagine St. David Ogilvy, the founder of the famed advertising firm Ogilvy & Mather, but St. Bernadine of Siena, the fifteenth-century Franciscan friar famed for his preaching and powers of conversion. He is also the patron saint of people with respiratory problems and uncontrolled gambling.

Mythology is a great fountainhead of brand names, especially Greek and Roman, as in *Ajax* cleanser, *Midas* mufflers, and *Titania* voltage converters. Brand names draw on the connotation of grace, charm, beauty, nobility, strength, or wisdom associated with mythological characters. Here are some that frequently occur:

Achilles	Cupid (Eros)	Orpheus
Adonis	Delphi	Pan
Amazon	Diana (Artemis)	Pantheon
Ambrosia	Hercules	Pegasus
Apollo	Hero	Phoenix
Arcadia	Iris	Saturn
Argo	Juno	Titan
Ariel	Jupiter (Zeus)	Trident
Atlas	Mars	Tristan
Aurora (Eos)	Mercury (Hermes)	Triton
Bacchus (Dionysus)	Minerva	Venus (Aphrodite)
Centaur	Neptune (Poseidon)	Vesper
Cerberus	Olympic or Olympus	Vulcan
Cherubim	Oracle	Zephyr

Other gods, myths, and creatures of legend and folklore bear attending to. The *Arabian Nights*, Holy Grail cycle, the Nibelungenlied saga, Arthurian romance, *Grimm's Fairy Tales*—Cinderella, Lancelot and Galahad, Robin Hood and his Merry Men, Charlemagne and his Paladins—are troves of potential brand names, some of which have come to pass, such as *Sea Nymph* and *Aladdin Thermos*. From many sources come such generic large and little folk as dwarfs, leprechauns, elves, pixies, gnomes, giants, and fabulous creatures like dragons and unicorns. Into the names of video and computer games will creep or storm monsters, ogres, creatures of the night like vampires, werewolves, or succubi, or paranormal phenomena like poltergeists and ghosts—all the camp followers of witches, wizards, and warlocks.

Proper names can also be drawn from the arts and popular culture, becoming mythological characters and then brand names: Don Juan, Sherlock Holmes, and Mickey Mouse. They can resonate far beyond their historical or geographical importance, though of course they could not have achieved their status without having loomed large historically or geographically. The names of people are already present in generic terms (*Nehru jacket, Shakespearean*). As the makers of *Victoria's Secret* undergarments realized, they can confer brand-name benefits (although in the case of Hitler and Stalin it's hard to imagine what they might be).

The symbolism of generic geographical features is well known: the island, the desert, the river, hill or mountain, the valley, the sea itself, but locations (corner and crossroads, the center or omphalos, nadir, and zenith) and directions (east, west, north, south, up, down, sideways, or right and left) have intrinsic meaning, too. But specific famous places, addresses, and locations can have names with extra symbolic dimensions (think, for example, of all the connotations of *America* or *American*. Thus brand names will climb Everest, explore the Amazon, sound Motown, or extol the homey merits of *Town Square* and *Village Green*.

The names of national, ethnic, or religious groups can do more than simply identify, because they will trail behind them stereotypes that range from abject flattery to outright racism. Of the former, one may cite the old slogan of Paillard Inc.: "Hermes means Swissmanship, a step beyond craftsmanship." The hundreds of product names in the IKEA catalog make up a gazetteer or phone directory of Nordic nomenclature, clotted with umlauts: the *Fägelbo* corner bed sofa, *Poläng* armchair, *Skärpt* knives, *Innervik* swivel chair, *Ekeberg* queen bedframe, *Svala* suite of children's furniture, and *Jutta Ruta* curtains.

The distinction between word and thing is especially acute in the case of color names. *Blue* is a highly emotive word ("Am I blue?") but also blue is part of the spectrum or part of a color scheme—a typical bag of fifty *M&M* candies contains, by the way, fifteen brown, ten red, ten yellow, five green, five orange, and five blue. Colors can be highly emotive culturally as well, as in the red, white, and blue of the United States or the green of Ireland. They can be used to gauge temperament, as in the widely used Lüscher Color Test, in which one chooses from a pack of cards in various shades. The key here is not strictly speaking the separate emotive color—purple is considered to indicate emotional instability—but the combination one makes with differently colored cards. They have even spawned a new vocational category—color consultants.

The *Color Me Beautiful* system, founded by Carole Jackson in the United States in 1974, helps women discover their natural beauty through color by using the metaphor of the four seasons. A person must be in harmony with her true color, and "color vitamins" are related to a range of positive and negative attributes. She has lots to work with: one dictionary of color terms lists more than three thousand.

In English, white connotes fairness and harmlessness *(white magic)*, professionalism *(white collar)*, surrender or peace *(white flag)*, and white as a skin color *(white slavery,* "the white man's burden"). Black is generally negative— evil, falsehood, error, grief, despair—but note there are also positives: *in the black* and *black belt*, not to mention black as a skin tone. Blue is extremely popular among phrase makers, and there is a William Gass novel called *On Being Blue.* Red is almost as favored: the universal color of blood and fire, it's acquired since the nineteenth century the cultural connotation of Communism—since it is a lucky color to the Chinese, it's no accident that it features in the flag of what used to be called Red China. Green has become the political color of ecology and environmental protectionism, although in English it is traditionally the color of envy. Not so in French, Italian, and German, in which envy is yellow.

Colors have all kinds of positive—and sometimes highly negative—connotations. For the latter, we have only to think of yellow as signifying cowardice and the infamous yellow star that Nazis forced European Jews to wear. Color is culture-dependent: black suggests death in the Western world, white suggests it to the Japanese and is the color of funeral attire among the Hindus. Yellow when not golden has negative associations, except of course, the yellow rose of Texas. Purple words are uncommon in other languages, but popular in English for the sense of pomp and royalty. The shipping company UPS promoted its corporate color, brown, as a nickname, "Brown," and asked, "What can Brown do for you?"

Pink has been for a girl, at least since World War I, and blue for a boy. Blue has the historical attributes of hope, piety, and sincerity. Pepsi offered a new fusion of berry and cola called *Pepsi Blue.* For U.S. restaurant names, blue has become a signature color. Here are some:

Amadeus Blue	Blue Chalk	Blue Moon	Deep Blue
Bistro Blue	The Blue Collar Grill	The Blue Owl	Dharma Blue
Black & Blue	Blue Grotto	Blue Peter's	French Blue
Bloo	Blue Heaven	Blue Sky	Le Blue
blu	The Blue Heron	Blue Smoke	Mt. Blue
Blue Agave	Bluehour	Blue Spruce	Red Hot & Blue
Blue Angels	Blue Iguana	Blue Whale	sixtyblue
Blue Bell	Blue Lagoon	Cactus Blue	Uni Blue
Blue Bird	The Blue Marlin	Cool Blue	Zanzibar Blue

As nouns, verbs, and adjectives, symbolic words appear in discourse, including but not exclusive to catchphrases, slogans, fables, folktales, proverbs, traditional and urban legends, the names or titles of songs, movies, TV programs, music groups, advertising theme lines and taglines—and, of course, brand names. Although they may be as small as an alphabetical letter ("an *A* student," "*X* marks the spot"), they are keywords, each dragging behind it a dense cluster of related derivatives. A word is not just a potent symbol in itself, but also a "word" linked with other words. *Brewer's Dictionary of Phrase and Fable* shows hundreds of such clusters.

Apart from versatility and flexibility, the other salient characteristic of symbols its their perpetuity. As Carol Moog says, "The psychological importance of heritage may derive from the power of being a participant in a continuous line that connects and bonds one to the right to be alive, to a history that one carries forward from the living past, through death and on into the next generation; the link is a link to immortality."

The Eternal Return is a important myth. In marketing, this can express itself in several ways. It may mean that a new brand name derives from a traditional one, as in *Chevette, Disprin, Electrolux, Kodachrome, Minolta,* **◁ Electrolux** *Polyfilla, Range Rover,* and *Victrola. Clarinex,* Schering-Plough's allergy medicine, kept the brand name of a popular drug, *Claritin,* alive for another generation. It may mean the creation of a family, as in the long *Ford* history of F-names. A boat company may first coin a meaningful neologism, the *Suncruiser* line, and then pick island names for individual boats—*Bimini, Tahiti, Trinidad.* It may also mean returning to roots. When *New Coke* failed in the marketplace, we heard again about old *Coke.*

The reader may conclude we mean that *anything* can be a symbol. If so, the reader would be right, because a symbol is not so much a thing in itself as the associations and connotations we bring to it. The year 1984 has come and gone, but as a symbolic year from the Orwell novel *1984* lives on. Those who would understand life in its fullness ignore symbols at their peril—as do marketers. The popularity of tattoos, of ear-, nose-, and tongue piercing, of body decoration of all sorts, is not just some whim of fashion, but a reversion to ancient tribal customs and their authenticity. Some might argue that the appropriation of symbols for commercial purposes devalues their content and betrays a long legacy of profound belief in what they tell us about life, death, and eternity. But it could equally be argued that brand names mark their recurrence in another form. People are putting money where their mind is.

12

NAMES HEARD ROUND THE WORLD

Contrary to appearances, all the world does not know English. As many as six thousand other languages are spoken, although it's sadly true that the number drops every year. In some respects languages are analogous to organisms like plants and animals. If, like plants and animals, their populations dwindle enough, they become extinct.

English is not on the endangered list. It ranks second among mother-tongue speakers and is the world's premier auxiliary language. A December 2000 survey found that 56 percent of fifteen European Union member countries spoke English, 40 percent as an acquired language. Nearly all countries' TV ads were partly in English. English is an official language in more than forty countries and an "associate" official language in India and Pakistan.

English-speaking countries, notably the United States and Britain, are sometimes accused of linguistic imperialism, even cultural genocide. But no matter how much English is used in business and the mass media, those who have it as a second language typically rely on their own tongue to communicate anything to do with family, friendship, and love. Although English is the dominant language of the Internet, it's been estimated that more than 60 percent of those online have a different first language.

Nonetheless, the dream of the nineteenth-century Polish medical doctor Ludovic Zamenhof has been fulfilled, but not in the way he hoped. Zamenhof invented Esperanto (from a Romance language root for "hope"), which was devoid of irregular verbs and almost free of tricky idioms. About three-quarters of its vocabulary derives from Romance languages. (An Esperanto sentence handy for customers is *"Mi preferas plendi, dankon,"* meaning "I prefer to complain, thanks.") Esperanto has about fifty thousand fluent speakers.

In the 1940s, C. K. Ogden and I. A. Richards compiled Basic English, a word list that consists of 850 words: one hundred for operations (*come, be*), four hundred for general things (*motion, mountain*), two hundred picturables (*angle, sail*), one hundred general qualities (*able, free*), fifty opposites (*bitter, loud, hard, soft*), with a few simple rules. But, although it strongly influenced language teaching, Basic English didn't fare any better than Esperanto in becoming a universal medium.

English is a juggernaut (from the Sanskrit *Jagannātha*, "Lord of the world"). Yet the head count of those who don't speak English as a first language dwarfs

143

native English speakers. By the year 2000, there were 874 million mother-tongue speakers of Mandarin, and for Chinese in general the number is even more impressive when it includes the speakers of other Sinitic varieties: the 77 million people who speak Wu (also called Shanghaiese) and 71 million who speak Yue (Cantonese). The 366 million speakers of Hindi outpace the 341 million speakers of English, with fourth-ranked Spanish coming up fast, somewhere between 322 million and 358 million. There are at least 18 million Spanish speakers in the United States. The rapid growth of Spanish domestically (especially in Florida, the New York City area, and the Southwest) so alarmed California Senator S. I. Hayakawa (who was Canadian-born) that in 1981 he proposed a constitutional amendment to make English the U.S. official language. The ELA (English Language Amendment) failed, but several states have since adopted similar measures.

Next in the world ranking are, in this order, Bengali, Arabic, Portuguese (mainly in Brazil), Russian (which has slipped in the ranking over the past few decades), Japanese, German, and Korean. French follows. Once the language of diplomacy and the indispensable auxiliary language for any cultivated person, French has faded badly over the centuries and now is chiefly spoken in France and its present and former colonies, in Belgium, Switzerland, and Québec, in pockets elsewhere in Canada, and in Louisiana. Trailing the pack, but with at least 70 million speakers each, are Javanese in Indonesia and the Telegu in southeastern India. About 225 languages today are spoken by at least two million people each. In a cosmopolitan mood, the U.S. Department of Education in 1985 published a list of 169 languages it considered to be "critical." Knowledge of them was deemed to promote scientific research or economic and security interests—though it was hard to see how Ciokwe, Kamba, and Wolof counted. Oddly enough, English was not included.

How languages handle grammar is one way of sorting them out. In analytic languages, words have no grammatical endings and express syntax through word order: Chinese, Vietnamese, Samoan. In inflecting languages, the changing internal structure of words express grammatical relationships, typically by endings that send several signals at once: Ancient Latin, current Greek, and Arabic. In agglutinative languages, words are built from a long sequence of units. Each unit sends a grammatical signal; a sequence of five affixes may express person, number, tense, voice, and mood: Turkish, Finnish, Japanese, Swahili. In polysynthetic languages, words are often lengthy and complex, and contain a mix of agglutinating and inflecting features. These are often indigenous or aboriginal languages: Inuktitut, Mohawk, Australian Aborigine.

English is a mongrel. It's comparable to a tree in which the trunk of grammar and the most commonly used vocabulary are Germanic, and most of the leaves are Greek, Latin, or French—with new buds sprouting every day in the form of loan words from languages across the world. English is sometimes accused of having no grammar, though the 1,020 pages of *A Grammar of Contemporary English* by Randolph Quirk et al. argue otherwise. It is a Germanic language, though with much vocabulary and some grammar from the Romance languages, and ultimately from Ancient Latin and Greek. Yet English is also an analytic language, like Chinese, in that the syntax of words, rather than their inflection, determines the grammar.

English mostly ignores gender of nouns, and there is no distinction between familiar and polite forms like the French *tu/vous* and the German *du/Sie*. Many languages use spatial terms to describe time. In English, time is strictly linear, as in "We're behind schedule" or "Let's move the meeting forward." In tonal languages like Chinese, it's almost impossible to adapt words to a Western melody and still preserve meaning. For the English-speaker, even languages containing many cognates—vocabulary look-alikes—can be rife with the shoals of *faux amis*, or false friends. In French *demander* is to request, not demand; *libeller* is to make out a check, not to libel; and *sensible* is sensitive, not sensible. The German *also* is "therefore," and in Spanish *constipado* is to have a head cold.

David Crystal has noted that many other languages don't have an equivalent for the many words we employ for the different sizes, types, and uses of motor vehicle. On the other hand, there is no general English word for a vehicle driver, though *mobilist* and *wheelist* have been tried. In English many words (more often spoken than written) signify things that temporarily elude speakers' minds, beginning with *doo-dad*. Contests and radio phone-in shows often invite people to fill lexical gaps in the language with newly minted "needed" words, such as *aginda* for a preconference drink, or *catfrontation* for a cat fight.

Language distinguishes social classes but ignores borders. In many countries, the largest linguistic group comprises less than half the population. More than one hundred languages are used in Britain. Millions around the world are driven into exile by reason of politics or war. Many millions more are migrant workers or toil at jobs that pay better than they do back home: Turks fill jobs in Germany; Africans in France; Indians, Pakistanis, and Filipinos in the Middle East and elsewhere; West Indians and Latin Americans in the United States and Canada.

When all is said and heard, English is our Latin, but with greater reach than the Romans ever managed. Some symptoms: In Japan, Yoshio Tesawara published a popular book called *Lack of English Ability Is Destroying Our Nation*. In the People's Republic of China, an estimated 300 million people have enrolled in government-sponsored English classes. In a thirty-country survey by RoperASW, a U.S.-based market consulting firm, 31 percent of sample respondents—representing nearly 2 billion people—said they have "some" spoken English fluency, up from 27 percent in 2000. The largest relative increase, no doubt a delayed consequence of the Iron Curtain's collapse, was in

Central and Eastern Europe. English is the *de facto* common language in the European Union. In the near future nearly all the Dutch may be bilingual, and the same process is under way in Scandinavia.

Another factor in erasing Babel is that technospeak for cars and electronics products is nearly universal. The scattered outlets of multinational chains like Boots, MacFisheries, Mövenpick, and Wienerwald, at least in Europe and the United Kingdom, offer many of the same products and brand names. Not coincidentally, many of these brand names are in English. In Finland, it sometimes pays not to translate a brand name. Crystal reports that in 1960 a Finnish firm distributed canned coffee using Finnish labels. Sales were bad. Then the firm had new labels made with a text in English on the same cans, and sales shot up. English marketing firms and other businesses make use of foreign languages to convey special effects—such as the use of French for the names of restaurants, nightclubs, and perfumes. Many Finns are already trilingual in Finnish, Swedish, and English, and the language trio may be found on many highway and store signs in and around Helsinki.

Store signage is a good gauge of linguistic macaronics—mixtures of languages. In the Slovenian city of Kranj a researcher found "MURA European Fashion Design Boutique Elita," and in Ljubljana "BIG BANG melodija." In Vienna there was "Last-Minute-Urlaub l'tur Software Dschungel," and in Trieste "Goielleria Orologeria Gold Emotion." A stretch of Regent Street in London included shop signs in French, Italian, and German, and mixed English-French, English-German, and English-Slavic. One could find the French of *Esprit* ("spirit") and *Aigle* and the Italian *Blunauta* (word formation of *blu*, "blue," and *nauta*, "ferryman"). There was something called *Triumph House Carree Blanc* and *Lloyds TSB Bureau de Change*. Then there was the roll call of international brand names: *Gucci, Viyella, Scholl, Jaeger,* and *Adolfo Dominguez*. A spot-check of the telephone directory under "Restaurants" showed that nearly half the names were in a language other than English.

Globalism and Its Discontents. At the turn of the twentieth century, the International Telegraph Convention decreed that coded telegrams could only be sent mixed or wholly in Dutch, English, French, German, Italian, Portuguese, Spanish, or Latin. Today, no one doubts that English is the dominant language of employment, business, communications, and popular culture.

In the collision between English and other languages in brand naming and marketing, the smashup can come from the use of an English brand in a foreign market, or the translation of the English brand into a foreign tongue. Brand names can symbolize much more than a product or service. For a tourist abroad, a familiar brand name may be a reassuring reminder of home. For a foreign consumer it may connote status or prestige. For a foreign businessperson it may signify profits; for a foreign worker it may represent a job. For geopolitical enemies or intellectual critics of the United States or any other big powerful Western country it may epitomize globalization, imperialism, or capitalism—so-called Coca-Colonization.

Some governments labor to preserve a cherished national identity. In Canada, Québec language laws for a time included legal trademarks among the English words to be stricken from the province's commercial signs, leading to such oddities as the purging of an apostrophe, as in *Wendys*. Trademarks were later exempted. In Greece, home of the 2004 Olympics, an Athens municipal law ordered that firms had to translate or be fined: *McDonald's* would become *MakNtonalts*; the Dutch-based furniture store Habitat something like *Xampitat*; and poor *Wendy's* call itself *Giouenti's*. Language  change can be an instrument of national policy. From 1928 into the 1930s the president of Turkey, Kemal Atatürk, made his country switch from Arabic script to a modified version of the Roman alphabet, purging Persian and Arabic words from the language and simplifying the literary style so that it was closer to colloquial speech. Atatürk's language reforms were unprecedented. But in scope it was minuscule compared to the huge twentieth-century language reforms in China, which involved, among much else, the promotion of Mandarin as a common language and the romanization of phonetic spelling as Pinyin, which is why we now we write *Beijing*, not *Peking*.

Wars and geopolitical events play havoc with language in general, and brand names in particular. France, Germany, and Canada were among the countries that declined to join the U.S.-led coalition that invaded Iraq in 2003. France-bashing became something of a U.S. domestic sport. Baltimore's Star Spangled Ice Cream Co. produced a line that included *I Hate the French Vanilla, Iraqi Road,* and *Smaller Government* and advertised its products at  *www.starspangledicecream.com*. Some 10 percent of U.S. consumers said they had found substitutes for German or Canadian products, and 15 percent boycotted French goods. Even the U.S.-owned *French's Mustard* suffered a drop in sales, despite its stout denials that it had anything to do with Paris. By the same token, since September 11, 2001, words like *America* and *U.S.* regained favor domestically, particularly for tech companies engaged in security and related fields. The reverse was true in Europe, especially in France, where the French have always regarded America with an odd mixture of envy, resentment, and admiration.

Even in peacetime, consumers often confuse national origins of products. It gets worse in a war. Wirthlin Worldwide, a division of Wirthlin-Hilliard, interviewed one thousand Americans in early April 2003 and found that, asked to link brand name with country of origin, some 80 percent of respondents recognized *Perrier* as French and 62 percent knew the same about *Christian Dior.* Some 87 percent knew *Volkswagen* was German and 76 percent knew *Mercedes-Benz* was. A reasonable recognition rate, but only 49 percent knew *Moosehead*

beer came from Canada, and only 25 percent thought *Molson* was Canadian—the same number thought it was German. Some 79 percent thought *Canadian Club* was Canadian: right and wrong; although distilled and bottled in Canada, it had British owners, as did *Canada Dry,* which 68 percent said was Canadian. *Labatt,* the beer maker, was recognized as Canadian by only 24 percent of Americans: 37 percent thought it was French. A mere 12 percent knew *Bombardier,* Montréal-based maker of jets and Ski-Doos, was Canadian;

15 percent thought it was U.S., and 14 percent considered it French.

Since 1990 cola-loving Iraqis had to rely on the likes of Baghdad Soft Drinks, which distributed its products in imported Pepsi bottles. In the wake of the invasion, Pepsi-Cola and Coca-Cola contemplated reentering the Iraq market. They might face competition, however, from the French-owned *Mecca-Cola,* launched in France and the Middle East in 2002, and *Qibla-Cola,* based in the United Kingdom and a success in Europe, as well as a presence in Bangladesh and Pakistan. Said a Quibba spokesperson: "Quibba transcends race, ethnicity, religion and language. It's a cola and product for all people of conscience."

Globalization involves complex issues, and proponents and opponents of it become heated in argument and sometimes even vandalize cars and storefronts. Yet if people want to buy goods produced outside their local communities, especially from a foreign country, they will require brand names and logos to identify them, and a vast system of communication and transportation to make them available. In any case, enemies of globalization might be surprised to learn that, in some respects, marketers can be on their side.

Since Theodore Levitt's seminal article, "The Globalization of Markets," was published in 1983, globalization has thematically dominated international business strategy. Seldom has one concept been so overused, misused, and—by its opponents—abused. It was a neat idea: A big company drives a global brand with one big differentiated idea, from Akron to Auckland. Its brand gets recognized on the shelf by travelers and natives alike. A single marketing team means it saves on staff and time. A single global name and design lowers production and manufacturing costs. The same pool of commercials used everywhere means it saves production dollars (and its ad agency does less work). Such was Levitt's counsel.

But the idea of marketing a standardized product with a uniform message around the world remains theoretical. Although a product concept may be universal, it must be adapted to differences in local culture, legislation, and even production capabilities. Consumers' interests and needs are not the same everywhere. Not even graphic signs are the same. In North America, graphical shorthand might include a stop sign to signify "stop," a mailbox or envelope to signify e-mail, an open hand to signify "help," an exclamation mark to draw attention to key text. But not all these icons translate into other cultural contexts. Not all mailboxes look the same the world over. The open-hand icon may be offensive. Not all languages use exclamation points.

In marketing, as with linguistic signs, the local, regional, or national context is vital. By the time a multinational shows up in Malaysia or Brazil, a local firm may have preempted a vital differentiating idea. Global strategy is often a mirage. Consumers' interests and needs are not the same everywhere. "Homogenization" is a myth, in its secondary meaning of "fallacy." Domestic markets everywhere are segmenting. True, *Oil of Olay* was the first beauty product to say a woman can be beautiful at any age, and that idea speaks to women the world over. And companies can turn their national origins and heritage into global identities. *Levi Strauss* and *Disney* export the American dream. *Chanel* and *Louis Vuitton* represent French chic. *Armani* represents Italian style. *Burberry* stands for solid British values. But for most marketing mortals who are chasing the "uniform market" and "one global village," the facts don't support the dream.

CHANEL

One global pioneer found there were limits. *Heineken* is a global premium beer brand and the world's second-largest brewer. It is meticulous about product consistency. All their breweries stick to the same recipe. To make sure the product is the same everywhere, every two weeks their breweries send samples to professional tasters in the Netherlands. They also buy back some bottles from small shops as far away as Shanghai for testing. Employees are not permitted to alter a single line on the label, lighten the packaging colors, or vary the shape of the bottle. Vary *any* component and you go to Heineken hell.

Standardizing the taste is one thing. Standardizing the marketing is another. Karel Vuursteen, Heineken's CEO, admits that it's impossible: "We don't believe you can communicate to all cultures in the same way. In the United States and Western Europe, beer is a normal part of life, it's thirst quenching. In Australia and New Zealand, it's very macho. In many Southeast Asian countries, it's almost a 'feminine' product—sophisticated. Thus, we give our local representatives a lot of freedom in sales and advertising."

Another would-be global brewer found to its dismay that its beer didn't travel well at all. *San Miguel* claimed something like 80 percent of the Philippines beer market. With that kind of share, growth had to come from elsewhere. So management built a brewery and bottling plants in China and Hong Kong in order to become a pan-Asian brand. Instead, it was *San Miguel* that got panned. They stumbled in Hong Kong by projecting the same brand image it had in the Philippines—a working-class beer consumed by the masses. One ad showed a group of San Miguel drinkers on a dusty construction site, ogling young women. They neglected the fact that Hong Kong had a huge number of young urban Asian professionals. The yuppies took one look and reached for a Heineken.

Nestlé has been a global company from its earliest days. In the 1860s, the Swiss pharmacist Henri Nestlé saw how many children were dying—at the time infant mortality was higher in Switzerland than in most emerging countries today. He developed the first Nestlé product, an infant cereal to help nourish them when mothers could not do it. Henri Nestlé had two visions. First, he went international at once. The product was in five European countries four months after launch. Second, he wanted his own brand on display everywhere.

Even with its global thrust, Nestlé came to realize that global brands alone couldn't win the marketing war. An analysis by the McKinsey consulting firm showed that the company regularly sends out different horses for different courses. *Nescafé* is Nestlé's top-selling coffee brand around the world, but in India, it had to create a special instant coffee named *Sunrise*, blended with chicory to give a strong, familiar flavor and please local taste buds. Sunrise out-sells Nescafé. Nestlé has several dozen worldwide brands, such as *Baci, Buitoni, Carnation, Kit Kat, Maggi, Mighty Dog*, and *Perrier*, more than a hundred regional brands, such as *Alpo, Contadina, Herta, Mackintosh*, and *Vittel*, and more than seven hundred local brands, such as *Brigadeiro, Solis*, and *Texicana*. But still, it's not even close to global.

The most consumed foods in the United States are dairy products, beef, and potatoes. A huge proportion of the world's population eats none of them, or has dietary prescriptions about how they should be mixed. McDonald's learned this in India. The golden arches wanted to think globally, but it was forced to act locally. In India, most consumers consider cows sacred and don't eat beef. So McDonald's served the *Maharajah Mac*—two all-mutton patties, special sauce, lettuce, cheese, pickles, onions on a sesame-seed bun—in place of the beefy Big Mac. In Germany, the second-largest market outside the United States, there were different challenges. Menus became much more varied *(Oriental Burgers)*, and there were more vegetarian offerings *(Veggie McNuggets)*. The international account director for the ad agency Leo Burnett, which handled the McDonald's brand in eighteen countries, has observed, "Marketing food is a tricky business precisely because everyone has an idea of what good food should be, and it's usually a different idea. The U.S. overtones of a McDonald's sandwich might be aspirational in Latin America or even some of the Asian markets but, by the same token, these overtones are guaranteed to make European hackles rise and trigger complaints about American culinary cultural imperialism."

Finns, among the world's heaviest coffee drinkers, con-
sume a yearly average of 160 liters per person. General Foods
targeted Finland with its Swedish coffee brand, *Gevalia*, a
blend of Colombian, East African, and Indonesian beans that
bragged on its label that it serves "His Majesty the King of
Sweden and the Royal Court." But the megamarketer's entry
was thwarted by the decades-old local brand, *Paulig*. The fact that Finland had
been a Swedish colony for nearly seven hundred years (until 1809) may have
had something to do with it, too. In any event, there was no room for a standardized coffee product with a universal message in Helsinki. Paulig, the home-
grown brew, kept perking along with a more than 50 percent market share.

The attributes of beer brews can vary, too. In Mexico, *Corona* is a humble,
low-rent beer. You can pick up a six-pack in a Mexico City *supermercado* for
about $2.50. But in the United States, Corona has a spring-break, palm-trees,
drink-it-with-a-lime upscale image. That same six-pack will cost more than
twice as much in Atlanta. Much to the bewilderment of Mexicans, Corona is now
the top-selling imported beer in the United States. Or, consider yogurt. In the
United States, yogurt is generally seen as a healthy food, and *Dannon* (known
internationally as *Danone*) celebrates that. But in France, Danone was seen as
too indulgent and pleasure-oriented. So the company created the Danone
Institute, a research center dedicated to food and education.

Kellogg's is a proud old name for cereal. Folks from Battle Creek, Michigan,
would be repelled in India, where hot food is preferred for breakfast because
 Indians believe heat infuses them with energy. Kellogg's
was out of luck in India. Unilever, which marketed *Lux*
throughout Asia, boosted its brand with commercials
with Demi Moore and Brooke Shields. But what was Lux?
In Indonesia, it was a soap. In China, Taiwan, and the Philippines, it was a
shampoo. In Japan, it was everything from soaps to shampoos. That was the
problem with all-out globalization. Tastes vary. Preferences vary. People vary.
You can differentiate anywhere. But you can't differentiate everywhere with
the same idea.

Some opponents of multinational culture would argue that localization, the
adapting of products for foreign markets, is only globalization in a new, more
sinister guise. What we can safely say is that globalization engenders a new,
heightened sensitivity to foreign manners, mores, and sensibilities.

Lost in the Linguistic Fun House. In tailoring brand names for overseas markets,
translators are the first cutters of the cloth. Besides their place in big business
firms and ad agencies, they work as in-house staff at national and international
organizations (the United Nations, the European Union) and government bodies (the majority of Canadians speak English but the federal government must

produce all documents in French as well). They create or use software, electronic products, and user guides in multiple languages.

Computational linguistics and translation-specific tools—the evolved offspring of research carried out during the Cold War—have created digital and online tools. The security fears that followed September 11, 2001, led to polylingual search software. The CIA and National Security Agency have been using products from Language Analysis Systems, one of which, NameClassifier, attempts to identify the cultural origins of a name, and another, NameHunter, searches forenames with the same linguistic parameters, such as whether affixes like -y and de la are used. Another company, Basis Technology, in Cambridge, Massachusetts, has developed a language analyzer, based on phonics, for translating Latinized names back into their original alphabets so they can be searched against lists in the original language. This is handy, since "Quaddafi" can be spelled at least sixty ways in the Latin alphabet.

Translation aids can range from simple glossaries of terms to the latest in speech-recognition devices. In this technofuture, machine translation ought to be the real-life answer to the "Babelfish" in Douglas Adams's *Hitchhiker's Guide to the Galaxy*, a creature that when inserted into an ear provided seamless translations from extraterrestrial speech. No, *nicht*, *non*, *nyet*. Machines can be as blooper-prone as people. It was a machine that translated into Russian the saying "The spirit is willing, but the flesh is weak" as "The vodka is good, but the steak is lousy." The name "Rob Malkin," when pronounced in Japanese as "Robu Marukin," was "parsed" (analyzed) by speech recognition software as *rokumaruchin*, which means "six Japanese spaniels." Mistranslation of numbers can lead to surprising discounts. "There is a Lufthansa flight at 4:40 P.M." was taken to be literally "There's a Lufthansa flight bed for 40 yen," producing the translation: "A Lufthansa Airlines flight will be available. That is 40 yen."

Humans do worse. The hapless business people who consult a pocket dictionary and hope for the best are staples of tourist humor. (Poland, on a restaurant menu: "Salad a firm's own make; Limpid red beet soup with cheesy dumplings in the form of a finger; roasted duck let loose; beef rashers beaten up in the country people's fashion.") Lest the English-speaker guffaw too much, we should remember that the locals are at least making an effort to communicate in a different language. Moreover, the English howlers that a local hotelier, restaurateur, or clerk may commit are nothing compared to the damage a visitor can do to a foreign tongue.

Latino Lapses. In a move that has become legendary for how not to market a brand, General Motors between 1972 and 1978 introduced to Latin America the Chevy *Nova*, which had hit the U.S. market as the *Chevy II* in 1962. (Not to be confused with a smaller, front wheel drive vehicle produced in 1985 as a joint venture between General Motors and Toyota and also called the Nova.) It was unaware that in Spanish *no va* means "it doesn't go." After GM figured out why it wasn't selling many cars, the company renamed the car the *Caribe*. At least this is how the story goes, though some have claimed that it is an urban legend—an appealingly plausible tale that becomes endlessly repeated. They point out that *nova* and *no va* don't sound alike in Spanish (the first places the accent on the first syllable, the second puts the accent on the second of two words). Moreover, speakers would more likely say *"no funciona,"* *"no marcha,"* or *"no camina."* In Mexico, Pemex (the government-owned oil monopoly) sold gasoline under the *Nova* brand without trouble. The Chevy Nova sold reasonably well, at least in Venezuela and in Mexico. A marketing analyst pointed out that *nova* was sufficiently accepted to mean "new" (as in "Bossa Nova") that there could be no confusion, adding that it "never ceases to surprise me is how Coca-Cola has never had a problem. *Coca* has drug connotations and *Cola* means 'tail'—yet no one thinks the worse of it."

According to debunkers, the story that Nestlé was unable to sell its instant coffee in Latin America because the name is understood as *No es café* ("It isn't coffee") is also untrue, since Nestlé not only sells instant coffee under its own name in Spain and Latin America, but also operates namesake coffee shops. Since vowels are typically distinct in Spanish, *Nes* was unlikely to be understood as *no es*.

In many cases it would take a congressional enquiry or a royal commission to tell the difference between an urban legend and an illustrative howler. But one can safely say there are more howlers than urban legends. Ford had a problem in Brazil when the *Pinto* got foot-in-mouth disease. Ford found out that pinto was Brazilian slang for "tiny male genitals." Ford pried all the nameplates off and substituted *Corcel*, which means "horse." The Toyota *Fiera* was problematic in Puerto Rico, where *fiera* translated as "ugly old woman." In the United States and Latin America, Mitsubishi's sports utility vehicle was named the *Montero*, and marketed in Europe as the *Shogun*. Named the *Pajero* in Asian countries, it would have amused a Spanish-speaking traveler. During a Rivkin & Associates naming workshop, a man said with a laugh: "You should look it up in any Spanish dictionary." We did.

Pajero [*vulg*] A masturbator or wanker.

Rivkin & Associates once alerted a client that a proposed name for a power tool with -*gage* in it (*DynaGage*, *PowerGage*) would probably be pronounced like the Spanish word *gajes*, which connotes an occupational hazard. Perdue Chickens, entering the Mexican market, attempted to translate an ad that read, "It takes a tough man to make a tender chicken" and got "It takes a virile man to make a chicken aroused." Parker Pen introduced its *Jotter* ballpoint pen in Latin American countries, only to find out the word is slang for "jockstrap." A food company named its giant burrito a *Burrada.* "A big mistake," which is what colloquially the word meant.

In Brazil, *self-service* and *center* are ubiquitous as loanwords, and *Coca-Cola Light* is the term for Diet Coke. Such usages do no harm. But, though it may not bother the Brazilians, it may distress the English-speaking visitor to see a fashion shop called *Stroke;* a cleaning-service contractor called *Master Limp* (not derived from English, but from the Portuguese *limpar,* "to clean"); a sandwich stand called *Donald Lanches;* and *Acne-aid* face wash.

In Latin America, the process of a trademark's turning itself into an unprotected generic term has been under way for decades. *Resistol,* the trademark of Mexico's Industras Resistol SA, comes from the English words "resist all" and Mexicans use it as a synonym for glue. The company was forced to come up with the slogan, "The product is adhesives, and the brand is Resistol." The 2001 edition of the *Dicionario de la Lengua Española,* published by the Madrid-based Real Academia Española, added forty-four brand names and trademarks, bringing the total to seventy-six. In 2003 it added Procter & Gamble's *Tampax* brand of tampons and Gillette's razor blades. Gillette has 80 percent of the razor market in Latin America, and in Buenos Aires people ask for razor blades as *gilettes,* which the dictionary defines as a "disposable razorblade." *Jacuzzi* was also added as *yacuzzi,* so spelled in Argentina, Brazil, and Uruguay. Based in Walnut Creek, California, *Jacuzzi,* though not *yacuzzi,* has practically cornered

the Latin American market for whirlpool baths. DuPont's *Teflon* got into the dictionary as *teflón,* a nonstick coating for waffle irons and electric grills, and *Lycra,* elastic-fiber brand for lingerie and swimwear, was added as well. To strengthen brand recognition, DuPont opened a Lycra Hotel in São Paulo, Brazil, which didn't provide overnight lodgings but made people aware of the brand.

In Chile people ask for *"un scotch"* when they want to buy any kind of adhesive tape: 3M, the maker of *Scotch Tape,* has a 60 percent market share there. The Mexican word used for adhesive tape, *diurex,* derived from products marketed by Durex México SA, founded in 1947 as a Mexican unit of 3M. Although the company never sold "Durex" tape, customers identified the product with the trade name. In the 1980s the company gave up and renamed itself 3M México. It considered registering Durex but abandoned the notion when it realized that *diurex* was so widespread that the capitalized brand name could not be revived. By the 1990s, it was marketing Scotch-brand adhesive tape as "the Real Diurex."

Eurogaffes. In some European countries, like Bulgaria, ads sometimes appear with no text, only an image and the brand name. A wrong brand name can thus go very wrong. If you were an Italian maker of battery chargers called *Powergen,* what would *you* name your Web site? Probably not *www.powergenitalia.com,* which is what the company named it. A British energy company, also called *Powergen,* was so dismayed that it issued a press release denying that the two businesses were connected.

Adrian Room calls Rolls-Royce brand names like *Silver Ghost, Silver Wraith,* and *Silver Phantom* "ethereal." Less than ethereal was *Silver Mist* when it appeared in Germany, because *der Mist* meant "dung or rubbish." It was renamed the *Silver Shadow.*

Estée Lauder also got the scent of trouble. It was set to export its *Country Mist* makeup line when German managers pointed out that they were being asked to sell manure. The name was rechristened *Country Moist.* Undaunted, another cosmetics company introduced a curling iron into Germany called *Mist Stick.* Nor was this the end of coprophilia. A few years ago Coca-Cola introduced a tonic water called *Nordic Mist* into Europe. The Norse gods wept.

Germany has a multinational corporation called SAP, but not all, or even most, Germans are saps. They noted that in 2003 the Swedish-based IKEA was marketing a new child's wooden bunk bed across Europe under the name *Gutvik,* which sounded in German like "good fuck." Alerted, an IKEA spokeswoman said, "It is the name of a tiny Swedish town. We did not realize that it could also be taken as something obscene." She also said that ten thousand items in the IKEA catalogue had the same names around the world. At this very moment, IKEA may be mouthing obscenities in a foreign language. Also in Scandinavia, the Norwegian branch of McDonald's introduced a new burger called *McAfrika,* which consisted of a beef patty and cheese slice supporting vegetables between tiles of pita bread. The name was said to derive from what African focus groups had told McDonald's was a traditional dish. Norwegians, mindful of the chronic famines devastating Africa, declined to indulge.

Germans weren't blameless, either. Rich ice cream is sometimes called "sinful," but a German company called Langnese went too far when, in 2003, it introduced a range of ice creams labeled after the Seven Deadly Sins. Volkswagen's *Vento* went over well in German, but in Italy it meant "fart." Volkswagen's 2003 SUV is called the *Touareg,* after a nomadic Saharan tribe known for its ability to survive in a hostile environment. Good for an SUV, right? Alas, the Touaregs were notorious slave owners until a century ago, which did not sit well with some VW dealers in the United States. Neither did the obscure, hard-to-pronounce moniker itself. The manufacturer *Foden* was named after its founder, Edwin Foden, who took control of the business in 1876, its first vehicle a steam tractor engine. In Portuguese, though, the name has the same connotation as the German *Fokker* aircraft or the Dutch gin *Fokink*

has in English. It became *Poden* in Portugal. In 1980 the company went into liq-
uidation and was acquired by a U.S. firm with a more decorous name, *Paccar*.

Finnish has always been a linguistic anomaly, part of a small language
family, Finno-Ugric, whose other main language is Hungarian. This, or unfa-
miliarity with English, may account for the fact that a Finnish lock deicing
compound was called *Super Piss*. North American export prospects look bleak.
But Americans did no better. When entering the Québec market, Hunt-Wesson
made a sporting attempt at translation by renaming its Big John products as
Gros Jos, which is Québécois slang for "big breasts." Sales didn't suffer, though.
When SC Johnson sold a furniture polish in The Netherlands under its
American name, *Pledge*, they were startled to learn that the word meant, not
promises, but urine.

Linguistic challenges in export and import abound. Successful local products include *Bimbo* bread (Spain), *Zit* soft drinks (Greece), and the French soft
drink *Pschitt*. In Spain, the state-owned banking corporation had to change its
name, *Argentaria* (later merged into BBVA Bank), derived from the Latin for
"silver." Many people misunderstood the name as Argentina. *Cona*, the coffee
machine, is named after its English founder, Alfred Cohn. In Portugal, though,
it had to be changed to *Acolon* since *cona* is the Portuguese slang for the female
pudenda; moreover, other languages have similar-sounding slang words for it—
including English itself. People will always default to what they know best, especially in pronunciation. The manufacturers of *Biro* first attempted to get the
British to pronounce the name the Hungarian way as "beero" but failed because
it didn't chime with words with which they were already familiar, like *autogiro*.

Car names seem especially susceptible to misunderstandings. It may be
fortunate that most people don't know Latin because *Volvo* means "I roll." For
2004, Buick planned to introduce its LaCrosse model in Canada to replace the
Regal. Then it learned that in Québec French the verb "*se crosser*" is slang for "to
masturbate" and that *LaCrosse* could be translated as "The Jerk-Off," akin to the
more general expression "*ils nous ont crossés*" ("they jerked us around"). The
Spanish car brand *Seat* had a model called *Malaga*, as in the city name, but in
Greece had to change the name to *Gredos*, the name of a Spanish mountain
chain. In Greek, it sounded like *malaika*, a favorite term of abuse for a masturbator. General Motors named a new Chevrolet model the *Beretta* without getting
permission from the Italian arms manufacturer. It cost GM $500,000 to settle
the lawsuit. Ford had a computer-devised, shortlisted name for the model that
became the *Corsair*. The name, *Copreta*, was dropped when it was discovered that
Greek *kopros* has the same meaning as German *Mist*.

Sometimes brand-naming is a misty business.

Asian Answers. When the country then known as the Dominion of Pakistan
gained its political independence in 1949, it devised a label, *Pakmark*, for all its

products. Pakmark failed to take hold as a national identifier. But, as some variety in this sordid and scabrous tale of brand defaming and misnaming, here are a couple of success stories. Both involve smile-provoking names that, on closer examination, are made of the right stuff.

One of India's favorite teas has the offbeat name *Wagh Bakri*, which translates as "Tiger Goat." It is a century-old brand of select Assam teas whose market share ranges up to 90 percent in the country's highest tea-consumption regions. It is India's third-largest tea purveyor.

At Wagh Bakri's headquarters in downtown Ahmedabad, one wall of the conference room is taken up by a reproduction of a certificate given to the group's founder by Mahatma Gandhi. The certificate attests to the fact that the Mahatma "knows Narandas Desai to be an honest and experienced tea estate owner in South Africa." Whether this letter of recommendation actually helped Desai when he returned to India to start a tea business isn't known, but it does give a clue about the brand name's Gandhian qualities. The name symbolizes the gathering of the weak and strong, the bold and timid, the rich and poor—over a cup of tea. Once the name might have seemed provincial. Today it emblematizes the brand's heritage of coexistence and harmony. The name is—in the words of the sixty-five-year-old grandson of Wagh Bakri's founder—"cool."

Two new Indian banks are called *Yes* and *Egg*. A private bank announced in June 2003 that it would set up in partnership between Indian partners and Rabobank of the Netherlands, and call itself the *Yes Bank*. The *Rabobank* name had little brand recall in India. The firm had a presence for several years, but its visibility has been restricted to corporate and financial services in Mumbai (formerly Bombay), the financial capital.

The decision to adopt *Yes* could have been inspired by *Egg*, the online bank of Prudential, launched in 1998. Egg provided a fast, effective way for Prudential to move into sectors where it was little known. Its services include mortgages, savings accounts, personal loans, and credit cards. Online Egg gained 1.75 million hits in the first week alone. In its first eight months, it built an affluent customer base of 550,000.

"The funniest stuff happens when you're not paying attention to cultural differences," says Russ Meyer, head of the naming division of Landor Associates. "We came up with a name [for a company], *Telemon*. It was wonderful—until we went to Thailand, where it means 'intercourse with your mother.'" Also in Thailand, the office of the ad agency Leo Burnett alerted a client that their proposed name for a motor oil phonetically read as *Tight Virgin*. There's no getting away from the anatomical in brand names. Gulf Oil wanted to use its *No-Nox* name to brand its gasoline in Indonesia. After all, Americans understood there would be "no knocks" in the engine when they used the brand. However, after *Gulf* started using the name in Indonesia, it found that No-Nox sounded like the Bahasa Indonesia word *nonok*, slang for female genitals.

Chinese Choices. A mother of languages, Chinese originally provided the characters for Japanese and Korean. Except Japanese, no language is as fraught with problems of transliteration and translation. Chinese characters are composed of strokes, called radicals. Both characters and radicals can convey meaning. Of the fifty thousand Chinese characters, about seven thousand are in general use. In Chinese, each character stands for something that has no particular relationship to the sound of the word. Moreover, Chinese is a tonal language in which four different tones are used to distinguish words: the word *ma* can mean "mother," "horse," "hemp," or "to curse." The pronunciation of *gong* corresponds to at least ten distinct characters, all with different meanings.

To translate a brand name spelled in English (Coca-Cola, for instance), you can choose from several possible characters, and then decide what meaning to convey. Appropriate characters have to be picked. Most likely, the best translation will not sound at all like "Coca-Cola." In transliteration, the aim is to choose characters that sound closest to the original brand name but this, too, can be a trap. Those characters can have inappropriate connotations.

Which is exactly what happened with Coke's first marketing foray into China when the brand name was rendered in Mandarin. Shopkeepers created signs that combined characters whose pronunciations formed the string "ko-ka-ko-la" or "ke-kou-je-la." After printing thousands of signs, Coke discovered the phrase meant, roughly, "bite the wax tadpole." The character for "wax," pronounced "la," had been the trip wire. Coke then researched forty thousand Chinese characters and found a close phonetic equivalent ("ko-kou-ko-le"), which loosely translates as "make man mouth happy" or "happiness in the mouth." Pepsi-Cola was luckier from the start, understood as "a hundred happy things."

Not so lucky was Kentucky Fried Chicken's slogan "Finger-lickin' good," which came out as "So good you'll eat your fingers off." In Taiwan, the Pepsi tagline "Come alive with the Pepsi generation" was interpreted as "Pepsi will bring your ancestors back from the dead." Masterfoods, USA, the makers of M&Ms, were disconcerted to find that a W&W candy was popular in central China. Definitely not a translation, a Taiwanese beverage, bright yellow in color, with startling economy went by the name of *P.*

China, the world's most populous country, will one day be the world's largest consumer market. Marketers foresee lip-smacking rewards, but guarding the treasure are semantic and cultural tigers. In Mandarin, the concept of time lies on the vertical plane: you point down in pointing to the future, not straight ahead. The name itself is understood as a work of art, reinforced by the fact that calligraphy, the art of writing characters, has an ancient and hallowed history. Andy Chuang, whose company, *www.Goodcharacters.com* in

Fresno, California, specializes in Chinese naming and linguistic evaluation, points out that Americans typically choose existing first names for their babies, like *John*, *David*, or *Mary*. However, the Chinese pick some "good" characters and put them together to form a "good" meaning. The character *Ze* is a "pool" or a "benefaction." One might think that putting *Ze* and *Guo* (a "country" or a "nation") together would mean "benefit to the country." But *Ze-Guo* means "an inundated area."

One of Chuang's clients wanted to order a Chinese name seal as a gift for a friend named John. *John* is a Biblical name that is traditionally transliterated to *Yue Han* in Chinese. It does not sound as "John" is pronounced in English, but resembles the way it was when the Bible was first translated. The character *Yue* means "promise" and *Han* means "writing." *Yue Han* was fine as it stood. Later, however, the client mentioned that his friend was very athletic. Chuang's company thought of a better, though much less common, transliteration. They chose the character *Chiang* (*Qiang* in Pinyin) for "John." *Chiang* means "strong" in Chinese. It not only sounded much more like "John" in English but also created a springboard for athleticism.

In creating company names, transliteration, based on sound, is more common than translation, based on meaning. Chinese will want to remember a new English name by "converting" the sound into Chinese equivalents. In transliteration, the ideal is to create a Chinese name that both sounds closest to the original name and has positive associations.

Hewlett-Packard's Chinese brand is Hui-Pu. *Hui* is "kindness" and *Pu*, "universal." (A Chinese phrase, *Pu-Tien*, "universal" and "the sky," means "all over the world.") So Hui-Pu can mean "benefit to all," the right message for Hewlett-Packard. Some brands are **TOSHIBA** better translated than transliterated. Toshiba once had a commercial song in China that began, "Toshiba, Toshiba . . ." However, it turned out that "to-shi-ba" sounded like "let's steal it" (*tou-chu-ba*) in Mandarin. But Toshiba is a Japanese name and its corresponding characters, *Dong-zhi*, means "the East" and "nobility." Oracle launched itself in China as *Jia Gu Wen*. It sounded nothing like *Oracle*, but, uncannily, had the same name as an early form of Chinese written language, dating back more than three thousand years. Not only was it the most advanced way to store information in its time but was used for prophecy and forecasting. Nothing better could fit the profile Oracle wanted to present.

Chuang advises that even if a company isn't planning to launch a product in China, it should run a Chinese linguistic test before deciding on a new name to minimize the chance of creating a name that sounds profane or has negative connotations—political, social, historical, or psychological—in Chinese languages. In his view, the name should at least be tested under Mandarin, Taiwanese (also called Ming or Hokkien), and Cantonese (Yeuh). These are the three most widely spoken languages by Chinese in China and in countries that have a million or more Chinese residents—the United States, Canada, Malaysia, Indonesia, Singapore, and Thailand.

The brand entrant should also keep in mind that a Chinese name should confine itself to a name with two to three characters, and never more than five. In Chinese, the more characters in the name, the weaker it sounds and the less memorable it becomes. In order to qualify as a lucky Chinese name, a name must have balance of yin and yang: Yin characters are comprised of an even number of strokes, yang ones are made up of an odd number of strokes—a lucky name equals a lucky number of strokes. According to some, you want a name that is the opposite of your personality type in order to achieve a balance. If you are a yin, you would want a name that is full of yang. Stroke counting is done in Japan, too. A complication is that the same character can be written in slightly different ways and thus have different counts in Japan, China, and Taiwan. It's a matter of different strokes for different folks.

The Perils of Japlish. Some wag once said that Spanish is the best excuse anyone ever had for not learning Japanese. This may be unfair, but Spanish does have a simple, consistent grammar and largely phonetic spelling. Neither is a conspic-uous feature of Japanese. But the importance of Japan in manufacturing and technology cannot be gainsaid.

Modern Japanese has four writing systems, and corporate and brand names can be spelled in any one of them. Brands that use *kanji*, the oldest writing system, are perceived to be more traditional and appropriate for a product such as tea. Most high-tech products use *katakana*, the phonetic script developed to cope with foreign words, and hence right for foreign products. In a Tokyo residential area, McDonald's will appear not in Roman script (the Japanese *romaji*), as in South Korea, Hong Kong, Israel, and elsewhere, but Japanized in *katakana*. The made-in-Japan *katabana* often creates new combinations and meanings, such as "paper driver" (someone who has a driver's license but rarely drives), "golden time" (TV prime time), and "free dial" (toll-free phone numbers). *Hiragana*, a cursive script derived from *kanji*, is commonly used for beauty products and hair salons. One estimate has it that English loan-words represent 10 percent of Japanese. A sample of store signs revealed that 24 percent advertised English and Japanese names, and 26 percent English-only. One bar-restaurant was called *Manpuku*, a Roman transliteration from *kanji*, and meaning the sound of patting your stomach when you're full, "10,000," and "happiness." Worth a detour.

David Crystal has pointed out that Japanese is the culture that makes the most use of foreign languages in business and advertising. In car names, English is used in order to convey high quality and reliability (*Crown*). To con-note elegance, French (*Ballade*). A sports car may have an Italian name (*Leone*).

In TV commercials foreign words are left untranslated. Given this abundance and complexity, it's little wonder that Western brand names often hit reefs. Guess jeans placed the Japanese characters *ge* and *su* next to a model in Asian magazine ads, intending them to mean "Guess." But *gesu* actually translates to "vulgar," "low class," or even "mean-spirited." Guess changed the name. *Mos Burgers*, popular in Japan, likely would cause dyspepsia in North America. Japan's leading brand of coffee creamer is called *Creap*. A Japanese tourist agency, the *Kinki Nippon Tourist Company* (named after the Kinki district of western central Japan), was mystified when it entered English-speaking markets and began receiving requests for unusual sex tours. Conceding defeat in 1989, the officials in Osaka, the largest city in the district, announced that Kinki would no longer be used overseas because of connotations. An alternative geographical name, *Kansai*, would be used instead. The name of the *Kinki Research Complex* changed, as well as the English-language tourist magazine *Kinki*.

A shopping list of potential misunderstandings can be found on Japanese grocery shelves:

Trickle (gum)
Angel Relief (chocolate petits fours)
Slash (gum, whose slogan is "Shock Your Mouth!")
Naturot (low-calorie candy bar)
Baked Chunk
Creamy Ball
Mother Stick
Coming (chewy fruit bar)
Eye Power (blueberry tablets)

The Westerner will grin at such names. But these brands are not being targeted at Westerners; they're being sold to the Japanese. Just because a name looks or sounds funny outside its market does not mean it is ineffective within it.

English as a Foreign Language. Sometimes English is a foreign language even to English-speakers. Regional dialects, slang, as well as the jargon of trades, professionals, and technologies add their levels of obfuscation, as does register (how formal or informal it is, depending on who says something and where it's said). Some vocabulary items may be specific class markers, as in "U" and "Non-U" in British English, elaborated by A. S. C. Ross and popularized by Nancy Mitford. U people say, or used to say, *pudding* for dessert. Non-U people say *sweet*. U people gaze at themselves in a *looking glass* while the Non-U employ a *mirror*.

On occasion, the difference between high and low language or between Black and White in English seems as steep as that between the Brahmin and non-Brahmin speech in India. *Bad* can be good, or so the sales of Michael Jackson's 1987 album would suggest. But there was also a more commercial reason why bad could be good. The concept crossed over from the Mandingo language in West Africa: *a ka nyhi ko-jugu*, literally "it is good badly," meaning, "it is very good." This sense of *bad* was among the thousands of words and terms in "Black Talk," which the African American scholar Geneva Smitherman calls "the dynamic span of Black language" in her book of the same name.

National varieties of English also yield a harvest of confusions, some of them hilarious. A Canadian athletic team was at moments the laughingstock of the Sydney 2000 games, but it had nothing to do with its athletic prowess, or because its members said "zed" not "zee" for *z*, *icing* not *frosting*, *chocolate bar* not *candy bar*, and requested that a pizza be *all-dressed*. No, it was because their uniforms were emblazoned with the name and logo of their sponsor, the *Roots Canada* clothing chain. In Australia, "to root" is to have sexual intercourse.

If it's any comfort to Canadians, the Australians have had their problems, too. In the 1970s, when Australian beer began to be sold inter-nationally, the brewers of a well-known domestic brand called *XXXX* (pronounced "four ex") were puzzled as to why their competitor Fosters was so successful in the United States but XXXX flopped. The problem was the slogan "I feel a Four Ex coming on . . ." suggested more sex than suds.

Long before the spot of unpleasantness known as the Boston Tea Party, American English was busily diverging from its British parent. The current differences are not such that a New Yorker is likely to identify the Queen's English as the language spoken by cross-dressers at a Wigstock festival, but they still amount to the material for more than one book. The differences include idioms and expressions that *take the cake* (or take the British *biscuit*) and can make a reader *roll in the aisles* (or *fall about laughing*). In restrictive clauses, the British love to use "which," and the Americans prefer "that."

One can amuse oneself by imagining a surreal alternative planet in which the lexicon would consist entirely of the most cryptic, ambiguous, or hilarious names and terms in American and British English. A diner orders *buffalo wings* followed by *spotted dick*; a homemaker washes dishes with a *J-cloth* and *Fairy* liquid; a letter-writer addresses envelopes to *ME, IN,* and *MO* as well as to *Beds, Bucks,* and *Wilts*; a driver in a semi hits a *sleeping policeman*; a batter *grounds out* and then is *out leg before wicket* (in each case resuming a fielding position as a *backstop* or just *silly*); and a *stage-door Johnny* decides to *knock up* an old friend. These are mainly words for country-specific things, but there are also lots of different words for the same thing: an American *pharmacist* is a British *chemist*, a British *shopwalker* is an American *floorwalker*.

Apart from their slang, Americans are more euphemistic than the British, more politically correct, less ridden with class and other inherited distinctions, and, as befits their country's global reach, more effective in distributing their coinages. Each country has matching prejudices: British English can seem snobbish to Americans, American English philistine to Britons.

Many of these matters are discussed in Orin Hargraves's book *Mighty Fine Words and Smashing Expressions: Making Sense of Transatlantic English*. He notes that in Britspeak a *merchant bank* is a Yankspeak *investment bank*, a British *high street* has some common elements with a U.S. *main street*, and a British *launderette* is an American *laundromat*. More subtly, the English order a "white coffee," not "coffee with milk."

Here are some U.K. and U.S. brand names or generic terms with their equivalents across the pond.

UK	U.S.
Autocue	*TelePromTer*
Bulldog clip	sprung metal clip for holding papers; known but not a U.S. trademark
Calor gas	liquid propane in portable tanks
Chubb lock	deadbolt lock
camping light	*Coleman lantern*
skip	*Dumpster*
Erector set	*Meccano*
Mills & Boone	*Harlequin romance*
CS gas (not a trademark)	*Mace*
Rexine	*Naugahyde*
Perspex	*Plexiglas*
Portaloo	*Porta Potti*
claylike substance used as play material	*Silly Putty*
Strimmer	*Weed Whacker*
polystyrene	*Styrofoam*
Tannoy	public address system
wooden toy	*Tinkertoy*
Tipp-Ex	*Wite-Out*

Yet, despite the differences, it's arguably true that, thanks to TV satellites and the Internet, American and British English are closer than they've ever been. The language reforms that Noah Webster was famous for (*-or* and *-er* spellings rather than *-our* than *-re* ones, for example) commend themselves on the grounds of concision and sensible phonetics. Some countries follow American English spelling practices, some follow British, and a few mix both. In computing and medicine, American English spellings are becoming prevalent, but uniformity is far from the norm. One form or other may carry more cachet, but there will always be some degree of lexical distinctiveness in the specialized terms of local politics, business, culture, jobs, and natural history. There is much to be said for the quirks and vagaries of British English as a corrective to an oppressively rationalized and homogenized world. The same may be said about the other languages of the world. Brand names not only can live with, but thrive on, their differences.

What's a namer to do when confronted by such a gulf of difference, not only between languages, but even within what is technically the "same" language? The short answer is to never assume, always do your homework, and realize that one language doesn't fit all.

PART THREE

NAMERS

I would to God thou and I knew where a commodity of good names were to be bought.

—Shakespeare, *Henry IV, Part I*, I, 2.

13

AN UNLIKELY PROFESSION

Along with worm-picking and chicken de-beaking, the professional naming of products, services, and companies must be one of the odder ways to make a living. From one viewpoint, professional brand namers are symptoms of capitalistic decadence: pampered creatures battening off the blood, sweat, and tears of hard workers and their honest employers who, unlike the parasites, make real things in the real world. Surely a firm can name itself *Joe's Plumbing* without dropping a payload of cash on a greedy cabal of pseudo word-scientists.

Arguing against this view is David Aaker, Professor of Marketing Strategy at the University of California–Berkeley and the author of *Managing Brand Equity*, who cautioned:

> Name creation is too important to be relegated to a brainstorming session among a few insiders around a kitchen table or in an executive lunchroom. Excellent managers who would not dream of interjecting their opinions during decision-making sessions involving creative products or ads are for some reason tempted to take over during name-creation decisions, often in part because a working name is needed quickly, but also in part became name creation seems like the prerogative of the entrepreneur. Yet a name is much more permanent than most other elements of a marketing program. A package, price or advertising theme can be changed much more easily than a name.

Firms specializing in naming brands arose and prospered in the 1980s and 1990s out of a real, not just a perceived, need. An avalanche of new companies and products gave clients and consumers a staggering diversity of choice. In the auto industry alone, the consulting firm J. D. Power and Associates reported that there were 61 new or redesigned vehicles in 2004, up from 48 in 2003 and a mere 17 in 2002. Many called for a new name. In an October 2002 survey, Rivkin & Associates found that a record number of U.S. companies—87 percent—introduced a new name for a product, service, company, or division during the previous two years. Two-thirds reported that creating a new name was more difficult than in the past. The economy might have been slowing, but companies continued to introduce new names at a record rate. It was the highest percentage of new name introductions in twelve years of the survey. It became more necessary than ever to have a compelling brand name—one that shone out like a beacon in the crowded marketplace of goods and services.

William Safire pointed out that in ancient Rome a *nomenclator* was "the slave who called out the names of arriving guests." In keeping with this tradition, the people who started brand-naming firms emerged from advertising, marketing, and public relations. Only a few had training in linguistics, though the people they employed often did. The latter could be in-house staff, or they could be freelancers—most likely, it was a combination. The firms were occasionally divisions of an advertising agency, but more usually, they stood alone. Although everything they did affected the customer, theirs was a business-to-business operation. They were to be found in Europe, Asia, the Americas, and Australia. In the United States, they were dotted across the continent, but one thicket flourished around San Francisco Bay. They soon had a jargon of their own: "naming modules," "speechstream visibility" (how the customer would read the message), "phonetic transparency," and "multilingual functionality."

What signs did they put up to tout their services? Oddly enough, their names were not particularly innovative. Some relied on the surnames of their founders, principals, or partners: *Addison, Landor Associates, Ashton Brand Group, Rivkin & Associates,* and *Master-McNeil*. S. B. Master, a founder of Master-McNeil in Berkeley, California, told a reporter she'd added McNeil because "it had a substantial sound. From day one, potential clients have always assumed we were big and important, even though we weren't when we first started." Some firms sounded soulless, Slavic, or enigmatic, like *Luxon Cara, Igor,* or *Interbrand,* or baldly laudatory like *Enterprise IG* and the Belgian firm *Remarkable,* whose Web address was *www.remarkable.be*. Some, like *Lexicon, Idiom,* and *Metaphor,* Paris's *Nomen,* and Stockholm's *Skriptor,* appeared to borrow from a university's Language and Literature Department. One Web listing in 2003 showed nearly seventy employed "brand," "branding," "name," or "naming" companies, including *NameTrade, NameLab, Name-It, Namestormers,* and *The Naming Company*. It listed companies from *Absolute Brand* and *ABC Namebank* to *Trading Brands* and *Wise Name*.

The most evocative name for a namer was *A Hundred Monkeys* of Sausalito, California, responsible for *Raindance* (Web conferencing), *Jamcracker* (information technology), and *Ironweed* (a venture capital fund). The Monkeys' moniker was based on the apocryphal idea that if you parked a hundred monkeys in front of a hundred typewriters, they would *eventually* come up with all of Shakespeare. Or at least *Hamlet*. Or at least a good name. Like ad agencies, naming firms had high birth and divorce rates. In 2002, Steve Manning left the Monkeys and joined Jay Jurisich to found *Igor*.

Some firms, like Ashton Brand Group, Enterprise, Master-McNeil, Landor, and Interbrand, are both large and enduring. Interbrand is an integrated naming, corporate identity, design, and valuation firm. Landor, a division of Young & Rubicam, founded by Walter Landor in 1941 in San Francisco, has employees working in offices around the world, and its clients have included numerous airlines, not to mention France Telecom, Micro- soft, Pepsi-Cola, and Pizza Hut. Such firms dealt with many 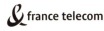 aspects of brand identity beyond the seminal name, and their clients were a cross section of the Fortune 500 list of giant corporations.

Each firm has its own modus operandi, culture, and set of tastes. A Hundred Monkeys tended to be the most gonzo: witness their creation of the brand name *Seven*. In December 2000, an entrepreneur named Bill Nguyen envisioned a global information network powered by his company's software, intended to unify cell phones, PDAs (Personal Digital Assistants), pagers, and other wireless devices. With a track record of successful company start-ups, he had lots of venture capital and employees—but no name. His launch date was two months away.

Nguyen picked the Monkeys to do the job. "If you went to a company trying to name their airline and gave them a choice between *Trans-AtlanticAir* and *Virgin*, they'd take Trans-Atlantic Air, because it sounds like something people would take seriously," Steve Manning said. "The problem is, with that name they become one of the trees in the forest." He pointed out that dozens of wire- less companies called themselves *Mobile*-something. *Mobile* was out. The Monkeys presented about fifty-odd names, including *Ironbit*, *Snafu*, *Gargoyle*, *Alpharay*, *Carbon8*, and *Blowfire*.

"Everyone says they want something unusual," commented Danny Altman, one of the Monkeys. "The classic line is, 'We want a name like Yahoo.' But when it comes down to it, the obstacle is always fear. We help them see that their fears aren't based on what happens to brands out in the world. It's like *Banana Republic*. People don't see the name and think, 'Whoa, an ugly racial slur—I'm not going to shop there.' It's all contextual." As it turned out, *Blowfire* and *Ironbit* were favored inside the company, but the Monkeys were touting *Gargoyle*. Then an outside candidate surfaced: *Seven*. Nguyen liked its arbitrary yet abstract quality, and connotations like good luck and "Seven Wonders of the World." A data language in the telecom industry was called *SS7*. For Nguyen, *Seven* was worth $75,000.

For some namers, the customer was always right. Others couldn't care less. The latter saw as their duty to provide what the customer *needed*, as opposed to what they wanted. Ruth Shalit quotes Ira Bachrach of NameLab as saying that his firm tends "to ignore the client's wishes."

Rick Bragdon, of Idiom, commented, "We actually prefer that clients don't fall in love with the name. If they fall in love with the name, it's a good sign there's something wrong with the name."

Ron Kapella, of *Enterprise*, relies on criteria. "By establishing criteria, and by developing names against those criteria, we've taken the arbitrariness out of the process. And so, when a client says, 'I don't like it,' I say, 'It doesn't matter whether you like it or not. The question is: Does it meet the criteria?'"

Firms often use software to generate names. Enterprise IG spun out thousands of names with its *NameMaker* software. Landor used its *BrandAsset Valuator*. Idiom used naming exercises, including "Blind Man's Brilliance," "Imagineering," "Synonym Explosion," and "Leap of Faith." Specialties developed. Brand Fidelity found a niche by creating online interactive tools for planning, screening, and registering brand names. Medibrand, a division of NameBase, was one of several that focused exclusively on naming new drugs and medical products.

However entrusted, the process of naming was expensive. A pharmaceutical company might spend as much as $2.25 million on a name for one drug. For Lucent and Agilent, Landor Associates charged more than $1 million each.

 Luxon Cara charged $70,000 for a syllable—in April 1997 *US Air* became *US Airways*. NameLab charged Infiniti. $75,000 for an alphabetical idea. As a bid for car-model distinctiveness, it recommended that the maker brand its models with little-used letters, notably *q* and *i*—one model became the Infiniti *J30*, another the *Q45*.

"We'd name a car for GM for free, if they'd just let us do something cool," Steve Manning said.

Danny Altman added, "No one names a car *Mustang* or *Thunderbird* or *Monte Carlo* anymore. Instead, you have *Acura. Alero. Xterra. Integra.* All thoroughly researched committee decisions. All emotionally empty."

As of the late 1990s, the cost of naming services varied wildly. For *98point6*, a project the Monkeys created for health-care Website MedicaLogic, they typically charged $65,000 per name and a month's worth of its naming process. At the low end, with a seven-day assignment turnaround, Name-It charged from $2,000 to $35,000, depending on whether their client was a small, locally based business, a larger regional or national company, or a corporation whose markets spanned the world. A one-day workshop conducted by a naming consultant could cost $7,500 plus expenses

Naming firms did not meet universal approval, especially at ad agencies and company marketing departments. One advertising executive said that the Monkeys' names were "these little creative pearls, and they're casting them before us swine." Marc Babej, a brand planner at Kirshenbaum, Bond & Partners, a New York ad agency, said that "The names have come to sound more and more alike. You can imagine how, at one time, *Livent* might have sounded new and hot . . . now we have *Lucent*. And we have *Aquent* and *Avilant* and *Agilent* and *Levilant* and *Naviant* and *Telegent*. What's next, *Coolent*?"

Namers were often their rivals' harshest critics. Naseem Javed, the president of ABC Namebank, noted that some "corporations are going out and spending five, ten, fifteen, twenty million dollars promoting these dumb names? And then going out and changing them to names that are even dumber?

As I see it, there is a real malpractice issue. If you've just developed a great stereo system, I can see paying $1 million for a great name—*Sony*. But what if you hire the same company for another naming project? And the names they come back with are *Bonyé Cony, Donyé Zony*? At what point do you say, forget it, this is not worth $1 million? This is not even worth five dollars."

Some companies, like the Web-based Yahoo!, took delight in conjuring their own names. "I love our name," Jeff Mallett, Yahoo!'s president and CEO, wrote in an industry newsletter. "It's fun, irreverent and consumer-focused. And it wasn't conjured up by Landor, or some huge naming agency."

Lu Cordova, president of *www.TixToGo.com*, an online booking, ticketing, and reservations service said, "We know who's in these big naming companies. We went to college with some of them. They say they're experts at this and experts at that. But they're really just our peers. They don't have any special mystical powers."

In 1999 Cordova had sought out a new name for her company. After some months, the namer she'd hired recommended *YourThing.com*. "The first ten people we mentioned it to all said, 'It sounds like your, um, thingy,'" Cordova noted. "So we said, whoops, OK, that one's gone." Banishing the naming firm, her company sponsored a contest. From more than 128,000 entries, a winner emerged, *Acteva*. Its nominee, a software engineer, won a Porsche Boxter. Of *Acteva*, Cordova said, "We love the name," she says. "And we're especially delighted it came from a civilian. . . . I had one guy from a naming firm ask me how I expected to get a name from a non-expert. He literally said, 'I charge $150,000 just to sneeze.'"

Given how much namers charged, companies might be forgiven if they tried other ways to come up with them. The fastest, cheapest (but not necessarily most effective) method was to rely on a boss's whim or inspiration. Usually, the boss's power was less absolute. In its 2002 survey, Rivkin & Associates found that the most commonly used methods to generate new names were internal task forces (used by 78 percent of respondents), extensions of existing names (50 percent), and advertising agencies (36 percent). At the bottom were naming consultants. But from the companies' standpoint, internal task forces were seen as most effective (by 66 percent of businesses), followed by advertising agencies (15 percent) and naming consultants (12 percent).

This was not exactly a sparkling report card for naming specialists, though the results might have been skewed by the relatively low number of clients who engaged the firms. If more had tried it, more might have liked it. Contests, whether staged among employees or among customers, ranked second to last in frequency (15 percent), and a mere 3 percent, dead last, in effectiveness. Contests had one problem. A contest has rules for judging a winner, and likely a prize for the winning entry. If a company hadn't set clear rules for entries or guidelines for how they would be judged, the contest failed in its primary aim.

Even more important, contestants might be eager, but they were untrained, undisciplined amateurs.

Once in a while, amid the slag, contests could hit pay dirt. Some famous names, like *Hovis*, have emerged from contests. In 1978, the marketing staff of the British car-maker Austin Morris assembled a list of 8,500 possible names for the company's new Mini. From these, a short list of three was submitted to the workforce of more than 19,000 employees. The winning name was the *Metro*, and the prize was the car itself. Binney & Smith, maker of Crayola products, used a naming contest as both marketing and a public relations opportunity to deal with an issue of political incorrectness. *Indian Red* was a popular Crayola color, but it had to be dropped after teachers complained that students thought it described the skin color of Native Americans. (*Indian red* actually was called after a reddish-brown pigment found on the Indian subcontinent.) Crayola's contest reaped 250,000 name suggestions. Working from careful criteria, the company selected *Chestnut*. Each winner received a "Certificate of Crayola Crayon Authorship" and an assortment of Crayola products. The new name started appearing on fifteen million crayons each year. Color the company happy.

In Las Cruces, New Mexico, a management team took the notion of choice in health care to a new level. They decided to let the people served by a new hospital determine its name. Community members helped to choose a name, a logo, and even influenced the architectural design for the hospital. Ads in the local newspaper announced the contest. Tables at a local Wal-Mart served as the voting booth. There was even a drawing with prizes: a weekend getaway at a local resort, and a donation to charity. More than one thousand local residents had their say. The winning name—*Mountain View Regional Medical Center*—got 67 percent of the votes.

In 2003 Boeing, for the first time in its history, encouraged people to name its newest airplane. In the process, the firm reaped a PR windfall. After tallying half a million votes in more than 160 countries, Boeing announced the winner at the Paris Air Show: *Dreamliner* was the new name of the Boeing 7E7. *Dreamliner* won over *eLiner*, *Global Cruiser*, and *Stratoclimber*, pruned from a list of one hundred names that consultants had come up with. Through a marketing alliance with AOL Time Warner, people placed votes at a Web site devoted to the new jetliner. Their choice reverted to the names of early Boeing passenger planes like the Boeing *Clipper*, the *Stratoliner*, and the *Stratocruiser*. Its jet-age planes, starting with the 707, going on to the 747 jumbo jet, and, most recently, the 777, had only had 7-series designations. The contest was designed to generate needed buzz for the new 250-seat, fuel-efficient plane. The hype happened. Boeing's hometown newspapers in Seattle were all over the story, but so were *Business Week*, the wire services, radio stations—and media worldwide. Breathless updates provided the play-by-play: "As of yesterday, more than 90,000 visitors to the site had voted, and *Global Cruiser* now has a slim lead."

To some extent, a comparison between uses of contests and naming firms illustrates the old conflict of democracy versus elitism. Yet democracy is not always what it seems. The Las Cruces citizenry, if not elitists, were at least contrarian. A Rivkin & Associates survey of one thousand respondents revealed that consumers preferred *Hospital* to *Medical Center*, believing that the former suggested a wider range of services, better quality medical care, and more up-to-date technologies and procedures. Yet the conventional wisdom for years had been that *Hospital* was tired and old-fashioned. As many hospitals expanded and moved beyond single buildings, increased their outpatient and home-health business, and partnered with physicians, they came to see themselves as "centers" of health care for their communities. *Medical center* also had an academic pedigree, conveying to some physicians and other practitioners more prestige. As a result, hundreds of hospitals dropped the word and renamed themselves *Medical Centers*. As is often the case, the conventional wisdom was wrong. The creation of HMOs (Health Maintenance Organizations) had trained tens of millions of Americans to select their physicians, so it was no surprise that more and more patients also expected to choose their hospital, and preferred one called precisely that.

Both the entrants in the Las Cruces contest and the respondents in the Rivkin & Associates survey were given a limited menu of choices. But the real dilemma facing anyone involved in any naming process was exactly the opposite: too many choices. Naming firms assumed most of the headaches—for a price. It might seem as if choosing a name ought to be a simple matter: assemble a list of names, pick one. But that is not the end of the process. It is not even the beginning.

14

MAKING A LIST

The imperative to create a new name can have many causes. Brand fatigue, slumping sales, new products—all require new names. Name changes may also happen more or less out of natural evolution. Palm virtually invented the handheld computer market with its *Palm Pilot.* That model was discontinued, though the original name became synonymous with any similar device. The devices are now simply called *Palms.* Among companies that changed their trade names, nearly half did so because a merger or acquisition required a new corporate identity. New competition may loom, effecting change at the top.

A successful family firm, Helmac Products, makers of lint removers, cedar clothing balls, potpourri, and other household items, got its name from the founder's wife and business partner, Helen McKay. After her death, and facing competition from 3M, the company approached Landor Associates for advice on their name. Landor showed Helmac a survey in which 12 percent associated *Helmac* with helmets, 11 percent with mayonnaise, and 9 percent with fire and brimstone. As part of a $500,000 fee, Landor came up with *Evercare,* establishing that consumers linked it with hygiene and cleaning supplies—although 7 percent did note a similarity to a rock band and a cheap liquor called *Everclear.* The brand name changed in 1999; the trade name in 2002. Competition combined with losses can result in serial name changes: the Woolworth's fabled five-and-dime retail chain changed its name to *Venator.* Then, in 2001, trying to focus on sports apparel, it took the name of a subsidiary, *Foot Locker.*

A public relations calamity may occur, as happened to Johnson & Johnson in the 1980s, when a psychopath laced Tylenol with poison (in this case the company did manage to salvage its brand name). World events can also cause name upheavals. In the early days of the U.S.-led coalition's invasion of Iraq in the spring of 2003, the Pentagon spoke of a "Shock and Awe" bombing campaign. A day after the invasion, Sony filed a trademark application for a *Shock and Awe* videogame. Sony later withdrew the filing, calling it an act of "regretable bad judgment." People applied for trademarks for *Shock and Awe* sauce, firework displays, T-shirts, bumper stickers, pens, toys, sporting goods, eyewear, housewares, restaurants, audio recordings, computer music files, and software. Two bids were made for the military campaign name, *Operation Iraqi*

Freedom, one for computer game software, the other for electric model toy trains. About "Shock and Awe," Glenn A. Gundersen, cochairman of the intellectual property group of the Dechert law firm said, "if you use it to suggest some connection to Iraq, it's misleading if you have nothing to do with the military, or if it doesn't have much independent trademark significance other than merely a reference to the action over there and it's not an independent brand name."

Gundersen noted that in the wake of "Desert Storm" in the Gulf War, and the turn of the millennium, people tried for related trademarks, "thinking that they're going to corner the market on commercial use of a phrase, and they quickly discover that they can't, and that these phrases have an extremely short shelf life. So the vast majority of these applications are abandoned." He pointed out that after September 11, 2001, some twenty-four applications had been filed for the phrase "Let's roll," a reference to the remark Todd M. Beamer, a passenger on one of four planes seized by terrorists, made when a group of passengers decided to fight back. In February 2002, the Todd M. Beamer Memorial Foundation won a trademark to use "Let's roll" for charitable fund-raising.

New names fluctuate with economic cycles and the waxing and waning of industries and stock markets. Gundersen's firm reported that in 2000, when the NASDAQ index (largely technology stocks) peaked, computer-related goods and services accounted for 81,100 new trademark applications. The next year the total dropped to 43,000, and then in 2002, plummeted to a mere two thousand. Applications for names of Internet-related stocks in 2000 totaled 41,900, the next year there were 17,300, and in 2002 only 11,400. The year 2002 was a bad one for mutual funds and investment and securities brokerage services, but applications for pharmaceutical goods and services were steady, and perfumes, cosmetics, clothing, food, and alcohol had modest growth.

Whatever the motive for a new or changed name, the first thing namers must understand about a product is what they're naming. They also have to know what company is hiring them to name the product and what the client proposes to sell to the public at large—often at very large. They have to acquire information and condense it into knowledge, creating an Identikit for a wanted brand name. This involves tapping the market research that the client has already done: more than half the companies in the Rivkin & Associates' 2002 survey used some form of research to test new names before they were unveiled. For companies that didn't test new names, it was usually because of the pressure to make rapid decisions and have goods and services reach the marketplace with equal speed.

For those who took the time to test and evaluate new names, there were plenty of ways to do it: qualitative research about imagery through focus groups online and in person, in single sessions or over an extended period of time, using screens and filters to select target audiences. Telephone interviews through call centers or one-on-one. Random interviews in shopping malls and at conventions. Telephone, Web, and e-mail surveys. Panels for consumers and for industry professionals like engineers and medical personnel, and for native speakers of different languages. The bigger naming firms tested for comprehension, memorability, ease of pronunciation, positive and negative associations and connotations, the fit with the marketing concept, and comparisons with competitors.

Each method had its own virtues, but not all met with the same esteem. "Focus-group testing is a complete waste of time," Steve Manning said. "I would take whatever name comes in dead last in the focus group and choose that one."

Some firms, including naming firms, were more intent on making a name pass an internal committee rather than please the truly vital audience, the public. Focus groups have their strengths and flaws. In picking from a list of names, a focus group will inevitably pick the most descriptive name, supposing that it will be most effective introduction to a product. Results have generally been more useful if the name was tested in context with the added elements of ad mock-ups, graphics, logos, package designs, and price level.

Luxon Cara spent 100 to 150 hours of interviews to determine that airlines whose names ended in "Air" were regarded as minor; hence *US Airways*, not *US Air*. In 1998, when the $8 billion computer hardware firm Hewlett-Packard decided to spin off its measuring instrument division into a separate company, they hired Landor Associates to come up with a new name. Landor staffers interviewed key executives for four months and came up with *Agilent*. But they also trotted the name past focus groups of business-to-business decision makers, combined with other research. The B2B crowd liked it, and so did the company employees. To test emotional responses to a name, Landor set up phone interviews in which the interviewer followed a tight script, with questions like "On a scale of one to ten, how strongly does the name *Agilent* communicate the following attributes: 'high quality,' 'very strong customer focus,' 'adapted to my needs,' 'truly cares about its customers'?" Results were fed into charts and graphs to wave in front of the client.

U·S AIRWAYS

Sometimes companies conduct their own testing. The German drug manufacturer Schering AG wanted a name for their new birth control pill that would both distinguish it from other oral contraceptives and convey a feminine feeling. Through its U.S. arm, Berlex Laboratories, it tested more than one hundred names on patients, pharmacists, and health care providers. The result was *Yasmin*.

The naming firm has to keep in mind how the new name will fit into a product line. This is where branding evaluation comes in. Old products may need to be repositioned. Some products may need names, not numbers. Some services, divisions, or subsidiaries should be branded, and a decision made about how well each trademark marches under the trade name banner. Sometimes this amounts to adopting a new family of names. Master-McNeil gave Holland America's cruise ships the suffixes -*oost* (East), -*zuid* (South), and -*dam* (ship), to complement its existing *Noordam* and *Westerdam* ship names, and grafted entire product lines for Apple, including the Macintosh *Pippin*, and for Sun Microystems, the *Sun Ray* enterprise appliances, *Sun Blade* workstations, and the *Sun Fire* family of servers. For Disney, NameTrade relied on a well-known rodent to found a family of school supplies: *Stick-With-Mickey Glue*, *Mickey's Chuckle Chalk*, *Mickey's Cooler Ruler*, and *Mickey Clicky Pen*.

The profile the naming team works with can embrace every relevant fact about the potential customers; what marketing, sales, and promotion a company anticipates; the length of time a product is going to be around; demographic data about the target age group, gender, and lifestyle; a list of its main competitors; its sales territory; and what existing names the client loves or loathes. More intangible, but equally important, is how the client hopes his company will be perceived. The trouble is, most companies come up with the same bundle of attributes. "We've done this process with hundreds of companies," David Redhill, an executive director at Landor, told Ruth Shalit, "They all say, 'We want to be perceived as strong, innovative, dynamic and caring.'"

Let's observe this profiling process in action. In the wholly fictitious example below, "Meerkat" is the code name for a naming project.

PROJECT MEERKAT Name Development Project

Background & Overview:

In Greece, Turkey, the Middle East, and many other parts of the world worry beads are common—a string of beads that people finger to alleviate stress, boredom, or anxiety.

The new company, as yet unnamed, aims to bring worry beads to mainstream America. The challenge is to conceive a name for the product. Headquartered in Pacifica, California, the client will manufacture, market, and distribute worry beads under its own brand. The worry beads will be sold in drugstores, supermarkets, and discount outlets, and its manufacturer's slogan will be "Rub Worry Away." The strung beads will be marketed in a wide selection of bead sizes and attractive colors.

Tranquilizers and antianxiety drugs represent a multibillion dollar market and require years of highly expensive research and development, adding huge costs in health care at the consumer level. Worry beads are a viable, low-cost, ecologically sensitive alternative that does not entail chemical dependency. Though addiction to using them is possible, there are no harmful side effects. Worry beads will appeal not only to ordinary people, but to the Human Resources departments of corporations for distribution to employees.

Product Launch:
November 15, 2004

Image Criteria:
The name should communicate the following brand image characteristics to its target markets:

· All In One	· Economical
· Long-lasting	· Effective
· Lo-Tech	· All-purpose
· High-Performance	· Simple
· User-Friendly	· Robust
· Tactile	· Integrated
· Responsive	· Healthy

The product will have the following effects:

· Relieves fear, anxiety, stress, and boredom
· Focuses thoughts
· Avoids annoying or irritating behavior, e.g., shuffling feet, twiddling thumbs, twirling pens, smoking cigarettes
· Saves money otherwise spent on prescription and over-the-counter drugs
· Feels pleasurable

The name should be:

· Allusive
· Distinctive
· Simple
· Easy to pronounce, spell, and recall
· Without adverse connotations in such target languages as English, Spanish, French, German, Italian, Portuguese, Arabic, Japanese, Chinese, and Korean
· Appealing regionally, nationally, and internationally
· Easy to register as a trademark
· Available as a Web domain
· Not easily confused with competitors' brands

Customer Profile:
Anyone who worries, especially those awaiting job interviews, sitting in dentist and hospital waiting rooms, or aboard planes, trains, and buses

Competitors:
What, Me Worry? Beads (Fretting Corp.)
Beadles (Beadworks Inc.)
Fingerlings (Laid Back Co.)

Names the Client Likes:
Prozac
Viagra
Halcion

Names the Client Dislikes:
Chiclets
Hula-Hoop
Tastee-Freez

The profile that results from these and other methods forms the basis for generating long and short lists of names. Some naming firms use proprietary programs to generate names. They're based on natural language processing, NLP for short, and combine chunks of existing morphemes to create plausible words that look as if they could be found in an English dictionary or somehow got abducted from the vocabulary lists of some artificial tongue like Esperanto or Volopuk. More refined software adds filters and screens related to pronounceability, multilingual use, and semantic appropriateness.

Of course, one problem is that—apart from the GIGO (Garbage In Garbage Out) principle that applies to any form of software—even simple combinatory programs of the A+B, B+A type can generate a glut of names. When Coca-Cola introduced its first diet drink in 1963, an IBM Model 1401 was programmed to disgorge every four-letter combination containing a vowel. It came up with 250,000 combinations. Only six hundred were possibilities, and only twenty-four had no conflict with existing trademarks. One of them was *Tabb*, and even it had to be doctored: it was shortened to *Tab*.

We are glad to say that most naming firms compile lists with teams of human beings—sometimes freelance, sometimes in-house—who, armed with the client's profile, come up with names. Some team members may have expertise in some specialty, some may be intuitive, creative, whimsical, some excessively methodical and rational: it's part of their employer's skill to match the job to the temperament. Some may rely on a database of names or topical lists that they've set up; some wing it through brainstorming alone. (See Chapter 5.)

One compromise between hiring a firm to do a full-scale name hunt and coming up with a name internally is to hold a naming workshop run by a consultant. A naming workshop session in fact amounts to a concentrated version of what many naming firms do when they're separately contracted.

Supplied ahead of time are background material on the company and on the product or service to be named, customer profiles, marketing research, press clippings on the category of product and service category, and thematic mug shots of competitors. Between eight and twelve people take part, selected for their knowledge of the product or service, their ability to be good team players, and their verbal skills. They come from product management, sales, marketing and communications, and often from R&D (Research and Development), engineering, and senior management. They're armed with product samples or a service demo, materials from competitors, any potential names already in the hopper, and several dictionaries and thesauruses. As Rivkin & Associates does it, the team gets a two-hour training session on naming strategy, tactics, and techniques, followed by a six-hour name-generating or brainstorming session in which user scenarios, symbolism, adapted metaphors, and thought association get an airing.

Efforts to name a newsletter targeted to customers might yield the following:

Action Plan	Game Plan	Power Tools
Benchmarks	Getting Ahead	Priorities
Best Bets	Going Places	Productivity
Best Results	Good Company	Right Course
Better Ideas	Hands On	Success Maker
Building Profits	In The Black	Take Charge
Business First	Know How	To The Point
Capital Gains	Leading Edge	Up To Speed
Capital Ideas	Net Worth	Vantage Point
Cutting Edge	On Course	Ways & Means
Decision Maker	On The Money	Winning Edge
Foresight	Performance	Working Smart

Typically, several hundred possible names get produced, and the day's concluded with a simple protocol for sorting the group's ideas, and preliminary screening on trademark, corporate name, or Internet domain name availability on, say, the five top names. However it's done—separately by a hired naming firm or during a workshop session—a long list of names inevitably needs to be whittled down.

15

CHECKING IT TWICE

Even after the list of names is whittled down, there are miles to go before they keep. The choices have to be legally eligible. Plaintiffs and defendants have been wrangling about the use of trademarks for a long time: one court case concerning the improper use of a trademark occurred in England in 1618. In the United States, the first trademark legislation was passed in Michigan in 1842, the first federal law in 1870. Averill Paints was the first company to get trademark protection. Since then, a huge body of trademark and patent law has evolved, with one of its tenets being former U.S. Supreme Court Justice Felix Frankfurter's "The protection of trademarks is the law's recognition of the psychological function of symbols."

Walter Pater, the nineteenth-century English aesthete, wrote that all the arts aspire to the condition of music. It could also be said that all of capitalism aspires to the condition of monopoly. Yet one of capitalism's paradoxes is that monopoly would be the death of it. Governments enforce antimonopoly laws to protect consumers, but consider that one kind of monopoly, the trademark, is unambiguously good—and legal.

A trademark's primary function is to identify and distinguish a product or service from that of its competitors. It may be a brand name for a product, a service mark for a service, or a trade name for a business. It can be three-dimensional objects like McDonald's arches, the musical notes signifying NBC television, or Corning's pink fiberglass insulation.

A California cat breeder, Ann Baker, was able to trademark a feline breed, the large floppy *Ragdoll* cat, and, cornering the market, commanded a royalty fee for each kitten sold. Kellogg's, the breakfast cereal maker, sued Exxon, the oil company, for using Tony (the tiger on the boxes of Frosted Flakes) to advertise its service stations and Tiger Mart convenience food stores. Until 2002, Kellogg's blocked Weetabix from selling Fruit Dots in Canada, arguing that the name for the small colored balls of cereal was confusingly similar to *Froot Loops*, which had been around since 1964. (Weetabix, the biggest cereal maker in the United Kingdom, had trademarked *Fruit Dots* in the United States in 1988.) But the Federal Court of Canada overruled trademark officials, saying that the brands were not alike, nor their names confusing to customers. The court said that some cereal trademarks already included *fruit*, such as *Fruit Rings*, *Fruit*

Whirls, Fruitful Bran, and *Tootie Fruities,* and that it, or its phonetic equivalent *(Froot)* was merely descriptive of the products' flavoring. *Dots* and *Loops* merely described the shape of the product and "do not enhance any inherent distinctiveness of the trademarks."

Dotty or loopy, a trademark is valuable. One former Commissioner of the U.S. Patent & Trademark Office (PTO) noted that a trademark is "frequently a more valuable asset of a business than all other assets combined."

The PTO sorts out trademarks into forty-five classifications of goods and services used around the world, ranging from chemicals to social services. (For the complete list, see Appendix.) This is not idle list-making: the type of product can determine what protection it gets. Protection typically extends only to the category of goods or services in which you register the mark. It's quite possible to have *Apple,* the computer maker, and *Apple,* the record label. In one celebrated case, Amstar Corp., the maker of *Domino* sugar, sued Domino's Pizza for trademark violations. In 1980 a U.S. Federal court ruled that the pizza chain was not in violation. You might open a chain of shoe repair shops called *McDonald's,* but God—and the law—forbid that you apply it to burger joints, much less Big Macs. Even this was disputable. In a California case, McDonald's the fast food chain was able to stop a computer company from calling itself *McDonald's,* even though its owner had the surname, and there seemed little confusability between bites and bytes. Pulling this kind of weight is the prerogative of big companies who possess what in law is known as a "famous mark."

In 2003 McDonald's pulled weight in the United Kingdom, telling Mary Blair, the Scottish proprietor of *McMunchies* sandwich shop in Fenny Stratford, near Milton Keynes, Buckinghamshire, to remove her sign or face legal action. McDonald's told Blair that it was the registered user of *Mc-* as a prefix. Mrs. Blair, who did not sell burgers or chips, said she chose the name because she liked the word *munchies* and wanted to remind sandwich consumers of Scotland, reinforced by her sign, which bore a Scottish thistle and a St Andrew's flag. As a reporter for *The Independent* newspaper noted, "Telling the Scots that they cannot use the prefix Mc is like someone registering the name Singh and then banning its use in India."

Legal protection may extend beyond the category of goods and services in a particular international class. Protection may also extend to goods and services that are in the "zone of natural expansion" of a company's goods and services. Simply put, these are products or services related to the initial product or service and are the natural extension of an existing market. As trademark attorney Tara L. Benson points out, this concept is one of the reasons that a trademark search does not merely look for marks in the identical classes, but instead searches for related goods and services. Sporting equipment can be considered the natural extension of sneakers *(Nike)*, or prepackaged alcoholic beverages the natural expansion of restaurant services *(TGI Friday)*.

As noted above, the registered marks Apple for computers and Apple the record label coexist. But it is foreseeable that these marks may come into conflict as Apple computers expands into providing music to listeners via its machines and iTunes online music store, and Apple Records expands to offer devices that enable users to listen to Apple Records' artists. Such expansion arguably would be within each owner's "zone," even though the developments might create overlap and confusion.

A U.S. law—the Lanham Act—decrees that in order for a trademark conflict to exist, there must be:

a. a likelihood of customer confusion between the goods and services offered by owners of two marks.

b. a likelihood of customer confusion as to the source or origin of goods or services offered by the owners of one mark.

c. a likelihood that there will be "dilution" of a well-known brand, in that the reputation or quality of the brand will be degraded by another's use even if the context does not involve customer confusion.

Trademark rights are established by using the trademark in connection with the goods and services, not just by deciding to adopt or filing to register it. Only actual usage establishes a right to the mark. As a common-law measure, the symbol ™ can be used to put everyone on notice that the owner is claiming trademark rights. The ® can only be used if the trademark is federally registered and provided with nationwide trademark rights. So even if a company starts out in just one state, federal registration safeguards future expansion, prevents others from using confusingly similar marks, and, in a dispute, gives access to federal courts, considered more predictable than state courts. If a service is offered, ᔆᴹ is a clue that the service mark is not registered with the PTO. If it is registered, ® or "Reg. U.S. Pat. & Tm. Off." follows the trademark.

In the United States, trademark lawyers would not be gainfully employed were not the Lanham Act subject to various interpretations. It's been a windfall for them. Is *Office Max* too easily confused with *Office Depot*? What about the cosmetics names *Moonglow* and *Moonglaze*? Or the brand-name accessory with the brand name *Xsre*? Such is the swirl of trademark law.

Here are a few representative cases. Kenner Parker Toys Inc., the owner of the *Play-Doh* trademark, sued Rose Art Industries Inc., which had sought registration in 1986 for *Fundough* to mark its own modeling compound. The court noted that *play* and *fun* were "single syllable words associated closely in meaning. Particularly in the context of a child's toy, the concepts of fun and play tend to merge." Moreover, the suffixes *-doh* and *-dough* sounded the same. "In light of a modern trend to simplify the spelling of *-gh* words, consumers may even perceive one as an interchangeable abbreviation for the other."

 One celebrated case had a different outcome. Häagen Dazs filed against producers and distributors of another ice cream brand, Frusen Glädje. Häagen Dazs claimed that Frusen Glädje had infringed on its "unique Scandinavian marketing theme" and sought an injunction to prevent its continuing to use its container. The plaintiff seemed to have a strong case. Frusen Glädje's container had duplicated Häagen Dazs phraseology; described the way in which the ice cream was to be eaten to enhance its flavor; was a two-word, Nordic- or Germanic-sounding name with an umlaut over the letter *a*; had a map of Scandinavia. . . . However, the court rejected the injunction, ruling that Häagen Dazs's trademark was for its name, and that it neither held nor could hold a trademark on the "unique Scandinavian marketing theme," which was "simply a vehicle by which the plaintiff has chosen to market its product." It ruled that the two brands were clearly distinguishable. Yes, both names contained two words to identify an ice cream product, but this wasn't unusual. Both names seemed to be of Swedish origin (actually both were invented) and an umlaut appeared over *a* but this a matter of grammar only (actually, orthography); and the containers' coloring, designs, and shape were so different "that only the most unobservant and careless consumer would mistake one product for the other."

Sometimes the zeal of big firms to protect their brand names seems tantamount to bullying. The Santa Clara, California, based Intel Corporation was listed in 2003 as owning the world's fifth most valuable global name—worth $31 billion if accounting rules permitted the value of brand names to go on balance sheets. That year it sued Intel Financial Inc., a ten-employee financial services firm in Kelowna, British Columbia, for trademark infringement. Intel Financial filed a counterclaim, denying that Intel was the owner "of any famous trademarks," and requested an injunction to prevent Intel Corporation from using Intel in association with financial services and analysis. Intel Financial said that it had been using some form of its name in Canada as early as 1970. Moreover, it was in an entirely different market: "our clients call us to get a mortgage, not to buy computers."

Intel Corporation's lawyers were busy. In 2002, they accused Intel-Data, a printing company in Buffalo, New York, of copying the brand name. In business since the 1980s, Intel-Data decided to change its name rather than get buried by legal fees. Another Intel-Data, a Washington company that had five employees compared to Intel Corporation's 86,100, also yielded, becoming *IDG Resources*.

The computer-chip maker was also protective of its "Intel Inside" slogan. It threatened to sue Art Inside, a six-member art society in Shelbourne Falls, Massachusetts, a move that the *Boston Globe* called "silly." When Yoga Inside, a three-year-old Los Angeles group that taught yoga to imprisoned teenagers, applied for a trademark, Intel's lawyers descended. The yoga group became *Yoga on the Inside Foundation*.

In its claims of trademark infringement Starbucks was equally zealous, though less effective. In the spring of 2003, it launched a lawsuit against HaidaBucks, a restaurant in the small town of Masset, British Columbia, on the far edge of the remote Queen Charlotte Islands. Three of the original owners of the café were Haida, and another was married to a Haida; a cup of coffee sold for a buck. Canadian native peoples were hardened to courtroom exposure, since, in Canada, lawsuits concerning land claims as well as fishing and logging rights are perennial. HaidaBucks wasn't about to back down. It argued that *bucks* was a colloquial expression (equivalent to *dudes*) that young Haida men used among themselves. After HaidaBucks launched a Web campaign to promote its cause, Starbucks withdrew its claim.

On occasion native peoples or their advocates can be the plaintiffs. In 1992 the Stroh Brewing Company put on the market a malt liquor called *Crazy Horse*. After a vigorous campaign was mounted against it, the brewer apologized to the Crazy Horse Defense Project, defenders of the good name of the famed Sioux warrior. The science and technology writer James Gleick points out that, elsewhere, *Crazy Horse* can signify "France's leading nude dance revue and nightclub. When a Parisian buys a Crazy Horse baseball cap, T-shirt, cigarette lighter or dressing gown, Native American tradition doesn't enter into it."

Unlike Crazy Horse's defenders, Victoria's Secret fell short in its legal efforts. In 1998 the tony lingerie maker sued Victor's Little Secret, a Kentucky sex-novelty shop, for besmirching its trademark by selling pornographic material. The case reached the U.S. Supreme Court and in March 2003, the justices unanimously ruled that actual harm, and not the mere likelihood of harm, is required to impose liability under the U.S. Federal Trademark Dilution Act.

Individuals, not just companies, can go to court. One recurring book publisher's nightmare is an onslaught of readers who claim that they were libeled when their names were given to characters in novels. Trademark holders are sometimes subject to similar assaults. In 2003, a Swedish family named *Urge* maintained that Coca-Cola's caffeine-loaded citrus drink *Urge* (called *Surge* in the United States) violated their name, though a Swedish court ruled that the English word *urge* was more commonly known than the family name.

For businesses large and small, lawsuits are costly. Labatt Breweries of Canada sued the big U.S. brewer Anheuser-Busch, which had introduced a brand called *Ice Draft*, for $61 million, claiming that the terms *ice beer, ice brewing,* and *ice brewed* were its trademarks and that it had invented the process of brewing beer at lower temperatures so that ice crystals would form, allegedly improving the flavor. In early 1995 a jury of the U.S. District Court of St. Louis, Missouri, ruled against Labatt.

A trademark-infringing company may be liable for damages and all profits from sales caused by the infringement. In 1996 the clothing designer Tommy Hilfiger was judicially held to have been in bad faith by marketing sportswear with the name and symbol *Star Class*—both of which were owned by a nonprofit yachting group. Tommy Hilfiger had not performed a full trademark search, despite advice from counsel, and even when it found out about the yachting group's trademark, it continued to sell its products because it expected to win in court. Wrong. A U.S. Court of Appeals said the company was liable for $4 million in profits, legal fees, and interest. Tommy also lost in August 2002. A company called Nature Labs had been making a perfume for dogs named *Timmy Holedigger,* whose packaging used Hilfiger-like side-by-side yellow and red triangles as a label. This didn't smell right to the licensers of Tommy Hilfiger's name for cologne, but a federal judge ruled that Timmy's perfume parody of Tommy did not infringe on the trademark. The judge stressed that the maker of *Holedigger* sold other parody fragrances for pets, including *Bono Sports* (think: Ralph Lauren's *Polo Sport*) and *Miss Claybone* (*Liz Claiborne*). The perfumes bore slogans like "strong enough for a man, but made for a Chihuahua." Polo and Liz Claiborne had been smart not to challenge names for the doggie scents. Said the judge: "Most of the companies that purvey these expensive human fragrances have chosen either to accept the implied compliment in this parody—that the mere association of their high-end brand names with a product for animals is enough to raise a smile—or, if they have taken offense, to suffer in silence." The judge had other bones to pick. "Even if a dense and humorless consumer could mistakenly conclude that plaintiff itself sponsored the humorous line of fragrances," the products were sold in different stores at different prices. He called Hilfiger's position "dour," and suggested that a designer label had nothing to lose from association with pets, "particularly where the entire association is a light-hearted if somewhat heavy-handed parody."

Some cases could be guaranteed to run for years, and the same pattern of suit and countersuit occurred in other countries. Every nation has its own laws concerning trademarks and separate forms of interpretation. Aspirin has been called the twentieth century's only true miracle drug: the benefits of acetylsalicylic acid go far beyond headache relief, and may help prevent strokes, heart attacks, and even some forms of cancer. The name derives from the German *acetylerte Spirsäure,* "acetylated salicylic acid," with the suffix *-in* added. The element "*-spir-*" comes from the plant genus name *Spiraea,* and North American native peoples had long scraped bark from such plants for medicinal purposes. "Chew on the bark of a willow tree," an early medicine man might have said, "and call me in the morning."

The United Kingdom and France never recognized Bayer's use of *Aspirin* as a trademark after the tablet hit the market in 1914. The United States, not at war with Germany at the time, recognized it initially. In 1917, when it entered the war, the United States stripped Bayer of all its U.S. assets as an enemy alien corporation, and Sterling Drug bought **BAYER** Bayer's U.S. facilities and trademarks at government auction. After the war, Bayer was allowed to sell its products in the United States, but it couldn't use the names *Bayer* or *Aspirin*, which belonged to Sterling. The *Bayer Aspirin* that Sterling sold in the United States was not made by Bayer. In 1921, the U.S. Supreme Court ruled that *aspirin* had lost its distinctiveness, and Sterling lost its exclusive right to the brand name. Then the story took another twist. In the 1990s, Bayer bought Sterling, reacquiring the right to use its own name. That was all right for *Bayer*, but what about *Aspirin?* In a court decision many years earlier, a judge focused on the manufacturer's label, wherein Bayer had stated the tablets were its make of the drug known as *aspirin*, thus making it a generic term. But the decision didn't stand in all countries. In Canada, *Aspirin* is still protected, and to ease their throbbing heads the makers of generic versions have to make do with *ASA*.

In Canada, federal registrations are handled by the Canadian Intellectual Property Office. In 1997, the *Coffee Time* chain forced a rival, *Coffee Team*, to change its name. "Just changing one letter isn't enough," said Patrizia Banducci, an intellectual property lawyer, "The whole principle here is: What would an average consumer think?" Courts sometimes have trouble putting themselves inside the average consumer's head. In 1988 *Sunlife Fresh Juice* was ordered by the Supreme Court of Ontario to change its name after *Sun Life Insurance* argued that Ontarians would confuse fruit juice with insurance policies. On the other hand, or hip, when a jeans manufacturer branded a line *F.B.I. Blue Jeans*, the U.S. government sued and lost: a judge ruled that nobody would think the Federal Bureau of Investigation had got into the blue jeans game.

In protecting trademarks, a prudent company must tread stately steps. Some of these are outlined in a valuable booklet with a misleading title, *Life Cycle of a Trademark*, from the trademark research firm Thomson & Thomson's. The title is misleading because "life cycle" implies birth, growth, maturity, decline, and death. All marketers hope their trademarks will have eternal life.

After a brand name is developed, a list of possible trademarks is narrowed and screened by searching through online trademark research systems to eliminate those already taken. Companies and individuals can apply to register marks they intend to use months or years from now. So the tally of trademark applications reflects plans for new product and business launches, not just current brand-name use. The decade of the 1990s "demonstrated that the number of new trademark filings is a barometer of business optimism or pessimism about the public appetite for new products and services," according to the *National Law Journal*. In 2002, more than 213,000 trademark applications were filed in the United States. As of mid-2003, there were 1.6 million registered and pending trademarks in the United States. Another 1.8 million were segregated as abandoned, cancelled, or expired marks.

Outside the United States, the numbers are just as impressive. European trademarks total three million, according to some estimates. Year by the year, the onrush continues. The World Intellectual Property Organization tallies trademark activity in ninety-five countries. WIPO data for 2001 revealed 1,240,000 new trademarks were issued that year, with the top ten action centers being:

China	192,549	Mexico	49,741
Japan	94,832	Benelux	34,266
Spain	79,861	Korea	33,683
United Kingdom	67,362	Australia	31,244
Germany	66,245	Switzerland	25,112

Even the tiny nation of Andorra, nestled between France and Spain high in the Pyrenees, recorded 1,494 new trademarks in 2001—one for every forty-four people in the country, if you're keeping score.

A preliminary U.S. search, which can eliminate 90 percent of the names being considered, can involve using online or CD-ROM databases that cover federal and state applications and registrations. An online search service or a business investigation firm can be used. The WHOIS database covers Web domain names, and the U.S. Patent & Trademark Office offers a free search service at *USPTO.gov*—on its menu, TESS (Trademark Electronic Search System) offers her services. For company names, a check with the incorporation office in the state where the name is to be registered is a prudent minimum, as well as a check with a national business roster of company names to see if the same name is registered elsewhere: Dun & Bradstreet, for example, has a database of more than 10 million company names.

There's more. After a company has narrowed a list of potential trademarks, an outside searching service usually conducts a comprehensive search of permutations of the proposed name against U.S. state, federal, and common law databases, Dun & Bradstreet lists, telephone directories, business or trade directories, as well as those in foreign countries. Checks of global names can be made through WIPO, the ECT (European Community Trademark), and WISS (Worldwide Identical Screening Search) databases.

Trademark lawyers pronounce on whether surviving names stand a chance of being registered, after checking any confusingly similar marks in the relevant classes of goods and services, including phonetic equivalents, synonyms, homonyms (look-alikes and sound-alikes that have different meanings), marks using the same or a similar prefix, suffix, or root word, and even translations into other languages. The process may also involve searches of international company names, designs, and logos—as well as all U.S. trademarks. A seemingly conflicting trademark is investigated to see it's still in use, and what kind of problem it presents.

International agreements and disputes can raise obstacles. In August 2003, the European Union (EU) agreed on a list of forty-one geography-based food and beverage names for which they sought to gain global brand name protection under WTO (World Trade Organization) rules. The EU's allies included India (*Darjeeling* tea), Guatemala (*Antigua* coffee), and Morocco (*Argan* olive oil). This is the EU list:

Wines and Spirits

Beaujolais	Graves	Ouzo
Bordeaux	Jerez (Xerez)	Porto
Bourgogne	Liebfrau(en)milch	Rhine
Chablis	Madeira	Rioja
Champagne	Malaga	Rhone
Chianti	Marsala	Saint-Emilion
Cognac	Medoc	Sauternes
Grappa	Moselle	

Cheese

Asiago	Grana Padano	Pecorino Romano
Comte	Manchego	Queijo San Jorge
Feta	Mozarella di Bufala	Reebochon
Fontina	Campagna	Roquefort
Gorgonzola	Parmigiano Reggiano	

Cold Cuts and Other Products

Azafran de la Mancha (saffron)
Jijona y Turron de Alicante (almond candy)
Mortadella Bologna
Prosciutto

In South America, Peru accused Chile of misappropriating *pisco* when it applied the name to a clear, eighty-proof liquor distilled from Chilean grapes, much of it exported. Peru said that pisco, its national drink, originated near the town of Pisco, on the banks of the Pisco River in Peru. Tucked into the North America Free Trade Agreement (NAFTA) treaty, which encompasses the United States, Canada, and Mexico, is a clause that forbids the naming of a product with a "geographic brand name that is primarily misdescriptive." One consequence is that a brander could no longer count on the mystique of Idaho potatoes by calling its spuds *Boise Brand Mashed Potatoes*—unless they came from Boise.

There are about 12,000 different drugs on the U.S. market. Apart from the usual ordeal of finding and registering a conveyer belt of new names for pills and potions, drug companies face nonclinical trials. Apart from the USPTO, they must contend with the U.S. Food and Drug Administration, which rejects a third of the names it reviews. In 2001 the FDA stopped Eli Lilly & Co. from using *Zovant* for a drug to treat sepsis because it too closely resembled the names of other medicines. It's now called *Xigris*. Rejecting about a third of applications, the FDA regards coldly such syllables like *ultra*, *max*, or *new* in names, and those that sound like generic terms. The generic names for *Prozac* and *Paxil* are fluoxetine and paroxetine, so *-oxetine* is out. Trendy, ambiguous suffixes like *SR* (*sustained release* or *senior?*) or *XL* (*extra-long* or *excellent?*) also evoke displeasure. Extravagant promises are shunned. *Rogaine*'s first name was *Regain*, as in "regain hair," but the FDA ruled that the name in effect suggested that the preparation could cure baldness. Outside the United States, drug copiers are less constricted. Cipla markets its version of Viagra in India as *Silagra*, echoing its generic name, sildenafil citrate, and the sound of Viagra itself; in Latin America it's sold as *Eviva*, and in the Middle East as the forthright *Erecto*.

Some 15 percent of all reported medication errors in the United States between 1995 and 2000 involved some form of name mix-up. The painkiller *Celebrex* sounded similar to *Celexa*, the antidepressant, and to *Cerebyx*, the anticonvulsant. The FDA's reviewers examine how a doctor's script might sound or look when written, and can also rule out names if they seem too boastful. On occasion, the FDA has forced a company to change a name because of confusions: in 1994, *Levoxine*, a thyroid preparation, got mixed up with the heart medicine *Lanoxin*—leading to hospitalizations. Levoxine was changed to *Levoxyl*. When Schering AG settled on *Yasmin* as the name of its birth control product, it must have sighed collectively in relief: up to that point, the FDA's drug name list had no *Y*'s.

After a lawyer pronounces a blessing, the application is filed with the USPTO, based either on the trademark's actual use or on a good-faith intention to use the mark in commerce—the latter a liberalization of trademark laws that came in 1989. The application can go into either the Principal Register or the Supplementary Register. The Principal Register is preferred because the Supplementary only provides notice to intended users that the mark is already in use, and offers limited legal protection, although it does last for ten years and can be renewed for additional decades. After a trademark has been on the Supplementary Register for five years, the owner can petition to promote it to Primary.

Not relying on what the applicant's already done, the USPTO makes its own examination for possible conflicts. If none seem to exist, the application's published in its *Official Gazette* to see if anyone challenges it. Should a challenge occur, a Trademark Trial and Appeals Board rules on it. If no opposition is filed, or the opposition is overcome, the application will proceed. In the case of "Intent-to-Use" applications, documented use of the trademark must exist before registration can take place.

Once a trademark is approved, it's up to its owner to protect, maintain, and enhance its value, often including a policing or watching process to show whether use of it infringes or dilutes its uniqueness and worth. This involves searching through *Official Gazettes*, trademark journals, databases, and industry publications—some service companies specialize in this. If a conflicting trademark is found, it's more work for the lawyers. Protection also includes standards and guidelines for how the trademark is issued within a company and among the public. Some specialist firms handle this, too.

The International Trademark Association (INTA) has issued what amounts to a style guide, noting that a trademark is a proper adjective or adverb, not a verb or noun. What is a noun, however, is the product's generic name, which the trademark modifies, such as *camera* after *Kodak*. The generic term should be used at least once in each written communication and, when appropriate, in broadcast matter, preferably the first time the mark appears. The same is true of old faithful ® or ™ . Typography should be used to ensure the mark is easily recognizable: all capitals, or at least initial capitals; italics, boldface, or a different color. Extra emphasis can be given by using the word *brand* after the mark. A hypothetical ideal might be "*SCOTCH* ® Brand transparent tape." A horrible counterexample: "Are you going to xerox those xeroxes any time soon?"

Because they're not nouns, trademarks shouldn't be used in the plural form, though those that end in s may be used with singular or plural generic nouns. But the s is not removed to make marks singular, for example, "A *Baggies* plastic bag" or "*Baggies* plastic bags," not "a Baggie." (Dennis Baron reports that the question of pluralization once so exercised McDonald's that it hired a public relations firm to ascertain the correct plural of the *Egg McMuffin*.) The possessive ('s) form should never be used unless the trademark itself is possessive, such as *Levi's* jeans or *Johnson's* baby shampoo. Although many companies use their trade names as trademarks, the two are quite distinct. As corporate or business names, trade names are proper nouns, can be used in the possessive form, don't require a generic term, and don't need a ™ symbol. The INTA's examples:

- Athletic shoes made by Reebok International Ltd.
- These athletic shoes are made by Reebok.
- Reebok's newest line of athletic shoes.
- Are you wearing REEBOK athletic shoes or another brand?

Consistency is paramount, says the INTA, and all variations should be shunned: abbreviations, changed spellings, inserted or deleted hyphens, or combinations with other words. In his book *Technobabble*, John A. Barry notes that "Corporate-legal insistence on adjectival use leads to useless nouns and redundancies, such as 'MS-DOS operating system,' meaning, 'Microsoft Disk Operating System operating system.'"

Typographical designers can also be their employers' worst enemy—the media sometimes has to impose standardization for them. Newspaper, magazine, and book editors like to use a normal capital-and-type style: *Pop-Tarts* instead of the trademark *pop-tarts*, *Scrabble* not *SCRABBLE*, *Adidas* not *adidas*, *Teleprompter* not *TelePrompTer* (though other midcaps, as in *AtEase* or *TrimSoft*, are left unmolested. The problem of a sentence beginning with a lowercase name like *eBay* or *iMac* is handled by rephrasing.

Changes in form can detract from the mark's status because they suggest to the consumer that it is just another word. This is precisely what trademark owners wish to avoid. Some have gone so far as to publish informational ads about proper use of their names:

- *"Kelly* is a brand name for temporary help services provided exclusively by Kelly Services Inc. The following are registered trademarks of Kelly Services Inc.: *Kelly*®, *Kelly Girl*®, *Kelly Services*®, Nobody Puts Temporaries to the Test like Kelly®."

 - "Don't confuse a weedeater with *Weed Eater*®. Sometimes people say they want a 'weedeater' when they really want a *Weed Eater*® brand trimmer. . . . It's America's number one brand of trimmer—the one people ask for time after time."

- *"Formica*® is a special brand. . . by properly using our name, whenever you ask for *Formica* brand, you'll be sure of getting the real *Formica* brand."

Xerox once ran an advertisement targeted to journalists and editors. Its headline: *There are two R's in Xerox.* (The second "R" was ®). *Xerox* also issued a witty, albeit gently sarcastic, rebuke in a letter to the editor of the *New York Times*, referring to a clue in a crossword puzzle the *Times* had published:

Dear *New York Times*: 8 Down has us puzzled. Let's see, 6 Across is W-A-X-Y. That leaves us with a five-letter word for "duplicate" beginning with the letter X. Obviously, it couldn't be X-E-R-O-X. That's because *Xerox* isn't a verb. It's our trademark. As a trademark it should only be used as a proper adjective followed by the descriptive term, like a *Xerox* copier, a *Xerox* printer, a *Xerox* typewriter, or a *Xerox* duplicator. But you probably know this already. You of all newspapers are a stickler for this sort of thing. Which still leaves us with the original problem . . . a five-letter word for "duplicate" beginning with "X."

Letters to the editor aren't the only tasks involved. Affidavits and other documents have to be kept up-to-date in order to keep a registration active. Once registered, trademark rights don't last forever, but are based on continued use. Between the fifth and sixth year of the initial ten-year registration term, a company has to file an affidavit that the trademark is being used in connection with the good or service. Then it has to file a renewal document every ten years from the registration date, along with an example of how the trademark is being used in commerce.

In many registration documents occur three sad words: *abandoned, canceled,* and *expired. Abandoned* means that the party filing a trademark application has decided not to pursue it for one of several reasons. The PTO might have challenged some aspect of a trademark application or found something unacceptable in it. The applicant might have failed to respond to a question or request for additional information. *Canceled* may pop up if a company fails to file an affidavit of continued use after five years. A trademark also may be canceled after a legal challenge to its rightful ownership. If a company chooses not to file an application for renewal of its trademark, the mark will be stricken from the active PTO Register and listed as *Expired*.

One big factor in preserving a trademark is its visibility. Commercial exploitation, the endgame for a trademark's creation, may involve licensing of the brand name or trade name or logo for merchandise unrelated to the original product or service. The name can appear on clothing, toys, food, collectibles like mugs and key chains, or publications. All this makes a trademark more enduring.

Not all brand names are created equally in trademark protection. Much of the quest for novelty in naming can be attributed to the vulnerability of purely descriptive names. Generally, descriptive terms cannot acquire U.S. federal registration and are not eligible for protection unless they establish secondary meaning. The latter can happen when the owner demonstrates an established association between the mark and a single source for a significant portion of the consumer market. Acquired rather than inherent, it's developed through continuous use of the mark with the product or service, demonstrated through substantial sales and advertising, and has been used so long that it becomes synonymous with the goods or services with which it is connected. To take on secondary meanings, descriptive marks usually take longer to establish goodwill.

A simple descriptive name may offer little legal or no protection: *West End Auto Sales, Bud's Appliances, Lo-Cal Diet Drink.* A generic name like *Chair* can have no protection unless it identifies some nonfurniture item like a brand of soft drink. *Cola* is not protectable because it describes an entire product class, beverages made from the kola nut. (However, in 1930 the U.S. Supreme Court ruled that Coca-Cola had exclusive use of *Coke*, a shortened form that the company had shunned in its early years, which became registered as a trademark in 1945. But in 1938 the Supreme Court also ruled that *Coke machine* was generic.) Descriptive names may be eligible if the term becomes distinctive by establishing a secondary meaning and becoming synonymous with a manufacturer or supplier. Once McDonald's acquired a secondary meaning related to burgers and fries, it became a protectable trademark. But though a trademark is famous, it can serve for a totally different business: *Nissan Dry Cleaners*.

Book titles usually don't get trademark protection, but a few do, such as *Gone with the Wind* and *Winnie-the-Pooh*. As for magazines, one exception to the rule against the use of descriptive trademarks is *TV Guide*, which has remained protected, in part because of its owner's diligence. On occasion, descriptive names need not be avoided, as in the case, for example, of retail products sold via infomercials. For such products the consumer needs to be educated, either through expensive TV advertising or, much more cheaply, by using descriptive names and marks on the packaging. Trademarks need to be strong, protectable, and enduring; weak, descriptive marks educate consumers. A workable compromise is to form hybrid trademarks by combining the two marks, using the strong mark as the main trademark and a weak, descriptive mark as a descriptor or tagline. Despite such exceptions, descriptive names raise warning signs, and personal names, nicknames, surnames, and initials, attributes, and geographical locations can all be troublesome. So can names with bad translations or unfortunate homonyms, names with unintended connotations, or names too close to other well-known marks. Legally speaking, a unique mark is stronger.

Dictionary makers have an especially hard time with trademarks in balancing the claims of usage and legal protection. If a brand name has acquired generic status, they often run two entries with accompanying definitions: they run capitalize and punctuate trademarks according to the company's official form *(Levi's, Band-Aid)* and a second one, capitalized or not according to usage, to cover the generic or figurative form (Ronald Reagan, the *Teflon* President; *day-glo* pink). But problems abound.

In 1961, *Merriam-Webster* published its monumental *Webster's Third New International Dictionary of the English Language*. Plenty of trademarks were included: *B.V.D.* underwear, *Scuba*, *Hit Parade*, the *Phillips* screw, *Popsicle*, the *LP* recording format, *Blue Cross*, and *Tommy Gun*. The dictionary carried the disclaimer: "no definition in this Dictionary is to be regarded as affecting the validity of any trademark." They carried a part-of-speech label like any other main entry. Only in the etymology was the properly capitalized trademark given. This drew a barrage of protest from corporations, worried that their trademarks might suffer a generic fate the same as death, and hostile fire from the U.S. Trademark Association, whose executive director complained, "The only word capitalized was 'God.'" They were further alarmed by a prefatory note declaring that "Words that are believed to be trademarks have been investigated in the files of the U.S. Patent Office. Those that were originally trademarks before being taken over generically by usage and becoming lexical are recognized as such." The makers of Plexiglas claimed that *Merriam-Webster* had violated its trademark; *Advertising Age* reported that a random check of sixty-five trademarks revealed that forty-four were rendered as generic.

A polite panzer division from the Trademark Association arrived at the door of the dictionary's editor, Philip Gove, demanding changes. The association had its way and some three hundred entries were revised for a new edition. As Herbert C. Morton said, "In subsequent printings, hundreds of little gods of corporate productivity, trademarks, were capitalized as well." This offended lexical purists, who no doubt even had reservations about capitalizing *God.*

In the revised format, the initial letter was capitalized and the full name set in boldface type as a main entry, followed by a label, *trademark*. A lightface em dash indicated that the description was not a definition but a usage note.

Kleenex . . . *trademark*—used for a cleansing tissue.

The lexicographer Sidney Landau concludes that among all dictionaries, *Merriam-Webster* was "the most weaselly nonrecorders of generic meanings of trademark terms." Dictionaries try to shelter under disclaimers, like the one in the British-published *Collins English Dictionary* (2000):

> "Entered words that we have reason to believe constitute a trademark have been designated as such. However, neither the presence nor the absence of such designation should be regarded as affecting the legal status of any trademark."

Some, like the *Encarta World English Dictionary* (1999), took extra, even absurd, precautions, noting a trademark as both the label and the definition:

Kleen-ex /klée nèks/ *tdmk.* a trademark for a soft facial tissue.

We get the point.

16

SPINNING THE NAME WEB

Strictly speaking, domain names on the Internet are addresses like street addresses or locational clues like telephone numbers, rather than identifiers of a source of goods and services. It didn't take marketers long to realize that domains could be much more. Millions of Web sites exist, with thousands added every day. Web marketing sought to tap a world in which everyone was wired and had fat household incomes.

A huge body of people could be not just informed about a product or service, but could order it directly. Marketers wanted people surfing the Net to learn more about a product, and to purchase it. So a domain name that matched a product name was good for Web surfers who typed *www.YourProduct.com* into their Web browsers. A matching domain name was also good for remembering Web addresses, similar to the way people remembered *1-800-FLOWERS* as an 800-code telephone number. Before search engines, a one-to-one correspondence between the product name and the URL was ideal.

In the post-Google world, though, name length became less significant. After a user turned to a search engine, the domain name had little to no effect on the site's ability to be found. The first-time visitor browsed with a search engine, found a desired site, bookmarked its URL, and never had to type in the domain again. For their part, search engines catalog pages use many ranking formulas, and those formulas vary. Placing well on keyword searches is vital. Successful sites usually mixed a good·design, a memorable domain name, good search engine placement, online banner promotion, and promotion in such traditional media as print.

At first, marketers rushed madly to hoard domain names such as *www.jewelry.com* and *www.flowers.com*, popularizing the use of generic and descriptive marks. But from the angle of trademark protection, these were intrinsically weak marks even if they were registered as domains. Moreover, the existence of a similar trademark could block the use of a domain name. Generic and descriptive marks had their uses: Procter & Gamble has hundreds of domain names registered. Keyboarding *www.oldspice.com* brings you to Procter & Gamble's site, but so does *www.deodorant.com*.

In 1985, only six companies wanted to use *web* to describe their products, and 430 sought to use *net*. This soon changed. Filings from technology companies seeking to trademark names with *net, tech, power, cyber, link,* and *web* rose 30 percent a year since the start of the 1990s, but took an abrupt dive after the middle of the decade. The sizzle had become the fizzle. In their place came a new wave of Internet names with offbeat meanings (Yahoo!), typographic trickery (E*Trade, eBay), or a strong resemblance to a bowl of alphabet soup (PSINet). As though generic names came to seem too vague, other kinds of descriptiveness made a comeback. A Securities Data Corporation report of Internet companies with strong revenue growth—from semiconductor chips to new-age broadcast links—showed this. Many retailers in this group picked names like CDNow and Preview Travel, as logical for a bricks-and-mortar storefront as for a Web site.

Domain name availability began to be as important in deciding on a name as trademarkability. Internet names and addresses are managed through a U.S. corporation called ICANN, the Internet Corporation for Assigned Names and Numbers. ICANN in turn delegates the registration of domain names to more than 100 private companies, which agree to abide by a process for resolving disputes largely determined by WIPO, the World Intellectual Property Organization, an international body established by treaty among 180 nations.

The Tata Group, an Indian conglomerate based in Mumbai, sued the New Jersey Web site www.bodacious-tatas.com, purveyors of what the court called "sexually explicit material," arguing that it was exploiting the Tata Group's good name. In India, Tata won an injunction against the bodacious site in 1999 (which had no effect in New Jersey) and then filed a complaint with WIPO, requesting that the domain name be canceled. Sorting out whether tata and bodacious-tatas were "confusingly similar" the WIPO adjudicator ruled that bodacious (an informal term for excellent, admirable, or attractive) and the added s after tata "does not render the Domain Name less identical or less confusingly similar to a trade or service mark. Indeed, the opposite is true, particularly when one considers most of the meanings attributed to the word bodacious." Internet users might indeed think that the Tata Group was peddling pornography, he ruled, and canceled the domain name.

A company needed to know what was taken as an Internet address, and what legal repercussions might ensue from any real or presumed adaptations of them. One tool for searching addresses, especially those including the big three domains (.com, .net, and .org) is the online WHOIS database. If you were seeking to sell widgets over the net, searching widgets.com would show you not only the name, but who had it registered (in case you wanted to contact them and try to buy it). If "No Match For widgets.com" was returned, the name was available. If some domains popped up, a closer look was warranted. Just typing a hypothetical address on a browser and finding nothing appear wouldn't be enough since the domain name could be inactive but still registered.

Depending on whether you wanted simply registration or some grand strategy to make you master of your domain, a new URL could cost under $100 or more than $50,000. The number of domain names has swollen to bursting. In 1992, there were only seven thousand. By 1995, there were 170,000. Then came the Internet boom. More than 1.5 million URLs were on file by 1997, and two years later Network Solutions, the leading registrar of domain names, reported that it registered more names than it had in the prior six years combined, reaching a cumulative total of 8.1 million. One estimate for registered domain names in 2003 put them at 22 million. Nominet, the British nonprofit organization that acts as a registry for domain names and a trustee for *.uk* addresses, estimates that from 1996 to 2003 *.uk* registrations went from about 25,000 to 3.5 million.

Foreign domains are more complicated to tabulate, but pointers to their registries could be found on the Network Solutions, Inc. (InterNIC) Web page (*www.internic.net*). InterNIC manages the domain name system for the Internet's top-level domains (the last two or three letters of an Internet address following the last period). Domain names don't have to be registered in each country, but it was advisable to do so if a company didn't want it used by somebody else or if it did lots of business there. In any case, the huge number of addresses using the few Top Level Domains (TLDs) meant that something had to give. In 2001, ICANN approved seven new Internet extensions. The familiar *.com*, *.net*, and *.org* were joined by *.aero*, *.biz*, *.coop*, *.info*, *.museum*, *.name*, and *.pro*. Companies could apply for these new extensions through an ICANN-approved registrar or service provider. The new extensions came with limitations, though. The *.aero*, *.coop*, *.museum*, and *.pro* TLDs were for air carriers, cooperatives, museums, or professionals such as doctors and lawyers. The *.name* TLD was only for Web sites for individuals such as *www.JohnSmith.name*. That left only *.biz* and *.info* available to business generally. None of the new extensions gained the popularity of *.com*, *.net*, or *.org*.

For dot-biz domains, the Start-Up Trademark Opposition Policy (STOP) allowed trademark owners to register an intellectual property claim before Neulevel, the *.biz* registrar, actually recorded it. By registering this claim, the owners were entitled to later seek the transfer of a domain name to itself if it had been registered in bad faith. This is what happened with such generic-style domains as: *www.airport.biz*, *www.brands.biz*, *www.paint.biz*, and *www.parents.biz*. One Ottawa, Ontario, business domain was transferred back to Kalmar Industries USA, a Texas company that held a trademark for *Ottawa* in relation to truck tractors. Kalmar argued that the fact that Ottawa was a national capital was irrelevant. After a young university graduate registered *www.Canadian.biz* for an online business, Molson Breweries, which held a trademark for *Canadian* in connection with beer, a judge ruled that "simply because a domain name is identical or similar to a trademark name should not result in the transfer of the domain name to the trademark owner," and that "unless there is some evidence that the use of the domain name infringes on the use of the trademark name, a person other than the owner of the trademark should be able to continue to use the domain name." Moreover, if Molson were allowed to be the only one to register *www.Canadian.biz* without bad faith, it would give the company a monopoly on *any* Canadian-related online business. This added starch to the argument against STOP's name-dispute resolution policy that, as the intellectual property lawyer Michael Geist said, "Granted trademark holders far more rights online than offline and in the process effectively created a new super-trademark."

Owning the trademark on a company's name might help, but it didn't necessarily guarantee getting the associated Web site name. When WCI Cable started a Web site, it registered the untaken *www.WCICable.com.* When it tried to become *WCI.com* three years later, it was too late, leaving the company to fall back on *.biz* and *.info.* Even huge consumer-products companies can get caught short. Johnson & Johnson could not register its site as *www.J&J.com* because the ampersand symbol was not acceptable. Then it turned out that *www.jandj.com* was already registered by a financial consulting firm named Jordan & Jordan. Johnson & Johnson ended up as *www.JNJ.com.* Holiday Inns, with its thousands of lodges, was unable to register *www.holidayinn.com* because a single property—the Holiday Inn by the Falls in Niagara Falls, Ontario—had snared the domain name first and refused to transfer it to its parent. Holiday Inns had to cough up a hyphen and settle for *www.holiday-inn.com.*

These corporations could take comfort in the fact that, even with the new extensions, erosion of the value of *.com* was unlikely, since customers probably assumed that *.com* companies were in business longer than those in *.biz.* So companies guarded themselves in every possible way, hurrying to register every version of their business or product name with every possible new extension, and even common misspellings of their name. They registered their business nickname *(California Microwave* was well known as *Calmike).* Even a stock symbol would do.

The Internet itself is not a trademark. Or maybe it is, as in the case of Internet Inc., which had nothing to do with globally interlinked networks. In 1984, the Reston, Virginia, company, which ran a network of automated teller machines, federally registered the name—long before *Internet* became a household word. In 1997, the Internet Society and the Corporation for National Research Initiatives contended before the USPTO that *Internet* had become too widely used, could no longer be associated with a particular product, and that everyone should be free to use the word.

Sometimes popular indignation, not legal authority, is what counts. In 1992, Bell Canada, through its subsidiary Worldlinx Telecommunications, applied for a Canadian trademark, *The Net,* for its package of software and services. Internet users were outraged and the application was withdrawn. In the United States, however, Internet Inc., which had merged with another company to become Honor Technologies, wanted to retain its exclusive right to use and license the name. While the Trademark Office deliberated, hundreds of requests by companies wanting to use *Internet* to describe their products had to be delayed.

Courts, too, added another element to the complex mix. They weighed in on an online tiff concerning the use of "sucks" as part of a domain name, typically anchored to a well-known trademark, as in *www.LinuxSucks.com*. The courts ruled that such domain names did not infringe on trademark owners' rights since the "sucks" Web sites are unlikely to be confused with the original domain names. In effect, the courts were saying that some Web sites are successful, but others suck.

17

NAMING'S AFTERMATH

If a brand is trademarked, it can be bought, sold, or leased like any other property. Brand names are property, just like real estate—in fact, Web addresses are *called* "real estate." Webbed or not, there's plenty of precedent for commerce in names. In 1999, the personal computer maker Gateway decided not to try to revive its *Amiga* brand and sold its trademarks to Amino Development Corp. The beer maker Coors licensed the name of its upscale beer *Irish Red* from a long-defunct brewery. Yves St. Laurent bought the name of its fragrance *Opium* for only $200 from two elderly perfumers. Later, they paid $1 million for the rights to the name *Champagne*, which had already been cleared and registered in many countries. In 1999 the relaunch of National Airlines, which had been known for its sunny orange paint jobs and Florida flights before being bought by Pan Am in 1980, came about after Pan Am sold the name for $175,000 at a bankruptcy sale. Pan Am even sold its own name—for $1.3 million.

More than a trademark changes hands: the goodwill of a business the trademark represents is a major part of the package. Trademarks can also be licensed. But since competitors are not always in competition in every circumstance, and rights assigned can vary a great deal—in territory, in the period of time assigned—they sometimes buy rights from one another, usually through an intermediary. There are brokers for domain names just as there are for brand names, and the latter are even auctioned on eBay. Rivkin & Associates once helped a Fortune 500 company acquire the rights to an automation software name from a Japanese competitor.

Competition can also lead to preemptive registration strikes. The Web site *www.About.com*, which had several earlier incarnations, became by May 2000 the ninth most visited domain on the Web. No wonder. It had earlier bought more than four thousand domain names as an effort to control the *About.com* domain and all of the name's possible combinations. To protect itself, ChemConnect, a company that operated an Internet site at which chemical firms could buy and sell supplies, registered as many combinations and derivations of *chem* and *connect* as it could think of. But it didn't think of throwing -*dex* into the mix. Then a newly launched business-to-business entity legitimately named itself *Chemdex*. ChemConnect had committed an oversight. Not so in the case of the multinational media and database company the Thomson Corporation, which owned the Canadian national daily newspaper *The*

Globe and Mail. To head off readership and advertising incursions from Hollinger Corp., which was launching a rival daily, the Thomson Corporation registered a string of newspaper names. The tactic worked: Hollinger had to abandon its first choice, the *Times of Canada,* and settle for the *National Post.*

Cupidity came to woo. When Wal-Mart crossed the Canadian border in 1994, buying 122 Woolco stores from the Woolworth Corporation, it discovered that the Winnipeg businessmen Edward J. Nych and two partners had registered *Wal-Mart* earlier with the provincial government's corporations branch, which oversaw patents, incorporations, and registrations of businesses. Nych, unwilling to state what his business actually did, said the company was named after his cousins Walter and Martina, who had recently moved from Ukraine to Poland and were unavailable for comment. Nych hadn't told them about their namesake. True, *Walter* was not a common Ukraine name, but, well, it was anglicized from *Vladimir.* (So why not *Vlad-Mart?*) Wal-Mart paid a sum to Nych and his partner, not to mention Walter and Martina, to go away—without a corporate name.

The rise of the Internet led to a glut of registrations, sometimes by parties who had no intention of selling anything other than the names themselves. In 2000, of an estimated 22 million registered domain names, some 3 to 4 million were actually in use, and another 2 to 4 million were held in inventory never to be sold, for example, as preemptive misspellings or variants of names. Of those, a few million were actively marketed on Web sites like *www.greatdomains.com,* *www.register.com,* and *www.afternic.com,* and sold on a daily basis in the low $100 to $1,000 range.

This wasn't always the case: prices were once sky-high. The practice of registering and hoarding Web site names in the hope of forcing companies or individuals to buy back their names at a premium introduced a new term to the language: *cybersquatting.* In 2000, one hopeful Oregon man, Jerry Buys, offered *www.globaldotcom.com* on eBay, expecting to get $1 million for the name. Buys maintained that *.com* was the best TLD on the Internet and that *globaldotcom.com* "easily steals the prize as the world's premier *.com* domain," he said in a press release. (Perhaps Buys should have called himself Sells.) In any event, Ron Wiener, the chief executive of Portland, Oregon, based SnapNames, a domain name protection company that began in 1999, told a reporter that there were 1,000 domain names for sale for every one that's sold. Perhaps Jerry Buys had been inspired by the legendary Marc Ostrofsky, who purchased *www.business.com* in 1997, on special from a British Internet service provider for $150,000. Ostrofsky, who owned one hundred domain names, sold it for $7.5 million to eCompanies of Santa Clara, California. eCompanies claimed the purchase was "prudent." James Gleick recounts the story of Jeff Burgar, who lives in the small Alberta town of High Prairie. About 1994 Burgar, who denied that he was a cybersquatter but rather claimed to be a freedom-minded publisher or collector, discovered that domain names could be registered free.

During the subsequent decade he registered, among other sites, *jrrtolkien.com* and *brucespringsteen.com*. A WIPO panel ruled that, concerning the latter, the famous rock musician had rights to his own name but that Burgar, who'd registered the domain name on behalf of the "Bruce Springsteen Club," was not acting in bad faith. Gleick reports that in conflicts between trademark holders and cybersquatters, WIPO usually decided in favor of the former. Time Warner won a case involving 108 variations on the theme of Harry Potter. Telia, the Swedish telecommunications company, succeeded in winning back all but one of 204 variations of its name. The singer Madonna Ciccone yanked *madonna.com* from its domain owner, though the latter disclaimed affiliation with the Catholic Church, Madonna College, Madonna Hospital, the Madonna Rehabilitation Hospital in Lincoln, Nebraska—or Madonna the singer. But when Giorgio Armani attempted to retrieve *armani.com*, owned by Anand Ramnath Mani, a graphic artist in Vancouver, WIPO rejected the complaint and even declared that the company had abused the process, even though Mr. Mani hadn't set up a Web site using the name.

The introduction of new top-level domains like *.biz* and *.info* was a boon to cybersquatters. Some small countries reaped an unexpected harvest thanks to the handy implications of their domains' national extensions. Step forward, Tuvulu and Moldavia. Moldavia, a former Soviet Union satellite, could license *.md*, its TLD, to cybersquatters for $299 a year and a share of royalties. The cybersquatters could then resell it to doctors, health care providers, or any others who might like a nice, neat two-letter domain. A plastic surgeon in Florida registered *www.facelift.md;* an ophthalmology clinic was at *www.eye.md.* Tuvalu's *.tv* was also on the market, as well as Tonga's *.to*. A new opportunity arose when the Canadian Internet Registration Authority (CIRA) said it would no longer reserve the names of townships, cities, or regions that no longer existed as a result of amalgamations. Addresses such as *www.rocky-mountain-house.ca* would be sold—along with about two thousand other names—for $20 on a first come, first served basis.

Cybersquatting became viewed with increasing alarm, and measures were taken to quell such rampant capitalism. The Internet Corporation for Assigned Names and Numbers (ICANN) had regulations against cybersquatting, but the definitive move against the squatters was made by the Anticybersquatting Consumer Protection Act passed by the U.S. Congress in 1999. Under the act, it became illegal to register specific Web site names and sit on a trademark that properly belonged to someone else with "bad faith intent to profit." Likewise, it became an infringement to register the misspelling or distortion of a well-known trademark for the same fell purpose. The latter practice supplied another new word to English—"typo-squatting."

In the age of global communication, national laws can only have a limited effect. In response to trademark owners' protests regarding cybersquatting,

WIPO put in place the Uniform Dispute Resolution Policy (UDRP), a mechanism that allows trademark owners to stop piracy and online consumer fraud. Each domain name registrant has, by virtue of its registering a domain name, contractually agreed to submit itself to the UDRP. A trademark owner can bring an action under the UDRP if it can show that a domain name is identical or confusingly similar to its trademark or service mark, that the registrant has no rights or legitimate interests in respect of the domain name, or that the domain name has been registered and is being used in bad faith. "Bad faith" includes such things as cybersquatting, intent to direct traffic to the registrant's Web site, or intent to disrupt business of the trademark owner. UDRP proceedings are conducted by arbitrators who review the evidence.

Whether brand names are bought, sold, leased, or hoarded, they can have great inherent value that is sometimes sluggish in being realized. Marvel, publisher of comic books and cards with characters like *Spider-Man, The X-Men, The Incredible Hulk, Daredevil,* and *Captain America,* had 70 percent of the market for such things in the 1980s and early 1990s, driven largely by collectors. It pumped out 150 million comic books: supply began to drastically exceed demand. In 1996 Marvel filed for bankruptcy protection, citing a debt of $1.2 billion. In 1998 a new owner, the toy maker Ike Perlmutter, began to license forty-seven hundred characters to moviemakers, including *Spider-Man, X-Men,* and in the summer of 2003, *The Incredible Hulk.* In 2002, the company made a profit of $22.6 million, and was heading higher. The pioneering video game brand Atari (its arcade game *Pong* was so popular that machines sometimes jammed because they were glutted with quarters) died in 1996 but has lately been resurrected. In 2003 a Franco-American company that bought the rights to the name from Hasbro announced that it would adopt the brand for its new name, forsaking its less scintillating *Inforgrames* [sic]. The company was set to launch a new *Matrix 2* movie tie-in computer game, *Enter the Matrix,* which would join the company's popular *Godzilla: Destroy All Monsters Melee* on game-store shelves.

Naming is only one stage in marketing, the complex process of getting products and services from producers and providers to other businesses or to consumers. Gauging customer response is so complex that trademark checks aren't the last torture-test a new name or family of names undergoes. Once a short list of names is chosen and checked, it meets the public for the first time. It's tested within an inch of its shelf life in conjunction with packaging, logos, taglines, and graphics. Any new name doesn't always meet quick acceptance. In fact, some consumers may hate a new name. "We tell our clients to prepare for the backlash," said Steven Addis, chief executive of the San Francisco–based branding firm Addis. Tony Spaeth, an independent identity consultant, noted that "The best names sound bad at first because they're distinctive."

One key to a successful new name often lay in the pride that an organization felt when it changed identity. Those who compromised or backed into an embarrassing new name tended to be sheepish. A proud outfit was willing to take the time and spend the money to vigorously herald its new name. It previewed it internally, giving employees the first glimpse—ahead of customers and investors—of the new identity and the rationale behind it. These people had to be supportive, so it was important to make them fans at once. This entailed holding employee meetings to announce with fanfare the new name and its meaning. It meant distributing advertising preprints for the campaign that will launch the new name, and supplying coffee mugs and key rings to make it tangible.

This matter of tangibility is worth a moment's pause, if only to consider the many ways an appellation can sail forth:

Stationery

Letterhead	Memorandums	E-mail addresses
Envelopes	News releases	Internet addresses
Mailing labels	Postal meters	Cable codes
Calling cards	Fax answerbacks	

Listings and Certificates

Stock certificates	Who's Who
Certificates of incorporation	Credit certificates
Stock ticker symbols	Licenses
Business directories	Permits

Employee Communications

Recruiting materials	Credit union materials	Service awards
Benefits books	Pension plans	
ID cards	Medical plans	

Business Forms

Invoices	Statements	Corporate checks
Purchase orders	Payroll checks	Message forms

Business Affairs

Lease agreements	Computer entry codes
Insurance policies	Foreign exchange agreements

Advertising and Promotion

Advertisements	Yellow Pages	Apparel
Sales literature	Packaging	Novelty items
Presentation formats	Binders	

Signage

Buildings	Windows	Exhibit booths
Doorways	Directional cues	Rolling stock

This visible face was only part of the educational process. The media was told the reasons and background for switching names. If a company's name was changed, it was important that investment analysts started to use its new handle as quickly as possible, and avoid such locutions as "the former Blickstein Company." After a new name was announced in a news release and in advertising, organizations had to ensure the comfort of customers, clients, and suppliers, and confirm that each was conversant with the new moniker. Some CEOs wrote personally to each major customer, and any client grousing, "I didn't see anything wrong with the old name," got an immediate response. Thoughtful companies created a manual with simple guidelines for using the new name and logo. If conflicts over name usage were allowed to linger, they tended to become arguments for keeping the old name in play.

 Both a bad and a good way of orchestrating name change was shown by First Union, a North Carolina bank. First Union, which first took its name in 1958, bought its rival Wachovia ("wa-KO-vee-yah") in April 2001, adopted the name of the bank it took over, and unleashed a branding makeover. From the early 1980s until 1997, First Union had prospered through acquiring numerous small to medium-sized banks on the East Coast but suffered reverses when it paid too much for CoreStates Financial, Pennsylvania's second-largest bank. They tried to recoup by closing branches and firing staff, but lost customers and suffered a drop in its stock price. Jokes had it that First Union's acronym, *FU*, stood for something else. For their new acquisition, it took a different tack, hiring Interbrand to change every aspect of name, logo, and design. Disdaining the usual banking names of *First, Commerce,* or *Community,* it opted for something distinctive. Interbrand conducted in-depth question and answer sessions with employees, customers, and senior management. This led to a new slogan, "Uncommon Wisdom for Shared Success," which became linked to a blue and green box logo with silver lines cascading from one side to the other. In creating it, Interbrand was drawn to the historical origin of *Wachovia*—the Latin form of the name *Wachau,* the place of water, the name that eighteenth-century settlers had given to the tract of land in North Carolina, after the Wachau region, a pretty stretch of the mighty Danube river in Austria. In the name and logo were linked the idea of a community nourished by one source, a river, and a flow of communications and capital.

Marketing is a symbiotic process in which a name constantly interacts with every other element of a campaign, including slogan, taglines, and logos like the Polo pony and the Izod Lacoste alligator, as well as the object itself. Marketing might also involve sub-branding, which may entail using a big typeface for a product and a smaller one for its maker, for example, *Dustbuster* in big type, *Black & Decker* in small type, which can appeal to both corporate interests and to customers because a potentially confusing name (Black & Decker is better known for power tools)  is relegated to a lower billing. In ads, *V8 Juice* is bigger than *Campbell*, and *Courtyard* and *Residence Inns* more prominent than *Marriott*. Some names become synonymous with the object itself, as in the transparent plastics and pastel shades of the iMac computer series introduced in 1998, the simple, streamlined contours of Braun household devices, and Herman Miller ergonomic office furniture.

Apple, Braun, and *Herman Miller* are familiar names. A new name can carve a clearer path into the mind, and avoids the mess of locking an old name that already means something into a new product or service that stands for something else. Always the objective is to isolate the brand, not the generic, as in such slogans of yesteryear as "Don't ask for 'polish,' demand *Brite-Lite*," "If it isn't an *Eastman*, it isn't a *Kodak*," "*Foster's*. Australian for beer," and "Don't be vague . . . ask for *Haig and Haig*."

Both old and new brand names are highly visible and unconfusable on an American Express Web site that lists its trademarks and service marks:

AMERICAN EXPRESS®

AMERICAN EXPRESS Box Logo®

AMERICAN EXPRESS Card Design®

AMERICAN EXPRESS BUSINESS
  Card Design®

AMERICAN EXPRESS CORPORATE
  Card Design®

AMERICAN EXPRESS CORPORATE
  PURCHASING Card Design®

AMERICAN EXPRESS Travelers
  Cheque Design®

AMERICAN EXPRESS WORLD SER-
  VICE & Design®

AMEX®

AMEXMAIL SERVICES®

BLUE FOR BUSINESS [SM]

BLUE FOR STUDENTS [SM]

BLUE FROM AMERICAN
  EXPRESS [SM]

BLUE FROM AMERICAN EXPRESS
  Card Design [SM]

BLUE TOOLS®

BLUE ZONE®

BLUELOOT®

CENTURION®

CHEQUES FOR TWO®

COOLBLUEOFFERS®

DATAMEX®

do more®

DO YOU KNOW ME?®

DON'T LEAVE HOME WITHOUT IT®

DON'T LEAVE HOME WITHOUT
  THEM®

DON'T LEAVE HOME WITHOUT
  US®

DON'T LEAVE HOMEPAGES WITH-
  OUT IT®

EMPRESS®	PLATINUM Card Design®
EXPRESS APPROVAL Design®	Private Payments^{SM}
EXPRESSNET®	PRIVILEGED ASSETS®
FOOD & WINE®	REWARDSMANAGER®
Gladiator Head Design®	SHOPAMEX^{SM}
GLOBAL ASSIST®	SIGN & TRAVEL®
ID KEEPER^{SM}	SKYGUIDE®
IDS®	SMARTDATA®
MAKE LIFE REWARDING^{SM}	SMARTPARTNERS®
MEMBERSHIP B@NKING®	SMARTSOURCE®
MEMBERSHIP REWARDS®	TRAVEL + LEISURE®
OFFER ZONE®	TRAVEL IMPRESSIONS®
OPTIMA®	TRUE GRACE®
OPTIMA Card Design®	Wall Street Wise. Main Street Smart.®
OPTIMA TRUE GRACE®	YOUR COMPANY®
PLATINUM CARD®	

The site does double duty. It promotes American Express brands and also warns the unwary—or potential violators—that listed trademarks have been spoken for.

American Express's site is partly defensive. But names are also tied into aggressive marketing campaigns that are sometimes interactive. Niketown promotional showplaces—the first one opened in Chicago—became what John Heskett has called "a theatre of consumer testing." What other regions know as *ATM*s, some northeastern U.S. banks called *MAC* (*Money Access Center*), and personalized the technology: "Go see MAC!" Brand promotion may include what Ruth Shalit calls "spokescharacters." Certainly, it's become hard to imagine Green Giant without its Jolly Green Giant ("Ho Ho Ho! Green Giant") or Pillsbury without the Pillsbury Dough Boy. In the multicolored world of marketing, names can even find themselves associated with new hues and shapes.

Nike became linked with the Swoosh, an apostrophe-like shape that a college student created in 1971 for $35.

Pills took on new guises: Viagra was light blue (presumably for old boys); Zibeta, a heart drug, was heart-shaped; Zocor, an anticholesterol pill, was shield-shaped, Valium had a *V* cut through each pill. Drugs took on names that reflected not just medical needs but lifestyle choices. This was especially so in the case of generic drugs, where there might be little to distinguish one pill from another. Names became the sugar that made the medicine go down, like Flintstones, the children's vitamins. Flintstones, augmented by its design, built on the fame of its namesake cartoon show and virtually came across as candy. Kids found the pills so appealing that they forgot that vitamins were good for them.

Namers ride the crest of marketing trends, surfing fashion and styles. Nike began selling shoes in the 1960s but only hit its stride with the onset of the jogging craze. When mass jogging began to slow in the mid-1980s, Reebok cornered the market for aerobics shoes, and Adidas also cut into its sales, Nike transformed itself into a sports and fitness company. It branded itself as a lifestyle, as did The Gap, which cluster-bombed neighborhoods with multiple outlets of *The Gap, Baby Gap, Gap Kids, Old Navy, Banana Republic,* and *Gap Body* chains. There were brand stores, department-store brand boutiques, and branded holiday destinations. In the 1980s The Body Shop became a watchword for ecologically sensitive cosmetics. Conglomerates contracted out or spun off their manufacturing divisions. In 1997, Sara Lee, the frozen-food company, which also marketed *Hanes* underwear, *Wonderbra, Champion* sports apparel, *Kiwi* shoe polish, and *Ball Park Franks,* sold its plants to contractors who then became its suppliers. Consumers might not have aware of that, but they were sure to notice that some celebrities—Martha Stewart, Michael Jordan, Oprah—had gone way beyond endorsements and become brand names themselves. They even had namesake magazines like *Martha Stewart Living* and *O: The Oprah Magazine.*

During the 1990s two trends were at work. At one end were big-box stores in which house or no-name brands, such as Loblaw's *President's Choice,* Wal-Mart's *Great Value,* and Marks and Spencer's *St Michael* prepared foods, multiplied their market share in North America and Europe. At the other end were "attitude" lifestyle brands like Calvin Klein and Benetton. The spread of craft or boutique enterprises like small breweries or wineries made such inroads into big companies' sales that they resorted to creating faux-indie labels of their own.

Kraft can hardly be called an indie label. After Nestlé, it is the world's largest food and beverage company and credibly says that its products are in 99 percent of U.S. homes. Over the decades, its famous brand names have included *Kraft Miracle Whip* and *Kraft Dinner* (the 1930s), *Kraft Processed Cheese Slices* and *Tang* breakfast beverage crystals (1950s), and *Lunchables* (1980s). In 2003 it pledged to reduce fat and sugar in its products and put nutrition labels on them even when law didn't require it, and vowed to get the trans fatty acids, or trans fats, out of

Oreo cookies after a consumer group sued to force the company to remove them—the lawsuit was dropped after Kraft said it would bring the trans fat content of all of its products to under 0.5 per serving. Trans fats, the partially hydrogenated shortenings and oils used in many food products, had become implicated in an increased risk of heart disease. This latest health scare had food companies falling over themselves to get rid of them. Under mounting public pressure, Kellogg promised to reformulate its products by 2006. McCain with its Superfries and PepsiCo with its Frito-Lay chips, Ruffles, Doritos, and Cheetos promoted their products as  "trans fat free." In the United Kingdom, Mars and Snickers candy bars began to be made without partially hydrogenated oils, and The Nestlé Company and Cadbury Trebor Bassett planned to eliminate trans fats from their candy bars.

The manufacturers' motives were evidently twofold. One megatrend of the 1990s and early 2000s was toward the consumption of fat- and sugar-reduced food and drink, which may have been part of Kentucky Fried Chicken's decision to call itself *KFC*. At the same time, obesity as a public health concern had followed in quick succession much concern about the cancer-causing properties of tobacco use. A $12.5 million lawsuit had succeeded against McDonald's because the hamburger chain had failed to tell customers it was flavoring fries with beef tallow a decade previously, after announcing that it had begun to fry them in vegetable oil. Moreover, successful lawsuits had levied billions in awards against the big tobacco companies. If cigarettes were a health risk, what about sugar and fat?

Some marketing megatrends are quite explicable. *Time* reported that pet products and services in the United States were expected to top $31 billion in 2003, up from $17 billion ten years earlier—there was even a trade show called *Woofstock*. Other trends baffle understanding. Who would have supposed that the youth-culture market for teas and bottled waters would take off? During the 1980s the huge popularity of minivans was perfectly understandable: with children themselves, the Baby Boomers needed enough room to drop off the kids at the soccer game or load up on Saturday morning at the mall. But who could have predicted for the next decade the huge demand for SUVs—expensive, gas-guzzling, sometimes unstable, and virtually armor-plated? They looked as if they should be shoving aside boulders on a mountain road but were seldom driven outside the mall parking lot. They bore names like *Explorer, Navigator, Pathfinder,* and *TrailBlazer.* SUVs might have been related to the urban camping phenomenon: teenagers lugging around what appeared to be backpacks full of rubble, or about to launch an assault on Mount Everest. Senior citizens outfitted themselves as if about to set off on an overland safari. Was that predictable? For the marketers and namers who tracked such changes, success often consisted not in having fifteen minutes of fame, but in being fifteen minutes ahead of their time.

DO NAMES HAVE A FUTURE?

Zounds, I was never so bethump'd with words
Since I first called my brother's father dad.
—Shakespeare, King John, 2.1

"Never make forecasts, especially about the future," the American movie mogul Samuel Goldwyn sagely advised.

Goldwyn had a point. The track record of prognostication—whether it be about political campaigns, horse races, new products, or even naming trends—is dicey. History is filled with fearless forecasts that flopped. William Thomson, Lord Kelvin (1824–1907), the president of the Royal Society, predicted that heavier-than-air machines were impossible, X rays would prove to be a hoax, and that radio had no future. "Who the hell wants to hear actors talk?" asked Harry Warner of Warner Brothers in 1927. Decca Records rejected the Beatles in 1962, noting that groups of guitars were on the way out. In 1977 Kenneth Olsen, founder of Digital Equipment Corporation, could see no reason why anyone would have a computer in their home.

Eminent scientists, bankers, and entrepreneurs have stumbled, so should those in the naming business fear to gaze upon the future? "No," say we, because for something as mobile and changeable as the English language, there is always a future. In truth, there can be no afterword, only an overview. The same holds true for brand names.

We've created a typology of names. The initialized and acronymic world of *IBM*, *GM*, and *Alcoa*. The descriptive family of persons, places, and positive attributes. The vivid cohort of imaginatively allusive names (if you shave with a *Mach 3* razor you do not shave at three times the speed of sound) and their bewildering cousins, arbitrary names (you byte, you don't bite into an *Apple*), and the host of wholly synthetic coined names that draw on all the resources of language.

We've told how, on the macrocosmic level, brand names so surround and saturate every part of our society and culture that landscape becomes brand-scape. On the microscopic level are those creatures the brand words themselves. We've tried to show what kind of linguistic units they are, and how they pillage and enrich the language.

We've discussed the practical techniques involved in forging new names, a process that's equal parts inspiration and perspiration. We've populated a

Heaven and Hell for brand names that, respectively, work well or dismally, noting that *Star* soap, U.S. Trademark No. 9, remains a star. We've taken brand names apart and put them back together, showing how suffixes, prefixes, and other combining forms can be mixed and matched. We've auditioned the rhetoric of brandspeak, and lent the other ear to the music and metrics of their sounds. In the densest—we hope in a good way—chapter of the book, we've circled and perhaps corralled the topic of brand names' symbolism, their emotional impact, and their benefits. We've unpacked brand names from luggage taken around the world, and picked up a number of souvenirs from lands and peoples near and far.

We've sketched the odd profession of brand namers, what namers bring to their job, and how they connect with their clients. We've sketched the long and the short of creating lists of brand name and trade name nominees, how names get trademarked and stay protected, how they get bought, sold, and cornered in every sense, what happens to them when they become entangled in the World Wide Web, and taken a glimpse at how they remain themselves in a crowded marketplace.

But the implicit question of this Afterword's title remains: What is the future of brand names? To hazard a guess, insofar as we're willing to make any guesses at all, we can glance at the past, on the presumption that what's past is prologue and a signpost for the future. As in everything else, the naming of companies and products follows fashion and style, and both reflect the era in which they flourished.

At the start, brand names tended to be descriptive, combining three basic motives: the valued name of owner or founder, the locale of a business, or a description of goods or services. By the turn of the twentieth century, dozens of automobile companies tacked *Motor* or *Motors* to their family surnames. At the time of World War I, *-ine* became popular because of its Latin roots, which could translate across widening European markets—at least until another war struck. As marketing and advertising became more sophisticated, companies began to choose names that expressed positive, specific attributes. *Greyhound Bus Lines* suggested swift service, *Fidelity Investments* implied trustworthy financial advice, and *Tastee-Freez* was exactly what you wanted in ice cream.

Revolutionary changes in naming businesses came during the 1960s, the age of mergers and conglomerates when companies began to expand and diversify. In 1959, International Telephone & Telegraph suggested the international telecommunications business. Over the next two decades, it acquired numerous companies, becoming the world's largest conglomerate and changing itself to the intentionally nondescript *ITT*. The tidal wave of mergers and acquisitions swamped long-cherished brands and names. One naming trend pointed to expansion, like *AOL Time Warner*, the other to contraction, as in three successive name changes: *Citibank* became *Citicorp*, then *Citigroup*.

The evolution of naming speeded up in the hi-tech sector, when engineers and software programmers concluded that, since they were creating a new industry with unheard-of products, they should also concoct fresh names. During the space race of the 1960s and 1970s, many companies found -*tron* too tempting to resist. In 1968, three engineers formed a semiconductor company whose products would help electronic machines function more intelligently: it was *Intel*. In 1975, when Bill Gates and Paul Allen formed a company to make software for microcomputers, they melded the two to create *Micro-Soft*. The next year, realizing that hyphens had become outmoded, they dropped the hyphen and the uppercase *S*. Today's fashion in spatial punctuation jams two names together.

During the 1990s, one of the hottest trademark categories became *Class 9*, an "electrical and scientific apparatus." Innumerable companies reinvented themselves on the World Wide Web—especially telecom and e-commerce companies. Bring on *Amazon*, *eBay*, and *Yahoo!* In 1999, one registrar of e-names registered 8.1 million of them. This entailed new naming complications. Namers had to think of names on and off the Web. The Web name was as important as the print name, and could be quite different. Many names were created so they could be registered as a memorable, one-word e-mail address, or URL. Because so many common words were already taken, many companies coined their own words, in part to stake claim to an unoccupied URL. Some old rules had to be rethought. Since users often only had to click on, rather than type a word, the shorter-is-better dictum lost force. Some namers added trendy numbers to the mix, sounding futuristic, or coined a host of suffix-based names, such as *Unisys*. Others tended toward the whimsical or tacked on hip and edgy buzzwords that, seeking younger, technology-literate consumer, produced names resembling those of rock bands. The names of high-tech companies, like the companies themselves, often suffered instant obsolescence.

UNiSYS

Consider the fascination with these four building blocks of the era: *info* for information, *sys* for systems, *comm* for communications, and *data*. Meaningful terms, yes. Distinctive terms, no. The databases of the U.S. Patent and Trademark Office bulge with the filings of companies and their brands using these commoners:

Filings using

INFO	8,819	DATA	7,850
SYS	1,866	COMM	18,317

Lurks there a corporation named *InfoSysDataComm*? It would be the grand slam of obviousness.

The same herd instinct was true of biotech companies during the revolution caused by genetics breakthroughs. Throughout the 1990s, medicines to treat

everything from high blood pressure to depression flooded the market, and doctors and patients needed a way to navigate them. Companies started developing
names early in clinical testing, years before drugs are eligible for regulatory
approval. Pills (and names) were no longer just synthetic compounds in a form
that could be swallowed, but part of lifestyle choices. Pharmaceutical companies
that used to thrive or perish on the strength of their clinical studies now had to
differentiate themselves, especially with generic drugs. Small nonclinical details
differed, and these had to be highlighted. With so many versions of the same drug
on the market, companies hunted for ways to make their version stand out. At the
same time, new drugs were coming to market in bigger numbers. The focus
became consumer preference, not professional expertise. Suddenly pills, or at
least vitamin tablets like Flintstones, could sound like fun.

New companies needed new names for themselves, and old companies,
seeking a new look, wanted new names, too. However, changing an established
company's name can weaken brand awareness. The ostensibly boring Borland
software maker changed its name to *Inprise*, thinking it would connote *Internet*
and *enterprise*. Two and a half years later it reverted to *Borland.* By the early 2000s,
names moved away from initializations and technology-driven hybrids—the
ubiquitous *i-*, *e-*, *.com*, *.net*, or *-sys*—in favor of more resonant real words or
coinages. The stock market crash of dot-com companies took the shine off
names associated with the Internet.

Market upheavals shook up names. *Lucent Technologies* had been *Bell
Laboratories*, *Nortel* had been *Northern Telecom*, and before that, *Northern Electric.*
NORTEL In their most recent incarnations, both lost huge amounts
NETWORKS with the stock market collapse of telecom companies. In
2003, less than four years after buying Network Solutions for
$21 billion, VeriSign sold the dotcom-registration business for $100 million. In
1989 *Time*, the magazine publisher, linked itself to Warner Communications,
which included the Warner Brothers movie studio, then some years later it
merged with AOL, formerly American Online. In 2002, AOL Time Warner wrote
off $54 billion in assets, giving it the largest one-year corporate loss in history.
The next year its name reverted to *Time Warner*, which it had been called prior to
its merger with AOL in 2000. Even its stock symbol changed, from *AOL* to *TWX*.
The same year WorldCom, the U.S. telecom giant, in bankruptcy protection,
renamed itself *MCI*—the name of the long-distance carrier that it swallowed up
in 1997. Edgar Bronfman Jr. sold the liquor and entertainment company
Seagram to France's utility Vivendi Universal in 2000 in exchange for shares,
and promptly shed billions in shareholder value. It was all rather like the title of
a 1985 hit from Universal Studios, *Back to the Future.*

Where do we go from here, and can we get anywhere at all? True knowledge
begins with knowing what it is one doesn't know, and being aware that what
one thinks one knows may not be so. We know that currently the people in the

developed world are older on average, and those of the Third World are younger. We know that the population of some of the major European countries is shrinking, and that the global population has at last leveled off. But what the case will be in a few decades, we don't know. We also don't know whether global warming will persist or increase, causing catastrophic changes in the biosphere. We probably won't run out of fossil fuels soon, but we may run out of fresh water. We don't even know what we'll eat next year, and for some, whether we will eat at all. Who could have predicted that the British diet, notorious for its blandness, would start to favor incendiary curries, or that salsa would outsell ketchup in the United States?

Stuart Berg Flexner once wrote that "After Prohibition 700 companies were making beer; in 1976, after consolidations and mergers, only fifty-four brewers existed. How long will we talk about Rhode Island's *Narragansett* or New York's and New Jersey's *Ballantine* now that St. Louis' *Falstaff* has bought them? of Washington State's *Olympia*, now owned by St. Paul's *Hamms*; of *Schmidt's*, now owned by *Blatz*? Today five large brewers make up 'the big five': Anheuser Busch (*Budweiser* and *Michelob*), Joseph Schlitz, Pabst, Coors, and Miller." But neither Berg nor we could have predicted the rise of minibrewers and self-brewing pubs, or that some giant breweries would produce labels posing as small breweries, often enough the same old brew with a new name.

If we couldn't guess that, we certainly don't know what advances in genetics and biotechnology will happen next, and if human cloning will become commonplace. We don't know whether terrorism against Western powers will mount or subside. We don't know what we'll find in outer space, and how much that might affect us. We know that in 2002 Coca-Cola beat out Microsoft Corporation as the world's most valuable brand, though the value of the ninety biggest brands fell 5 percent. But if we knew whether and when the economy will slide into recession or depression we would be rich right now (or at least very shortly).

One twentieth-century revolution at least we are sure will be consolidated: the dramatic tilt in social, political, legal, and economic relations between the sexes. Beginning with the gain of the women's vote, strengthened by the home-front women's work force during World War II, we have learned to think in a new way about the opposite—or same—sex. We became feminist, and then postfeminist. Yet, despite androgynous personal names—"Gary" for a girl—and unisex hair styling, males still prefer masculine names and females feminine names. The differences even extend to conceptions of what makes a masculine or feminine name attractive. In a study published in the *Journal of Educational Psychology*, "Name Stereotypes and Teachers' Expectations," a pair of psychologists showed that a grade-school essay titled "What I Did Last Sunday" when said to have been written by a "David" or a "Lisa" consistently got a better grade than it did when said to have been written by an "Elmer" or a "Bertha." In 1980, researchers at Tulane University published a study on the effect of women's first names on how others perceive their attractiveness. The researchers randomly attached three "desirable" names *(Kathy, Jennifer,* and *Christine)* and three "undesirable" names *(Ethel, Harriet,* and *Gertrude)* to photographs of six women who in an earlier study had been judged to be equally attractive. Then, renting a booth at the Tulane Student Center, they asked passersby to choose a local beauty queen. THEY ARE ALL SO PRETTY WE CAN'T DECIDE, read a sign on the booth. PLEASE HELP US BY VOTING FOR YOUR CHOICE. *Kathy, Jennifer,* and *Christine* won.

Significant others and significant differences: *Psychology Today* reports that women "learn to speak earlier, know more words, recall them better, pause less and glide through tongue twisters." Even more impressively, they produce half as much saliva as men. Obviously, marketing and naming cannot ignore half the human race or confine itself only to the droolers.

Answers to the social questions we've asked profoundly affect what goods and services will be offered to the public, how they will be marketed, and what they will be called. A few people have made sporting bets. In 2002, Interbrand ran an online survey on *www.brandchannel.com* of marketing and branding professions across a range of industries around the world, most of whom were directly involved in a naming project. An open-ended question about naming trends got such answers as "increasing cross-culture and legal issues, requiring the expertise of outside specialists," "More real names will come into use, fewer whimsical ones," "Simplification will result from companies listening to the wishes of their customers," and "Ensuring [that a] name is identifiable with product/service, while maintaining differentiation in the marketplace." The more specific question "As a marketing professional, where do you think the future of names lies?" resulted in the following prophecies, in rounded-off percentages of responses:

Made-up, but meaningful compound names	
(jetBlue, MasterCard)	38
More "real" names *(Target, Apple)*	19
More "coined" names *(Accenture, Verizon)*	19
More "legacy" names *(Wyeth, Braxton)*	9

As the British linguist Tony Thorne has noted, the backlash against the *e-* and *.com* trend is plainly in full force: companies like eDistrict and eCentric changed their names to, respectively, *umedia* and *Capital Management.* Impelled by the millennium to make changes, namers and their clients were at the same time beset by worries, furrowing brows after the burst of the stock market bubble in telecom and e-com companies, and the fiscal implosion of mega-corporations and such big names as Enron and WorldCom a.k.a. MCI. Even typographical trickery and alphabet-soup namings were less common on the

Internet than one might have supposed. Gateway companies such as *Excite* and *Infoseek* chose descriptive or suggestive names. Security software firms such as *CheckPoint* or *Cylink* adopted appropriate word fusions or neologisms. Network services outfits did much the same: *Concentric Network, EarthLink,* and *Metricom.* Elsewhere, company names retreated to safety and retrenchment: in Britain, the old and old-fashioned Stanley Gibbons stamp company returned to its former name, and DeBeers, the diamond miners and sellers, decided not to change its name.

No one knows what will happen next, but a few constants are in force. One constant is the law, and how it continues to impact naming. Effective November 2, 2003, the United States joined the Madrid Protocol Relating to the Madrid Agreement ("the Madrid Protocol" for short). This change makes it easier for a trademark owner to file and maintain foreign applications and registrations. It enables a U.S. trademark applicant to seek trademark protection in up to fifty-seven different member nations at the same time. Similarly, the Madrid Protocol enables trademark applicants in member nations to seek protection in the U.S. under the same system. The likely result: a flood of foreign trademark applications in the U.S.

Store brand names are becoming more powerful. One of five items sold in U.S. stores is store-branded. In Europe, the percentage is even higher. Wal-Mart's brand of dog food, *Ol' Roy* (named for the founder's pooch), has quietly passed Purina as the world's top-selling dog chow. (Wal-Mart's wide wall of brands, such as *Great Value* bleach, *Sam's Choice* tuna, *Spring Valley* vitamins, and *Equate* analgesics, make up 40 percent of total store sales.) At the grocery goliath Kroger, there are more than four thousand privately branded food and drink items. 7-Eleven has launched its own beer, dubbed *Santiago*, to steal share from the Mexican import, Corona. At the French marketer Carrefour, a major internal branding program emphasizes quality, image, and innovation. These store brands are not designed to sell merely on the basis of price. They are carefully named and positioned to elbow others off the shelf. Expect more and better house-brand names.

A third constant in force is the fact that fashions in naming are like any other kind of fashion. For example, there is increasing consumer backlash against global megabrands and their ubiquitous advertising. Perhaps this will spur naming strategies that rely less on ties to an existing "family" of marks. (Instead of a new "McSandwich" in some form, McDonald's might invent a name that stands apart.)

Apart from the predictable shape of marketing cycles, there are even more important constants. Some 200,000 years ago, modern *Homo sapiens* evolved in an area of sub-Saharan Africa. Walking more or less upright, they acquired new physical equipment, including the capacity for complex speech. They began to use simple tools, though they did not seem simple at the time. About 40,000 years ago, they migrated to Europe, getting a cold welcome since that continent was then in the last throes of the Ice Age. They vanquished a rival species, the big, slow, and unfortunately for them, stupid Neanderthals. As Robin Dunbar, a British scholar has noted, "it was our ability to exchange complex data—shelter and sources of food among many of our fellow humans—that gave us a critical advantage in those harsh days." After this, the planet belonged to us. About 10,000 years ago, we invented agriculture and we began to write down words to keep track of the harvests and livestock. With it came our propensity for creating social ranks, acquiring possessions, buying and selling, and waging organized war.

What remains stable is our nosy interest in each other. Robin Dunbar monitored common-room chat at his university in Liverpool and discovered that 86 percent of daily conversations—at least in Britain—were about personal relationships and experiences: peoples' love lives, favorite TV programs, and jokes. Liverpudlian students seemingly couldn't care less about quantum mechanics or whether the deconstructionism of Jacques Derrida had a future. They, like many of us, were absorbed by chitchat, gossip, and what brand names to buy.

Language is an inextricable part of any activity inside or outside the common room. As we've noted, it's safe to say that English is unstoppable as a world language. One legacy of the British Empire is English's prevalence in many nations' governing bodies and agencies, their public service, legal system, religious groups, schools and universities, and all their related outpourings such as textbooks and the records of transactions of every kind. As a lingua franca, English has become a neutral communications medium between varied ethnic groups, and a local variety can even become a symbol of national or even international unity. In 1970 the grammarian Randolph Quirk predicted that, "by 1990 everyone in Europe may be using, or exposed to, English for some part of every day." He was right. Studies in the 1980s showed a rapid rise in the frequency with which English loanwords appeared in foreign language publications. As David Crystal reports in the *Cambridge Encyclopedia of the English Language*, one researcher, S. A. Vesterhus, found that in German car advertising brochures and model descriptions, there were 7,190 nouns from English in 8,459 pages—the leading two were *Design* and *Cockpit*, followed by *Spoiler*, *Styling*, *Limit*, *Star*, *Display*, *Power*, *Know-how*, *Output*, and *Tuning*. The use of English in print, broadcast, and Internet media is further enlarged by the United States's dominant rank in international business and markets. The tourist and advertising industries depend on English, and it is the language of international air traffic control, steadily expanding into maritime transport, policing, security, and emergency services. It is the lead language of multinational business and academic conferences. Most of the scientific, technical, and academic information in the world is in English, as is the great bulk of data stored in electronic retrieval systems. English provides access to authors of every other tongue. It is the main language of pop culture, satellite broadcasting, home computers, and video games. Less salubriously, it is the principal language of pornography and the illicit drug trades. No wonder that the *Reader's Digest* column "It Pays to Enrich Your Word Power" has been run continuously since 1954.

Even as he sums up the scarcely-to-be-underestimated impact of English, David Crystal points out that, "Each country where English is a first language is aware of its linguistic identity, and is anxious to preserve it from the influence of others. New Zealanders do not want to be Australians; Canadians do not want to be 'American'; and Americanism is perceived as a danger signal by usage guardians everywhere (except in the USA)." The open question about English is not whether it will proliferate, a foregone conclusion, but whether eventually it will branch off, like Latin, into separate vernaculars.

Given how much it borrows words from other languages, English is already polyglot. The speediness of global communications only hastens the process. On October 4, 1957, the Soviet Union launched *Sputnik*, the first artificial satellite, into space. Other than among Soviet space scientists, the word *Sputnik* was unknown on October 3. By the evening of October 4, it had entered hundreds of languages.

The fear of an industrial and technological "Japanese invasion" of thirty years ago has lessened, but Japanese still makes linguistic incursions, especially in pop culture. These include *manga*, the graphic novel–based black-and-white comics with titles like *Sailor Moon* and *Digimon;* anime, movie and TV animation, typically with a science-fiction theme; and *hentai*, which combines both, with explicit sexual content. *Hitachi, Hyundai,* and *Toshiba* can be recognized in every strip and megamall. In fact, the syllabic speech and writing systems of Japanese have even influenced corporate acronyms like Amoco and Texaco. Will the impact of Japanese increase yet more? Again, we don't know.

However, we can deduce that brand names themselves, whatever their national origins, have become something of a universal language. Partial results from an ongoing study done in 2003 by the French firm Nomen, which had coined the brand names *Vivendi* and *Vinci,* indicated that they account for two out of every three words an average French speaker knows. Nomen's team read small sections from 100,000 words in a French dictionary and 20,000 brand names. According to Marcel Botton, Nomen's chief executive, "The distinction between brand names and ordinary words is becoming quite blurred. This is bad news for companies that have invested a lot of money in branding a product, but for the general public I see advantages. Brand names are more international than words and they are creating a new Esperanto, which I rather like." To Botton, "it seemed people knew more and more brands and fewer words."

Google, the Internet's premier search engine, annually reports its ten most popular searches in various categories. Among corporate names, it's notable how many are those of multinational companies.

In Brand Names:

2003	2002	2001
Ferrari	Ferrari	Nokia
Sony	Sony	Sony
BMW	Nokia	BMW
Disney	Disney	Palm
Ryanair	IKEA	Adobe
HP	Dell	Dell
Dell	Ryanair	Oracle
easyJet	Microsoft	Ferrari
Last Minute	Porsche	Honda
Wal-Mart	HP	Canon

The relative importance of international names in any marketplace is further reflected in a sampling of brand names in commercials during the prime time hours of 8 P.M. and 10 P.M. on CITY-TV, Channel 57 in Toronto:

Local

Bad Boy (furniture and appliance stores)
Bridlewood Mall (location of used car sale)
Leon (furniture and appliance stores)
Oliver Jewellery

Regional and National

LCBO (Liquor Control Board of Ontario) with MADD (Mothers Against Drunk
     Driving, international organization)
Millionaires Month (lottery)
Molson Canadian (beer)
Optimax Gold
Six Flags (amusement park)
Swiss Chalet (restaurant chain)

International

Always (sanitary napkins)
Bacardi Superior
Budlight Collections (greeting cards)
Coors Light

Febreze (air freshener)
Ford Focus and Windstar
Heineken
Hyundai Accent GS, Elatia GL, and Turbitron
Nissan Sentra
Palmolive Aroma Therapy and Softsoap Aroma Therapy
Smirnoff Ice Triple Black
Volkswagen Touareg
Wal-Mart
Whirlpool (in cross-promotion with Future Shop, national electronics chain,
  and Petro Canada (national oil company)

The same mix of brand names can be found in any large market. We know that. We also know that sometimes the naming answer comes from overseas. When Häagen-Dazs wanted a new ice cream flavor to stimulate sales, it opted not to spend a year commissioning chefs to come up with exotic flavors. It opted not to run thousands of taste tests. Instead, it asked a simple question: "What is the best-selling ice cream flavor outside the U.S.?" The answer came from Buenos Aires. It was Dulce de Leche, a caramelized mix of sugar and whole milk. For Häagen-Dazs, now only vanilla sells better than the favorite of Argentina and Uruguay. Add *Dulce de Leche* to the English word stock.

Most of the 5,000 to 6,000 words we add to our language each year are derived from other words. How big is the overall word stock that namers can draw on? It depends on who's talking. Are we talking about the vocabulary of words that people know and use, or just the ones that they actually use, an individual's own idiolect? Some figures have been trotted out. There are said to be 13,000 words in a six-year-old's vocabulary, 25,000 words in an "average" speaker's repertoire (but 60,000 words in an eighteen-year-old's working vocabulary). (If that last figure is reliable, the eighteen-year-old outdoes Shakespeare, who was shown in a 1968 study to only come up with less than 20,000 lexemes—basic words that exclude inflections and different forms of verbs.) Who, or what, is "average" anyway?

Suffice it to say the word stock that everyone can dip into is big, and getting bigger. A typical college dictionary may have about 125,000 entries. The 1992 integrated edition of the *Oxford English Dictionary* claimed 500,000 entries, and the revision and expansion of it now under way will be much larger. It's now within the scope of electronic technology to produce a superdictionary whose contents would combine all existing dictionaries, including such giants as the *Merriam-Webster's* and the *OED* together with every specialized dictionary going, whether legal, technical, or scientific, and fully search-accessible online. We'll wait for that.

The linguistic kit that namers resort to comprises not just the total word-stock, but linguistic blueprints based on the rules of English. Brand names are typically short, so perhaps *Scrabble* may help. There are 106 two-letter words (*AA* to *ZO*) in the official Scrabble word-lists published by the *Chambers* dictionary people, and eighteen four-letter words using letter Q (*AQUA* to *SUQS*). But a list of the most commonly occurring words in English may be more useful. In order, they are:

Written	Spoken	Written	Spoken
the	the	on	is
of	and	at	yes
to	I	he	was
in	to	with	this
and	of	by	but
a	a	be	on
for	you	it	well
was	that	as	have
is	in	his	for
that	it		

As the above indicates, the most frequently used words in English are monosyllabic. One linguistic law, Zipf's Law, named after its discoverer, G. K. Zipf, dictates that statistically the first fifteen different words of a text, say of two hundred words or more, will account for 25 percent of all the words. They are likely to be short words. By contrast, the longest word in English is said to be a chemical name with thirty-six hundred letters describing bovine NADP-specific glutamate dehydrogenase, which contains five hundred amino acids—well ahead of that old favorite "antidisestablishmentarianism" and Mary Poppins's "supercalifragilisticexpialidocious"—which, for a brevity-loving brand-namer, may amount to *floccinaucinihilipilification*, meaning "the action or habit of estimating something as worthless."

Namers can also tap such innovators or virtuosos of vocabulary as the novelists Charles Dickens, Lewis Carroll, James Joyce, Vladimir Nabokov, and Nicholson Baker, or poets like Thomas Hardy, Gerard Manley Hopkins, E. E. Cummings, and Dylan Thomas. But perhaps best of all is to go back to the first fifty words of a toddler's vocabulary. Children have a spoken vocabulary of at least fifty words by the age of eighteen months. In a British study on language acquisition study done in the 1980s, "Will" only took six and a half months to reach his half-century. Excluding personal names (only one of those, *Muriel*, ranking last as it happens), purely imitative ones (*quack-quack, oink-oink, beep beep, meow, moo,* and *hoo hoo*), and exclamations (*uh-oh, grrr, heehaw*), they are, in order of frequency:

all done	up	bump
light	coat	out
down	keys	heehaw
shoes	circle	eat
baby	mama	sit
don't throw	daddy	bee
moo	more	tree
bite	off	yack-yack
three	tick tock	bye-bye
hi	ball	doll
cheese	go	kite

"Will" did OK. So will namers if they can summon the innocence and learning abilities of a small child.

There are said to be millions of insects already described, and several million more awaiting descriptions—and names. Since millions of brand names do actually exist, a final question arises. "Is it possible to run out of names?" Well, consider a small dictionary of 80,000 entries. If we combine each entry with itself and every one of the other 79,999 entries, we arrive at a total of 64,000,000,000 possible combinations. Even if we eliminate such brand-name non-starters as *AardwolfZit* and *ZeoliteAargh*, the number should still be enough to go on with.

The making of names will most certainly go on—extending the balancing act between business strategy and common sense, between marketing art and everyday science, between linguistic skill and legal competency. As to the total process, we would humbly suggest that the future of names and naming is limited only by the ingenuity of the human mind.

APPENDIX

INTERNATIONAL TRADEMARK CLASSES OF GOODS AND SERVICES

GOODS

Class	Description
1 (Chemicals)	Chemicals used in industry, science and photography, as well as in agriculture, horticulture and forestry; unprocessed artificial resins, unprocessed plastics; manures; fire extinguishing compositions; tempering and soldering preparations; chemical substances for preserving foodstuffs; tanning substances; adhesives used in industry.
2 (Paints)	Paints, varnishes, lacquers; preservatives against rust and against deterioration of wood; colorants; mordants; raw natural resins; metals in foil and powder form for painters, decorators, printers and artists.
3 (Cosmetics and cleaning preparations)	Bleaching preparations and other substances for laundry use; cleaning, polishing, scouring and abrasive preparations; soaps; perfumery, essential oils, cosmetics, hair lotions; dentifrices.
4 (Lubricants and fuels)	Industrial oils and greases; lubricants; dust absorbing, wetting and binding compositions; fuels (including motor spirit) and illuminants; candles, wicks.
5 (Pharmaceuticals)	Pharmaceutical, veterinary and sanitary preparations; dietetic substances adapted for medical use, food for babies; plasters, materials for dressings; material for stopping teeth, dental wax; disinfectants; preparations for destroying vermin; fungicides, herbicides.
6 (Metal goods)	Common metals and their alloys; metal building materials; transportable buildings of metal; materials of metal for railway tracks; non-electric cables and wires of common metal; ironmongery, small items of metal hardware; pipes and tubes of metal; safes; goods of common metal not included in other classes; ores.

7 (Machinery)   Machines and machine tools; motors and engines (except for land vehicles); machine coupling and transmission components (except for land vehicles); agricultural implements; incubators for eggs.

8 (Hand tools)   Hand tools and implements (hand operated); cutlery; side arms; razors.

9 (Electrical and   Scientific, nautical, surveying, electric, photo-
  scientific apparatus)   graphic, cinematographer, optical, weighing, measuring, signaling, checking (supervision), life-saving and teaching apparatus and instruments; apparatus for recording, transmission or reproduction of sound or images; magnetic data carriers, recording discs; automatic vending machines and mechanisms for coin-operated apparatus; cash registers, calculating machines, data processing equipment and computers; fire-extinguishing apparatus.

10 (Medical apparatus)   Surgical, medical, dental and veterinary apparatus and instruments, artificial limbs, eyes and teeth; orthopedic articles; suture materials.

11 (Environmental   Apparatus for lighting, heating, steam generating,
  control apparatus)   cooking, refrigerating, drying, ventilating, water supply and sanitary purposes.

12 (Vehicles)   Vehicles; apparatus for locomotion by land, air or water.

13 (Firearms)   Firearms; ammunition and projectiles; explosives; fireworks.

14 (Jewelry)   Precious metals and their alloys and goods in precious metals or coated therewith, not included in other classes; jewelry, precious stones; horological and chronometric instruments.

15 (Musical instruments)   Musical instruments.

16 (Paper goods and   Paper, cardboard and goods made from these mate-
  printed matter).   rials, not included in other classes; printed matter; book binding material; photographs; stationery; adhesives for stationery or household purposes; artists' materials; paint brushes; typewriters and office requisites (except furniture); instructional and teaching material (except apparatus); plastic material for packaging (not included in other classes); playing cards; printers' type; printing blocks.

17 (Rubber goods)	Rubber, gutta-percha, gum, asbestos, mica and goods made from these materials and not included in other classes; plastics in extruded form for use in manufacture; packing, stopping and insulating materials; flexible pipes, not of metal.
18 (Leather goods)	Leather and imitations of leather, and goods made of these materials and not included in other classes; animal skins, hides; trunks and traveling bags; umbrellas, parasols and walking sticks; whips, harness and saddlery.
19 (Non-metallic building materials)	Building materials (non-metallic); non-metallic rigid pipes for building; asphalt, pitch and bitumen; non-metallic transportable buildings; monuments, not of metal.
20 (Furniture and articles not otherwise classified)	Furniture, mirrors, picture frames; goods (not included in other classes) of wood, cork, reed, cane, wicker, horn, bone, ivory, whalebone, shell, amber, mother-of-pearl, meerschaum and substitutes for all these materials, or of plastics.
21 (Housewares and glass)	Household or kitchen utensils and containers (not of precious metal or coated therewith); combs and sponges; brushes (except paint brushes); brush-making materials; articles for cleaning purposes; steel wool; unworked or semi-worked glass (except glass used in building); glass-ware, porcelain and earthenware not included in other classes.
22 (Cordage and fibers)	Ropes, string, nets, tents, awnings, tarpaulins, sails, sacks and bags (not included in other classes); padding and stuffing materials (except of rubber or plastics); raw fibrous textile materials.
23 (Yarns and threads)	Yarns and threads, for textile use.
24 (Fabrics)	Textiles and textile goods, not included in other classes; bed and table covers.
25 (Clothing)	Clothing, footwear, headgear.
26 (Fancy goods)	Lace and embroidery, ribbons and braid; buttons, hooks and eyes, pins and needles; artificial flowers.
27 (Floor coverings)	Carpets, rugs, mats and matting, linoleum and other materials for covering existing floors; wall hangings (non-textile).
28 (Toys and sporting goods)	Games and playthings; gymnastic and sporting articles not included in other classes; decorations for Christmas trees.

29 (Meats and processed foods)	Meat, fish, poultry and game; meat extracts; preserved, dried and cooked fruits and vegetables; jellies, jams, fruit sauces; eggs, milk and milk products; edible oils and fats.
30 (Staple foods)	Coffee, tea, cocoa, sugar, rice, tapioca, sago, artificial coffee; flour and preparations made from cereals, bread, pastry and confectionery, ices; honey, treacle; yeast, baking-powder, salt, mustard; vinegar, sauces (condiments); spices; ice.
31 (Natural agricultural products)	Agricultural, horticultural and forestry products and grains not included in other classes; live animals; fresh fruits and vegetables; seeds, natural plants and flowers; foodstuffs for animals, malt.
32 (Light beverages)	Beers; mineral and aerated waters and other non-alcoholic drinks; fruit drinks and fruit juices; syrups and other preparations for making beverages.
33 (Wines and spirits)	Alcoholic beverages (except beers).
34 (Smokers' articles)	Tobacco; smokers' articles; matches.

SERVICES

Class	Description
35 (Advertising and business services)	Advertising; business management; business administration; office functions.
36 (Insurance and financial services)	Insurance; financial affairs; monetary affairs; real estate affairs.
37 (Construction and repair services)	Building construction; repair; installation services.
38 (Communication . services)	Telecommunications.
39 (Transportation and storage services)	Transport; packaging and storage of goods; travel arrangement.
40 (Material treatment services)	Treatment of materials.
41 (Education and entertainment services)	Education; providing of training; entertainment; sporting and cultural activities.
42 (Scientific and technological services; Legal services)	Scientific and technological services and research and design relating thereto: industrial analysis and research services; design and development of computer hardware and software; legal services.

43 (Restaurant and Hospitality services)	Services provided by persons or establishments whose aim is to prepare food and drink for consumption and services provided to obtain bed and board in hotels, boarding houses or other establishments providing temporary accommodations.
44 (Medical care, hygienic and beauty care)	Medical care, hygienic and beauty care given by persons or establishments to human beings and animals; it also includes services relating to the fields of agriculture, horticulture and forestry.
45 (Social services; Security services)	Personal and social services rendered by others to meet the needs of individuals; security services for the protection of property and individuals.

SOURCES AND RESOURCES

We intend the following references not only to show the sources we've drawn on to do this book, but as resources for anyone interested in brand names, naming, and namers—and the contexts in which they live and work.

BOOKS ON NAMING

Books specifically about the naming of companies, products, and services are few and far between, which is why we think our book is timely, topical, and badly needed. Henri Charmasson's *The Name Is the Game* and Javed Naseem's *Naming for Power*, both by naming practitioners, contain some useful information and tips, but the former is badly dated and the latter somewhat self-promotional. The title of Adrian Room's *Trade Name Origins* is a little misleading—it covers brand names as well as trade (corporate) names. It's essentially an alphabetical-format reference book, emphasizing British and European brands, including rich biographical background. The introduction is valuable, too, as is an appendix on letters and suffixes. The business journalist Alex Frankel's *Wordcraft* emphasizes branding in general as much as naming in particular.

Charmasson, Henri. *The Name Is the Game: How to Name a Company or Product*. Homewood: Dow Jones-Irwin, 1988.
Frankel, Alex. *Wordcraft: The Art of Turning Little Words into Big Business*. New York: Random House, 2004.
Javed, Naseem. *Naming for Power: Creating Successful Names for the Business World*. Toronto and New York: Linkwood, 1993.
Room, Adrian. *Trade Name Origins*. Chicago: NTC, 1982

REFERENCE BOOKS

David Crystal's *Cambridge Encyclopedia of Language* and *Cambridge Encyclopedia of the English Language*, as well as Tom McArthur's *Oxford Companion to the English Language*, are excellent reference books and we've tapped them at many points. The *Encyclopedia of the English Language* especially is rich in tabular material from scholarly sources, some of which we've drawn on. Every dictionary has strengths and weaknesses, and how dictionaries handle brand names is of absorbing interest. Using a keyword like "Trademark," one can instantly summon lists of brand names in dictionaries that have searchable CD version. We've also used more specialized compendiums. For new words in the language, chronicled by decade, we've relied on John Ayto's *Twentieth Century Words*. For symbolism, we've found *Brewer's Dictionary of Phrase and Fable* to be most useful. Although it cries for updating, Laurence Urdang's and Ceila Dame Robbins's *Slogans* is a wonderful compilation of brand names as they burst forth in advertising slogans and taglines.The turn-of-the-twentieth-century *ABC Universal Commercial Electric Telegraphic Code* is unique in its abundance of wholly synthetic words. For words that have loomed large through more than two centuries of U.S. history, including car, aircraft, and brewery names, Stuart Berg Flexner's *I Hear America Talking* is lively and comprehensive. Of the thesauruses, our favorite is Robert L. Chapman's revision of *Roget's International Thesaurus*, but for the practical business of creating brand names J. I. Rodale's alphabetically arranged *The Synonym Finder* may be more fertile. Another excellent naming tool is the many topical lists in Stephen Glazier's *Random House Word Menu*.

Algeo, John, with the assistance of Adele S. Algeo. *Fifty Years among the New Words: A Dictionary of Neologisms, 1941–1991.* New York: Cambridge, 1991.

American Heritage Dictionary of the English Language. 4th ed. Boston and New York: Houghton Mifflin, 2000.

AP Stylebook and Briefing on Media Law. New York: Associated Press, 2003.

Ayto, John. *Twentieth Century Words.* Oxford: Oxford University Press, 1999.

Barnhart, Robert K., and Sol Steinmetz, with Clarence L. Barnhart. *The Third Barnhart Dictionary of New English.* New York: H. W. Wilson, 1990.

Brewer's Dictionary of Phrase and Fable. 16th ed. Revised by Adrian Room. New York: HarperCollins, 1999.

Chambers Dictionary. 9th ed. Edinburgh: Chambers Harrap, 2003.

Chambers Official Scrabble Words Dictionary. Edinburgh: Chambers Harrap, 2002.

Chapman, Robert L. *Roget's International Thesaurus.* 5th ed. New York: HarperCollins, 1992.

Chevalier, Jean, and Alain Gheerbrant. *A Dictionary of Symbols.* Trans. John Buchanan-Brown, Oxford: Blackwell, 1994.

Chicago Manual of Style. 15th ed. Chicago: University of Chicago Press, 2003.

Cirlot, J. E. *A Dictionary of Symbols.* Trans. Jack Sage. New York: Philosophical Library, 1962.

Clausen-Thue, W. *The ABC Universal Commercial Electric Telegraphic Code.* New York: American Code Company, 1901.

Collins English Dictionary. 6th ed. London: HarperCollins, 2003.

Concise Oxford English Dictionary. 10th ed. Oxford: Oxford, 2002.

CP Press Stylebook: A Guide for Writers and Editors. Ed. Peter Buckley. Toronto: Canadian Press, 1992.

Crystal, David. *Cambridge Encyclopedia of the English Language.* Cambridge: Cambridge University Press, 1995.

Crystal, David. *Cambridge Encyclopedia of Language*. Cambridge: Cambridge University Press, 1987.

Editing Canadian English. 2d ed. Toronto: Macfarlane Walter and Ross, 2000.

Encarta World English Dictionary. London: Bloomsbury, 1999, and New York: St. Martin's, 1999.

Encyclopedia Britannica Almanac 2004. Chicago: Encyclopedia Britannica, 2003.

Flexner, Stuart Berg. *I Hear America Talking: An Illustrated Treasury of American Words and Phrases*. New York: Van Nostrand Reinhold, 1976.

Glazier, Stephen. *Random House Word Menu*. New York: Random House, 1992.

Globe and Mail Style Book. Ed. J. A. (Sandy) McFarlane and Warren Clements. Toronto: Penguin, 1994.

McArthur, Tom, ed. *Oxford Companion to the English Language*. Oxford and New York: Oxford, 1992.

Merriam-Webster's Collegiate Dictionary. 11th ed. Springfield, Mass.: Merriam-Webster, 2003.

Morris, William, and Mary Morris. *Dictionary of Word and Phrase Origins*. 2d ed. New York: Harper, 1988.

New Fowler's Modern English Usage. 3d ed. Ed. R. W. Burchfield. Oxford: Clarendon, 1996.

New Oxford Dictionary of English. Ed. Judy Pearsall. Oxford: Clarendon, 2003.

New York Times Manual of Style and Usage. New York: New York Times, 2002.

Oxford Dictionary of English. CD-ROM searchable version. Oxford: Clarendon, 2002.

Oxford Dictionary of New Words. Comp. Sara Tulloch. Oxford and New York: Oxford, 1991.

Oxford Dictionary of Phrase and Fable. Ed. Elizabeth Knowles. Oxford: Oxford, 2000.

Oxford Guide to Canadian English Usage. Ed. Margery Fee and Janice McAlpine. Toronto: Oxford, 1997.

Quirk, Randolph, Sidney Greenbaum, Geoffrey Leech, and Jan Svartik. *A Grammar of Contemporary English*. London: Longman, 1972.

Random House Webster Compact Unabridged Dictionary. Special 2d ed. New York: Random House, 1996.

Room, Adrian. *Dictionary of Contrasting Pairs*. London and New York: Routledge, 1988.

21st Century Misspeller's Dictionary, comp. T. J. Demers. New York: Dell, 1993.

Urdang, Laurence, and Ceila Dame Robbins, eds. *Slogans*. Detroit: Gale, 1984.

Webster's New World College Dictionary. 3d ed. New York: Simon & Schuster, 1997.

Webster's Third New International Dictionary. Springfield, Mass.: Merriam-Webster, 1961.

World Almanac and Book of Facts 2003. New York: World Almanac, 2003.

OTHER BOOKS

We've taken a magpie approach to other books and include those on topics drawn from psychology, linguistics, culture, and business, as well as novels such as Kenneth Grahame's *The Wind in the Willows* and, a very different cup of tea, Brett Easton Ellis's *American Psycho*.

Aaker, David. *Building Strong Brands*. New York: The Free Press, 1995.
———. *Managing Brand Equity*. New York: The Free Press, 1991.
Adler, Alfred. *The Individual Psychology of Alfred Adler*. New York: Perennial, 1964.
Alsop, Ronald J. *The 18 Immutable Laws of Corporate Reputation: Creating, Protecting, and Repairing Your Most Valuable Asset*. New York: The Free Press, 2004.
Barry, John A. *Technobabble*. Cambridge: MIT, 1991.
Benbow, John. *Manuscript and Proof*. New York: Oxford, 1937.
Bono, Edward de. *New Think: The Use of Lateral Thinking in the Generation of New Ideas*. New York: Basic Books, 1967.
———. *Six Thinking Hats*. New York: Back Bay, 1999.
Bryson, Bill. *The Mother Tongue: English and How It Got That Way*. New York: HarperCollins, 1990.
Bodmer, Frederick. *The Loom of Language: A Guide to Foreign Languages for the Home Student*. Ed. and arranged by Lancelot Hogben. London: George Allen & Unwin, 1944.
Burgess, Anthony. *A Mouthful of Air: Language and Languages, Especially English*. Toronto: Stoddart, 1993.
Campbell, Joseph. *The Hero with a Thousand Faces*. Princeton: Princeton, 1972.
Carter, Ronald. *Vocabulary: Applied Linguistic Perspectives*. London: Allyn & Unwin, 1987.
Casselman, Bill. *Casselmania: More Wacky Canadian Words & Sayings*. Toronto: Little, Brown, 1996.
Csikszentmihalyi, Mihaly, and Eugene Rochberg-Halton. *The Meaning of Things: Domestic Symbols and the Self*. New York: Cambridge, 1981.
Cochrane, Robertson. *The Way We Word: Musing on the Meaning of Everyday English*. Saskatoon: Fifth House, 1993.
Dalby, Andrew. *Language in Danger: The Loss of Linguistic Diversity and the Threat to Our Future*. New York: Columbia, 2003.
Eisiminger, Sterling. "Colorful Language." In *Verbatim: Volumes V & VI*. Detroit: Gale Research, 1981, pp. 795–802.
Ellis, Brett Easton. *American Psycho*. New York: Vintage, 1991.
Espy, Willard R. *O Thou Improper, Thou Uncommon Noun*. New York: Clarkson N. Potter, 1978.
Federal Reserve Bank of Dallas, 1998 Annual Report.

Fones, Robert. *Anthromorphiks*. Toronto: Coach House, 1971.

Galef, David. "Short Cuts." In *Verbatim: Volumes V & VI*, pp. 965–67.

A Guide to Proper Trademark Use. International Trademark Association, n.d.

Gibson, Claire. *Signs & Symbols*. New York: Barnes & Noble, 1996.

Grahame, Kenneth. *The Wind in the Willows*. New York: Scribners, 1954.

Hager, Philip E. "Diplophrasis." In *Verbatim: Volumes III & IV*, Detroit: Gale Research, 1981, pp. 475–79.

Hargraves, Orin. *Mighty Fine Words and Smashing Expressions: Making Sense of Transatlantic English*. New York: Oxford, 2003.

Heskett, John. *Toothpicks and Logos: Design in Everyday Life*. New York: Oxford, 2002.

Ingram, Jay. *Talk Talk Talk: An Investigation into the Mystery of Speech*. Toronto: Viking, 1992.

Hornos, Axel. "'Ouch!' he said in Japanese." In *Verbatim: Volumes III & IV*, pp. 251–54.

Jung, C. G. *Man and His Symbols*. New York: Laureleaf, 1997.

——. *Memories, Dreams, and Reflections*. Ed. Aniela Jaffé. New York: Vintage, 1989.

——. *Psychological Types*. Collected Works of C. G. Jung. Vol. 6. Princeton: Princeton University, 1979.

Karges, Joann. "Rhyme and Jingle." In *Verbatim: Volumes V & VI*, pp. 918–20.

Klein, Naomi. *No Logo: Taking Aim at the Brand Bullies*. Toronto: Vintage, 2000.

Landau, Sidney. *Dictionaries: The Art and Craft of Lexicography*. 2d ed. Cambridge: Cambridge, 2001.

Lloyd, Paul M. "Binomials and Trinomials." *Verbatim: Volumes I & II*, pp. 17–18.

Martineau, Pierre. *Motivation in Advertising: Motives That Make People Buy*. New York: McGraw-Hill, 1971.

Maslow, Abraham. *Motivation and Personality*. 3d ed. New York: Addison-Wesley, 1987.

McLuhan, Marshall, Quentin Fiore, and Jerome Angel. *The Medium Is the Message: An Inventory of Effects*. New York: Bantam, 1967.

Mencken, H. L. *The American Language: An Enquiry into the Development of English in the United States*. 4th ed. New York: Alfred A. Knopf, 1937.

Metcalf, Allan. *Predicting New Words: The Secrets of Their Success*. Boston: Houghton Mifflin, 2002.

Metcalf, Allan. *The World in So Many Words*. Boston and New York: Houghton Mifflin, 1999.

Moorhouse, Geoffrey. *To the Frontier*. New York: Holt, Rinehart & Winston, 1984.

Morton, Herbert C. *The Story of Webster's Third: Philip Gove's Controversial Dictionary and Its Critics*. New York: Cambridge, 1994.

O'Grady, William and Michael Dobrovolsky. *Contemporary Linguistic Analysis.* Toronto: Copp Clark Pitman, 1987.

Pei, Mario. *The Story of Language.* Philadelphia: J. B. Lippincott, 1949.

Pinker, Steven. *The Language Instinct: How the Mind Creates Language.* New York: HarperCollins, 1994.

Price, Bruce D. "A Metalinguistic Inquiry into F." In *Verbatim: Volumes V & VI,* pp. 639–42.

Pulgram, Ernst. *Theory of Names.* Berkeley: American Name Society. University of California Press, 1954.

Ries, Al, and Jack Trout. *Positioning,* New York: McGraw-Hill, 1986.

Rivkin, Steve, and Fraser Seitel. *IdeaWise: How to Transform Your Ideas into Tomorrow's Innovations.* New York: John Wiley, 2002.

Robertson, Kim Reed. "Cognitive Processing of Brand Names." Ph.D. thesis, University of Oregon, December 1982.

Ross, A. S. C. "U and Non-U: An Essay in Sociological Linguistics." In Nancy Mitford, ed. *Noblesse Oblige.* London: Hamish Hamilton, 1956.

Safire, William. "Generic: What's in a Name?" In William Safire, *On Language.* New York: Times Books, 1980, pp. 106–08.

———. "No-Name Nomenclature?" In William Safire, *On Language,* New York: Times Books, 1980, pp. 177–79.

Sarenpa, Colleen M. *The Trademark Shuffle: Five Steps to Trademark Success,* Thomson & Thomson, 1994.

Schulz, Clair. "We Shall Know Them by Their Roots." *Verbatim: Volumes III & IV.* Detroit: Gale Research, 1981, pp. 475–79.

Searle, John R. *Speech Acts: An Essay in the Philosophy of Language.* New York: Cambridge, 1969.

Sears, Donald A. "Ameritalian." In *Verbatim: Volumes I & II.* Detroit: Gale, 1978.

Smitherman, Geneva. *Black Talk: Words and Phrases from the Hood to the Amen Corner.* New York: Houghton Mifflin, 2000.

Stern, Jane, and Michael Stern. *Jane & Michael Stern's Encyclopedia of Pop Culture.* New York: HarperCollins, 1992.

———. *Square Meals.* New York: Alfred A. Knopf, 1985.

Trout, Jack, with Steve Rivkin. *Differentiate or Die: Survival in the Era of Killer Competition.* New York: John Wiley, 2000.

———. *The New Positioning.* New York: McGraw-Hill, 1996.

Wescott, Roger W. "Word Chains in English." In *Verbatim: Volumes I & II,* pp. 6–7.

Woodbridge, Richard C., and Robert G. Shepherd. *Selecting and Protecting Your Trademark.* Booklet no. 2, 2d ed. Princeton: Matthews, Woodbridge & Collins, 1990.

Word Mysteries & Histories. Boston: Houghton Mifflin, 1974.

PERIODICALS

Among periodicals, we especially like *English Today* for its worldwide perspective on English. Also notable are *Names*, the journal of the American Name Society; *The Name Gleaner/La Glanure des Noms* from the Canadian Society for the Study of Names; and *Dictionaries*, the annual of the Dictionary Society of North America. We're fond of *Verbatim: TheLanguage Quarterly*, but also worth the browse is *The Vocabula Review*, whose motto is "A society is generally as lax as its language."

To save space, we have not listed the many news items we've had recourse to, except for especially significant ones. Stories on brand names in major newspapers and business magazines typically appear in the marketing pages, but sometimes graduate to the front page. To avoid clutter we've not listed URLs for pieces that appeared in print, but most of the latter have a Web presence and can be summoned by author and title through www.google.com or another search engine.

Adrangi, Sahim. "B.C. firm in pricey bout of name-calling." *Globe and Mail*, Aug. 23, 2003.

Agrell, Siri. "Thirst for an 'ethical" cola?" *National Post*, Jan. 17, 2004.

Akin, David. "Zero-Knowledge Learns a Valuable Lesson." *Globe and Mail*, May 13, 2002.

Baron, Dennis. "McLanguage Meets the Dictionary." *The Chronicle of Higher Education*, Dec. 19, 2003.

Begley, Sharon. "StrawBerry Is No BlackBerry: Building Brands Using Sound." *Wall Street Journal*, Aug. 26, 2002.

Bianchi, Alejandro, and Gabriel Sama. "Brands Enter Lexicon in Latin America." *Wall Street Journal*, May 7, 2003.

Boyle, Matthew. "Brand Killers," *Fortune*, Aug. 11, 2003.

Bremer, Catherine. "Brand Names Create Global Language. Reuters, Sept. 5, 2003.

"Brewing a Worldly Brand." *Outlook*. Andersen Consulting, June 1999.

Brozan, Nadine. "The High-Stakes Game of the Name." *New York Times*, July 27, 2003.

Buchholz, Garth. "The Eternal Cycle of Cool." *Globe and Mail*, Nov. 29, 2001.

Butters, Ron, and Jennifer Westerhaus. "Trademark, Metaphor, and Synecdoche in Dictionary Labeling: A Band-Aid Solution to the Genericness Question." Paper presented at the 14th Biennial Meeting, Dictionary Society of North America, Durham, N.C., May 29–31, 2003.

Caldwell, Rebecca. "'You Smell Like a Crocodile.'" *Globe and Mail*, Aug. 2, 2003.

Callan, Sara. "U.K. Postal Service Restores Its Old Name, Records a Loss." *Wall Street Journal*, June 14, 2002.

Campbell, Calvin. "Convenience, Japanese-style." *Globe and Mail*, Feb. 22, 2003.

Carrick, Rob. "A Bank by Any Other Name Is Confusing." *Globe and Mail*, Oct. 17, 2002.

"The Case for Better Measurement and Reporting of Marketing Performance." *Business Horizons*, Sept. 19, 1995.

Chartrand, Sandra. "Before Shock and Awe Can Go from Battlefield to Lunch Box, There Is a Stop at the Trademark Office." *New York Times*, April 21, 2003.

Clankie, Shawn M. "Why Bud Wiser Can Sell Cars (but Not Beer)." *Verbatim* 26, no. 3 (summer 2001): 3–4.

Considine, J. D. "Manga Mania Comes to the West." *Globe and Mail*, July 17, 2003, p. R3.

Dalby, David. "The Linguasphere: Kaleidoscope of the World's Languages." *English Today* 65 (17,1) (Jan. 2001): 22–26.

Daniel, Caroline. "Beyond Sugarcoating New Colors, Shapes and Names Are Cures for the Common Pill." *Washington Post*, Nov. 11, 1998.

Evans, Mark. "Don't Get Burnt Changing Net Brands." *Globe and Mail*, April 6, 2000.

Fisher, Jerry. "The Elements of a Great Name." *Entrepreneur*, Dec. 2001.

Flynn, Laurie J. "Spinoff Is Christened with Care by Hewlett." *New York Times*, Aug. 2, 1999.

Frankel, Alex. "On Language: Branded." *New York Times Magazine*, Sept. 2, 2001.

Friedrich, Patricia. "English in Advertising and Brand Naming: Sociolinguistic Considerations and the Case of Brazil." *English Today* 71 (18,3) (July 2002): 21–28.

Geist, Michael. "Domain Name Policy Absurd When It Comes to Trademarks." *Globe and Mail*, July 25, 2002.

Gill, Alexandra. "B.C. Natives Triumph in Battle of the 'Bucks.'" *Globe and Mail*, Aug. 29, 2003.

Girard, Kim. "Cozone in the Ozone." *Business 2.0*, June 2000.

Gleick, James. "Get Out of My Namespace." *New York Times Magazine*, March 21, 2004.

Gordon, Joanne. "Brushing Off Mom." *Forbes*, Feb. 3, 2003.

Griffin, Jeffrey L. "Global English Infiltrates Bulgaria." *English Today* 68 (17,4) (Oct. 2001): 54–60.

Harari, Herbert, and John W. McDavid. "Name Stereotypes and Teachers' Expectations." *Journal of Educational Psychology* 65 (1973): 222–225.

Heinrich, Susan. "Canadian Goods Evade U.S. Boycott Radar." *National Post*, April 19, 2003.

Heinzl, John. "Ads Rock the Baby Carriage." *Globe and Mail*, Aug. 28, 2002.

——. "The Attack of the Brand Flakes," *Globe and Mail*, Nov. 24, 2000.

——. "Brand Names That Can't Cross the Border." *Globe and Mail*, Dec. 21, 2000.

——. "Ford F-word Fetish Doesn't Fly with Some." *Globe and Mail*, Feb. 7, 2003.

——. "Four Renamed Dunlops Now Big Wheels." *Globe and Mail*, March 12, 2002.

——. "The Wizard of Ads Touts the Power of Words." *Globe and Mail*, Oct. 20, 2000.

"Hershey Home May Change Name." Associated Press, Oct. 15, 2002.

Horowitz, Adam, Mark Athitakis, Mark Lasswell, and Owen Thomas. "The 101 Dumbest Moments in Business." *Business 2.0*, Jan.–Feb. 2004.

"How McDonald's Tailors Its Brand Identity to Local Markets," *Campaign*, Aug. 1997.

Hulbert, Mark. "Want to Pump New Life into a Fund? Change Its Name." *New York Times*, Dec. 28, 2003.

Hutchinson, Brian. "Rogue Food Nation." *National Post*, June 21, 2003.

Kalman, Marira, and Rick Meyerowitz. "What's New in Pharmacology." *New Yorker*, Sept. 8, 2003.

Kapica, Jack. "High-tech Revival? It Depends on How You Say It." *Globe and Mail*, July 17, 2003.

Kapner, Suzanne. "Advertising" column. *New York Times*, April 11, 2002.

Keenan, Greg. "If Ford Calls It the Freestar, Will There Then Be a Fustang?" *Globe and Mail*, Feb. 4, 2003.

Kelly, Michael H. "Naming on the Bright Side of Life." *Names* 48:1 (March 2000): 3–26.

Kollias, Tania. "Greek Sign Law Forces English to Bite Tongue." *Globe and Mail*, Dec. 11, 2002.

Kumar, Nirmalya. "Kill a Brand, Keep a Customer." *Harvard Business Review*, Dec. 1, 2003.

Lang, Amanda. "Don't Dismiss Faithful Ask Jeeves." *Globe and Mail*, July 21, 2003.

Levitt, Theodore. "The Globalization of Markets." *Harvard Business Review*, May–June 1983.

Lewyckyj, Maryanna. "Slang Crosses Up GM." *Toronto Sun*, Oct. 16, 2003.

Locke, Nancy A. "Finding the Right Words." *Globe and Mail*, July 23, 2003.

MacGregor, Laura. "The Language of Shop Signs in Tokyo." *English Today*, Jan. 2003.

Marano, Hara Estroff. "The Opposite Sex." *Psychology Today*, July–Aug. 2003.

McArthur, Tom. "World English, Euro-English, Nordic English?" *English Today*, Jan. 2003.

McKenna, Barrie. "What Do You Call Yourself When Your Name Is Mud?" *Globe and Mail*, Feb. 23, 2002.

McKie, Robin. "Lost for Words? Teenagers Grunt and Adults Chat about Trivia, but Are Our Unique Verbal Skills Really in Danger of Disappearing? Robin McKie Thinks We Are Unlikely to Be Left Speechless." *The Observer*, Jan. 12, 2003.

McNeil, Donald G., Jr. "The Science of Naming Drugs (Sorry, 'Z' Is Already Taken)." *New York Times*, Dec. 28, 2003.

Meyerowitz, Steven A. "Surviving Assaults on Trademarks." *Marketing Management* 3, no. 1, pp. A8–A10.

Miller, George. "The Magical Number Seven, Plus or Minus Two: Some Limits on Our Capacity to Process Information." *Psychological Review* 63 (1956): 81–97.

Milstein, Sarah. "Taming the Task of Checking for Terrorists' Names." *New York Times*, Dec. 30, 2002.

Mistry, Bhavna. "On a Global Mission." *Marketing Event*, Oct. 9, 1997.

Mitchell, Alanna. "Fat: The Next Tobacco." *Globe and Mail*, July 5, 2003.

Morfitt, Ian. "The Cat Zamboni." *Globe and Mail*, June 23, 2003.

Motluk, Alison. "You Are What You Speak." *New Scientist*, Nov. 30, 2002.

Moyes, Jojo. "Big Mac Chews Out Little Mrs McMunchie." *The Independent*, Sept. 24, 1996.

Mullan, John. "John Mullan Deconstructs Ian Fleming's James Bond Series. Week Two: The Villain." *The Guardian*, Dec. 21, 2002.

Murray, Thomas E. "The Overlooked and Understudied Onomastic Hyphen." *Names* 50, no. 3 (Sept. 2002): 173–190.

"Name Games." *Saturday Night*, Sept. 23, 2000.

Neufeldt, Victoria. "A Civil but Untrammeled Tongue: Spontaneous Creativity in Language." *Dictionaries* 16 (1996): 19–31.

Nickell, Joe Ashbrook. "What's in a Name?" *Business 2.0*, May 2000.

Ono, Yumiko. "Marketers Seek the 'Naked' Truth in Consumer Psyches." *Wall Street Journal*, May 30, 1997.

Ortega, Paul. "Two Wal-Marts Fight for Right to Be Manitoba's One and Only." *Wall Street Journal*, March 23, 1994.

Patriquin, Martin. "The Running Shoe Fits for AdBusters." *Globe and Mail*, Aug. 20, 2003.

Petersen, Melody. "American Home Is Changing Name to Wyeth." *New York Times*, March 11, 2002.

Picard, André. "Companies Struggle to End Growing Threat of Trans Fats." *Globe and Mail*, Nov. 26, 2003.

Pitts, Gordon. "Every Old Name Is New Again as Tech Firms Try to Forget Bust." *Globe and Mail*, Aug. 18, 2003.

———. "Ignore the Brand Flakes." *Globe and Mail*, Aug. 28, 2001.

Quesada, Begonia, and David Brough. "EU Claims Rights to 41 Food Names." *Globe and Mail*, Aug. 29, 2003.

Raento, Pauliina, and William A. Douglass. "The Naming of Gaming."*Names* 49, no. 1 (March 2001): 1–35.

Renzetti, Elizabeth. "The Game of the Name." *R.O.B. Magazine*, Sept. 2001.

Robertson, Kim. "Strategically Desirable Brand Name Characteristics." *Journal of Marketing Research* 6, no. 4 (fall 1989): 61–71.

———. "Recall and Recognition Effects of Brand Name Imagery." *Psychology & Marketing* 4, no. 1 (spring 1987): 3–15.

Ross, Cecily. "Doggone It, I'm Pretty." *Globe and Mail*, June 23, 2003.

Rozin, Randall S. "A Good Name Is Better than Riches: Tips to Consider When Selecting New Brand Names." *The Advertiser*, June 2003.

Rottenberg, Josh. "How to Invent a Brand Name." *New York Times Sunday Magazine*, April 8, 2001.

Rutkowski, Mariusz. "Two Types of Descriptiveness in Names." *Onomastica Canadiana* 83, no. 1 (June 2001): 25–38.

Saunders, Doug. "English-language Boom Worldwide Draws Support and Condemnation." *Globe and Mail*, July 14, 2003.

Schlick, Maria. "The English of Shop Signs in Europe." *English Today*, Jan. 2003.

Smith, Elaine. "Hey, Baby—Let's Play the Name Game." *St. Catharines Standard*, Jan. 20, 2003.

Sternbergh, Adam. "Got Bub All up in the Huzzle, Yo!" *National Post*, March 15, 2003.

Syme, Fraser. "When Hot Sauce Gets Out of Control." *Globe and Mail*, June 30, 2003.

Tucker, D. K. "Distribution of Forenames, Surnames, and Forename-Surname Pairs in Canada." *Names* 50, no. 2 (June 2002): 105–32.

———. "Distribution of Forenames, Surnames, and Forename-Surname Pairs in the United States." *Names* 49, no. 2 (June 2001): 69–96.

Van Alphen, Tony. "Ford Plays Name Game with Popular Windstar Minivan," *Toronto Star*, Feb. 8, 2003.

Vesterhus, V. A. "Anglicisms in German Car Documents." *Language International* 3 (1991): 10–15.

Waldie, Paul. "Licensing Deals Revive Marvel." *Globe and Mail*, May 7, 2003.

———. "When Is a Fruit Dot Not a Froot Loop? The Federal Court Rules." *Globe and Mail*, July 5, 2002.

Wintrob, Suzanne. "The Name Game." *National Post*, Jan. 18, 2003.

Woolley, Scott. "What's in a Name." *Forbes*, Nov. 15, 1999.

Young, Amalie. "Welcome to half.com, Population 360," Associated Press, Jan. 20, 2000.

Young, Patricia and Anne McIlroy. "Why Aussies Root for Canada." *Globe and Mail*, Aug. 17, 2000.

WEB SITES FOR NAMING

Our single most important online resource was Rivkin & Associates' www.namingnewsletter.com. *The Naming Newsletter* is full of lively naming-related stories and analyses. The home pages for naming firms are often richly educational. For example, at www.namebase.com and its sister site www.medibrand.com, we found Richard Hacken's useful "Sample Linguistic Analysis: VIAGRA" and Jim Singer's "Teensy and Humongus Inc.," Julie Cottineau's "Ten Most Common Naming Mistakes" at www.brandchannel.com, and "Trademark 101" at www.thenamingcompany.com. From www.ahundredmonkeys.com came "Branding strategies of the blue and famous" and from www.metaphorname.com a useful "Trademark Primer." Some naming firms specialize, in the case of www.medibrand.com, in pharmaceuticals, and for www.goodcharacters.com, in Chinese languages.

A typical namer's Web site will include case studies and topical articles, as well as names of clients and a portfolio with sample work. It will give a biographical rundown on the firm's staff, sometimes a selection of media pieces—not only about the firm but about naming in general—sometimes a section of FAQs (frequently asked questions), and always contact information. For do-it-yourself namers there's www.wordlab.com, which calls itself a "universal think tank" and free resource for naming and branding, including databases of "nomencreations" and "lingoventions."

The list below is representative, but by no means inclusive. A word of caution about Web sites. At press time we made every effort to prove that each site was current. But Web sites are constantly being dismantled, reconstructed, or renamed, and we cannot guarantee can be summoned at a click.

Naming Firms
www.abcnamebank.com
www.ahundredmonkeys.com
www.ashtonbg.com
www.brandchannel.com
www.brandinstitute.com
www.catch-word.com
www.cintara.com
www.connotion.com
www.creatingnewnames.com
www.enterpriseig.com
www.Goodcharacters.com

www.haydengroup.com
www.igorinternational.com
www.interbrand.com
www.landor.com
www.lexicon-branding.com
www.medibrand.com
www.metaphorname.com
www.namebase.com
www.namedevelopment.com
www.nameit.com
www.namelab.com
www.namestormers.com
www.nametagintl.com
www.nametrade.com
www.naming.com
www.namingnewsletter.com
www.namix.com
www.nomen.com
www.remarkable.be
www.Rivkin.net
www.skriptor.com
www.thenamingcompany.com
www.wordforword.com
www.wordlab.com

Trademark Registration & Search Firms

These firms may act as sellers and brokers of names, research and monitor trademarks, or do legal searches prior to filing for them. At www.trademark.com, American Trademark Co. files and registers trademark applications, not to be confused with www.trademrk.com, which does extensive top-level domain searches and international trademarks. Of special note is www.brandfidelity, which allows you to search online for direct-hit trademark and .com, .net, and .org domain availability. The *WHOIS* database of Web domain names is at www.networksolutions.com, from Network Solutions, the first and largest registrar of domain names.

www.afternic.com
www.brandfidelity.com
www.buydomains.com
www.greatdomains.com
www.networksolutions.com
NameProtect.com

www.register.com
www.riobrand.com
www.trademark.com
www.trademrk.com

Selected Online Articles and Data about Naming and Names
Most article titles are self-explanatory, and all were useful, but we would
single out the "BBC Shoptalk" radio panel discussion, Neil Franklin's collection of humorous computer acronyms, and "Strange Names," the equally
humorous assortment of British pub names, as well as American Express's
listings of its own trademarks, and Ruth Shalit's witty and revealing "The
Name Game."

"BBC Shop Talk."
    www.bbc.co.uk/radio4/news/shoptalk/shoptalk_20021022.shtml
Cooper, Michael, P. Raghavendra Rau, and Huseyin Gulen. "Changing Names
    with Style: Mutual Fund Name Changes and Their Effects on Fund Flows."
    papers.ssrn.com/sol3/papers.cfm?abstract_id=423989
Franklin, Neil. "Neil Franklin's Jokes and Fun Page."
    neil.franklin.ch/Jokes_and_Fun
"Frequently Asked Questions." www.nameit.com/question.htm
Feuerstein, Adam. "Meet the Street: How to Name a Blockbuster Drug."
    www.thestreet.com/funds/meetthestreet/10003579.html
Gross, Daniel. "The Name Game." Attaché Archives.
    www.namebase.com/news_03.html
Johnston, David. "Trademarks: A History of a Billion-Dollar Business."
    www.infoplease.com/spot/trademarks1.html
Krauskopf, Lewis. "Naming New Drugs: Costly, Complex." North Jersey Media
    Group, Jan. 15, 2002. www.namebase.com/news_03.html
"Life Cycle of a Trademark." tdomino.thomson-
    thomson.com/www/Reference.nsf
Rozin, Randall. "A Good Name Is Better Than Riches."
    www.brandchannel.com/images/papers/rrozin.pdf
Shalit, Ruth. "The Inner Doughboy."
    http://dir.salon.com/media/col/shal/2000/03/23/doughboy/index.html?s
    id=700303
——. "The Name Game."
    http://dir.salon.com/media/col/shal/1999/11/30/naming/index.html?sid
    =474305
"Sloganalysis." www.adslogans.co.uk/sloganalysis/sloganalysis.html
"Strange Names." www.fatbadgers.co.uk/Britain/weird.htm
"Trademarks." www.AmericanExpress.com

Selected Naming-Related Websites

This is a variety pack of sites pertaining to brand, corporate, and domain names, many with helpful links. At Lucian James's www.agendainc.com may be found "American Brandstand," a chart based on the brands that appear in the lyrics of songs in the top 20 songs of the Billboard Hot 100. The law firm Brown & Michaels offers "Your Trademark: Do's and Don'ts" at www.bpmlegal.com. The site www.isoc.org concerns the activities of the Internet Society and the Internet Domain Name System (DNS): it deals with issues of content, privacy, taxation, intellectual property, and other aspects of Internet commerce. The site www.icann.org represents the Internet Corporation for Assigned Names and Numbers. That for www.internetmarken.de puts special emphasis on Germany but provides many useful links to trademark-related organizations worldwide, including the American Bar Association's intellectual property law section, the European Communities Trademark Association, the International Trademark Association, intellectual property offices, as well as patent attorneys, and online intellectual-property journals and magazines. Information regarding Internet domain name registration services is found at www.internic.net. For offline brands the United States Patent and Trademark Office, an agency of the U.S. Department of Commerce at www.uspto.gov is of course indispensable; at www.strategis.ic.gc.ca its Canadian equivalent is the Canadian Intellectual Property Office, which maintains a trademarks database. The World Intellectual Property Organization is at www.wipo.int and the International Trademark Association at www.inta.org. Both www.shinolas.com and www.wordlab.com offer cautionary case histories, www.borfl.org/chevrolet_mexico.html has a full account of the *Chevy Nova* controversy, and *The Design Conspiracy*'s www.whatbrandareyou.com gives comic relief.

www.agendainc.com
www.bpmlegal.com/tmdodont.html
www.borfl.org/chevrolet_mexico.html
www.isoc.org
www.icann.org
www.inta.org
www.internetmarken.de/links_e.htm
www.internic.net
www.shinolas.com
www.strategis.ic.gc.ca/sc_consu/trade-marks/engdoc/cover.html
www.uspto.gov
www.whatbrandareyou.com

Selected Online Language Resources

The World Wide Web has vast language resources. Ask Jeeves, found at Google.com's sister site www.about.com, can summon an impressive range of definitions for keyed-in words. The site www.acronymfinder.com calls itself the Web's most comprehensive dictionary of acronyms, abbreviations, and initialisms. The site www.onelook.com claims to be able to call up nearly 6 million words from 964 indexed dictionaries. At www.clres.com/dict.html, the Special Interest Group on the Lexicon of the Association for Computational Linguistics, may be found links to electronic dictionaries, and www.omnilex.com offers one-stop shopping for lexicographical resources, including the Dictionary Society of North America, the American Dialect Society, and the American Name Society. Word lists on every imaginable topic abound on the Web. At geography.about.com is much information about geographical names and toponyms, and links to the Geographic Names Information System, the official database for place-names in the United States, and the Canadian Permanent Committee on Geographical Names (CPCGN).

At www.cogsci.princeton.edu/~wn is WordNet, developed by the Cognitive Science Laboratory at Princeton University, an online lexical reference system in which nouns, verbs, adjectives, and adverbs are organized into synonym sets, each representing one underlying concept and linked by different relationships. Another way of connecting words is through the Lexical Free Net at www.lexfn.com, including words related by rhyme, spelling, supersets,and subsets.

For foreign languages, especially notable are www.ethnologue.com, the site of SIL International (formerly the Summer Institute of Linguistics), which provides many resources about languages and cultures of the world, and over twelve thousand citations spanning sixty years of research, and www.linguasphere.com, site of a transnational research institute "with increasing emphasis on the welfare and education of each of the world's speech communities." A translators' and interpreters' network is found at www.universaldialog.com, and www.yourdictionary.com offers word lookups in many languages.

Among personal, as opposed to institutional, Web sites we especially like Anu and Stuti Garg's "A Word a Day"—their book has the same title—at www.wordsmith.org and Michael Quinion's "World Wide Words" at www.quinion.com/words. An amusing page of mondegreens may be found at www.funwith-words.com. Though not specifically a word site, www.snopes.com debunks some urban legends about brand names.

www.about.com
www.acronymfinder.com
www.clres.com/dict.html
www.cogsci.princeton.edu/~wn

www.ethnologue.com
www.fun-with-words.com
www.geography.about.com/cs/toponyms/
www.lexfn.com
www.linguasphere.com
www.onelook.com
www.quinion.com/words
www.snopes.com
wordlist.sourceforge.net
www.universaldialog.com
www.yourdictionary.com

Index